Accidents in childhood and adolescence

The role of research

A French version of this work has been published by INSERM/Documentation française under the title *Les accidents de l'enfant et de l'adolescent: la place de la recherche* (available from: Documentation française, 29–31 quai Voltaire, 75340 Paris, France).

Accidents in childhood and adolescence

The role of research

Edited by
M. Manciaux
Professor of Public Health,
Faculty of Medicine,
University of Nancy,
Vandoeuvre-lès-Nancy,
France

&

C. J. Romer
Injury Prevention Programme,
World Health Organization,
Geneva, Switzerland

World Health Organization
Geneva
1991

Institut National de la Santé et de la Recherche Medicale

WHO Library Cataloguing in Publication Data

Accidents in childhood and adolescence : the role of research /
edited by M. Manciaux & C. J. Romer.

1.Accident prevention 2.Accidents – in adolescence 3.Accidents –
in infancy & childhood 4.Research 5.Wounds and injuries –
in adolescence 6.Wounds and injuries – in infancy & childhood
I.Manciaux, Michel II.Romer, Claude J.

ISBN 92 4 156119 X (WHO)   (NLM Classification: WA 250)
ISBN 2 85598 460 2 (INSERM)

Typeset in India
Printed in England

89/8307—Macmillan/Clays—4500

Contents

Acknowledgements

The editors wish to thank:

- the World Health Organization and the French National Institute of Health and Medical Research (INSERM), co-organizers of a seminar on research and action strategies for accident prevention in children and adolescents, which provided the impetus for the production of this book;
- the authors of the various chapters, who responded with good grace to the requirements of updating and editing;
- Mrs Annie Gudiksen, Injury Prevention Programme, World Health Organization, Geneva, Switzerland;
- Mrs Suzy Mouchet, Mrs Claudine Geynet, and others in the INSERM publications department;
- and especially Mrs Annie Croquin for secretarial help.

Foreword

When the subject of health is mentioned, people generally think first of all of the prevention and cure of diseases. However, the World Health Organization holds that health is not just the absence of disease but a state of complete physical, mental and social well-being. In this context, we do not always attach as much importance as we should to the close link between disease and infirmity.

The slogan "health for all by the year 2000" encapsulates WHO's vigorous efforts to stimulate all countries to make substantial efforts to improve human health by the end of this century. While we realize that we shall by no means have vanquished all diseases by the year 2000, there are grounds for greater optimism about the second kind of health impairment, i.e. infirmity or disability. In contrast to the situation with many diseases, we already possess the theoretical means to fight disabilities effectively. This applies in particular to disabilities resulting from avoidable accidents, especially accidents to children.

We know a great deal about the circumstances in which such accidents occur, the factors conducive to their occurrence, and the precautions that should be taken to reduce the risk. We know enough about them, in theory at least, to act. But we do not know everything, and above all we do not know exactly *how* we should act for maximum effect. In other words, in this as in many other health fields, it is essential to conduct research, preferably before taking action or, failing that, in close conjunction with action.

Research and action—two words often seen together; one area where research and action are urgently needed is the field of accident studies. What *action* can we take, among the general public, to ensure that the concept of risk is better defined, better understood, dealt with effectively and not just labelled as a bad thing? What can we do to get individuals and communities to pay attention to risks as a matter of course?

On the initiative of WHO, a seminar was held in Paris to stress the need for specific research on accidents, as a basis for further progress in understanding, knowledge and mastery of the problem of accidents among children. I am pleased that the National Institute of Health and Medical Research was able to contribute to the success of that undertaking, which was crucial for making progress towards prevention, undoubtedly the most appealing way of safeguarding health. I thank WHO for giving us this opportunity to display our great interest in the subject. And I thank all the organizers, speakers and listeners who made the seminar so rich in substance and so cordial in atmosphere; the very high quality of the exchanges between participants is sure to bear much fruit in future practice.

Philippe Lazar
Director-General,
French National Institute
of Health and Medical
Research (INSERM)

Preface

This publication is intended to stimulate medical research and public health bodies to take an active interest in a health problem that costs the economy more than cardiovascular diseases or cancer, but which receives only a very tiny portion of the funds allocated to medical research in general. In the United States of America, for example, the amount devoted to research on accidental injuries in 1983 by the National Institutes of Health totalled around US$ 35 million, less than 2% of the total research funds allocated to these Institutes. And although accidents in the USA are responsible for the loss of more years of productive life than cardiovascular diseases and cancers together, federal expenditure on accident research is only one-tenth of the research expenditure on cancer and less than one-fifth of research expenditure on diseases of the circulatory system.

Nevertheless, and contrary to many preconceived ideas, accidents or more precisely their sequelae, like any other health problem, can often be prevented if approached scientifically. There is every reason to believe that an increase in expenditure on accident research to take it well above the present levels, yet still below the amounts devoted to research on cancer and cardiovascular diseases, would lead to a substantial improvement in the situation.

There are a number of factors that give accidents a prominent position among public health problems. Analysis shows that there are few countries where accidents do not appear among the five leading causes of death. In the region of the Americas in particular, accidents are among the five leading causes of death in all countries, whatever their level of development.

The consequences for health are tremendous and greatly under-estimated by the public and even by the top-level decision-makers. Indeed, accidents are a major cause of demands on the health system, whether at the primary health care level or the hospital level. On average in the industrialized countries, and also in many developing countries, one hospital bed in ten is occupied by an accident victim. In the public welfare hospitals in Paris, for example, road accidents, occupational accidents, domestic or sports accidents and suicides or other forms of physical violence are responsible for over 10% of all admissions of children, and injuries represent the third most common cause of admission, immediately after infectious diseases and malformations. Accidents are also responsible for significant mortality among young people; moreover, there is marked excess male mortality from accidents, a characteristic feature that appears right from the first year of life. Finally, accidents are often responsible for severe disability. In the United States of America, for example, almost 80 000 patients are disabled as a result of head injuries each year and will remain disabled for the rest of their lives; similarly, about 6000 new cases of paraplegia or tetraplegia occur each year as a result of injury to the spinal column. Motor vehicle accidents are the leading cause of paraplegia in that country.

Traffic accidents are a major cause of severe injuries in most countries, whether developed or not, and are also the cause showing the most marked tendency to increase, particularly among young people because of accidents involving two-wheeled vehicles. The other major causes, such as drowning, falls, burns and poisoning, show a general downward trend, although their relative importance as causes of death and morbidity varies considerably according to region and country. Children, adolescents and young adults are among the target groups from which accidents take the heaviest toll and this is why WHO considers that action and research in this particular area are so important.

The seminar in Paris was the fourth meeting held since the establishment of the paediatric component of WHO's Injury Prevention Programme. Three previous meetings were held in Ankara, Manila and Havana, leading to the formulation of a master plan for the promotion of epidemiological research in a number of countries, particularly in the WHO Region of the Americas, where Brazil, Chile, Colombia, Cuba and Venezuela have decided to take part in this project. Four countries in the South-East Asia Region—India, Indonesia, Nepal and Sri Lanka—are in the process of joining this group and it is hoped that in the next few years all WHO regions will become involved.

This child/adolescent component of the WHO Programme has two main objectives:

- to promote epidemiological research on accidents to young people, particularly in countries where such research is negligible, in order to collect sufficient information on the nature and extent of the problem to establish prevention policies;
- to evaluate these policies periodically and make the evaluations available to the Member States of WHO so as to provide them with useful information on various national experiences and thus assist them in formulating their own policy and defining their priorities.

These two objectives are included in the general description of WHO's medium-term programme for the periods 1984–1989 and 1990–1994. The "accidents component" of this programme sets out to facilitate the implementation of national policies and strategies aimed at reducing the risks of accidents or minimizing their consequences from the public health viewpoint, by carrying out situation analyses, disseminating information, supporting research on safety technologies, and encouraging the application of techniques of proven efficacy.

This publication relates to the second of the stated objectives, in the particular area of research, and its aim is to contribute to an evaluation of policies for research on accidents among young people, to review the present state of knowledge provided by such research, to define the priority sectors needing a special effort, and to evaluate the application and utilization of such research.

There is a need to define strategies that will assign to accident research a more appropriate dimension, in terms of both quality and quantity, within public health research in general. It is equally important to devise mechanisms for the management of such research so as to give it an essentially multidisciplinary and intersectoral character. Accordingly the collaboration of research bodies such as INSERM can only strengthen the value and impact of WHO's programmes, and such collaboration is both vital and appreciated.

C. J. Romer
Injury Prevention Programme
World Health Organization

Introduction
Accidents in childhood and adolescence: a priority problem worldwide

C. J. ROMER & M. MANCIAUX

The problem

A priority problem

Any problem in public health can be considered a priority problem if it occurs frequently and/or is serious, and is amenable to measures for its treatment or, better still, its prevention.

Accidents are a frequent problem, although our knowledge of their frequency is poor and biased. They have potentially serious consequences in terms of mortality, morbidity and disabling sequelae. But there are real possibilities for treatment and also for prevention. Witness the reduction in mortality from accidents in a number of countries—mainly developed countries—at a time when the risks (in terms of total vehicle mileage, number of toxic substances and drugs on the market, etc.) are increasing year by year. It is not clear what this reduction in accident mortality can be attributed to, and the relative contributions of preventive measures and of improved treatment procedures are difficult to determine with accuracy.

The socioeconomic cost of the problem must also be taken into account when determining priorities. Accidents are expensive, certainly much more expensive than their prevention, even though the cost of prevention is generally greatly underestimated. But a large number of preventive and educational activities have been developed in various parts of the world without ever being evaluated, and it is to be feared that much money has been spent in vain on programmes of doubtful efficacy.

A universal problem

It was long believed, and still is believed by some, that accidents occur only in developed countries, being the price that has to be paid for industrialization, technology, urbanization and motorization. This is not true. In the developing countries, accidents are perhaps just as common, and their consequences are often more serious. The reasons for this are related to:

- living conditions in rural settings, where there are many dangers associated with an ill-controlled and frequently hostile environment;

1

- living conditions in or around vast urban areas with explosive and uncontrolled population growth;
- rapid socioeconomic changes: motorization, introduction of manufactured goods and technology;
- inadequate maintenance of machinery, equipment, roads, vehicles, etc.;
- inadequacy of specialized services (police, health) to take responsibility for, treat, and rehabilitate the injured.

But are accidents really a priority problem for the Third World? The answer depends partly on the level of development of the individual country and the success achieved in the control of other major causes of disease and death in children. Wherever such control is successful, injuries from accidents become a priority: this was the case during the 1970s in the oil-producing developing countries, and the same thing is happening in the countries currently undergoing rapid industrialization; it is better not to delay too long in introducing preventive measures (*1*).

A better-known problem

Our knowledge of the "accident phenomenon" is certainly advancing rapidly, largely because of mortality statistics, national and international. The European Communities, the Organisation for Economic Co-operation and Development, and the World Health Organization have made large contributions, particularly from the epidemiological viewpoint, to this greater awareness and to the resulting progress.

The situation is less satisfactory as regards accident morbidity: the few surveys available come mainly from developed countries and the majority are hospital-based and therefore biased. They are usually descriptive, rarely explanatory and almost never evaluative. Exceptions are a few studies (*1–8*) and several documents arising out of the Global Programme for Accident Prevention set up by WHO in 1978 (*9–12*).

The situation regarding the sequelae of accidental injuries is even worse; for example, it is impossible to tell whether or not the reduction in accident mortality observed in most industrialized countries is accompanied by an increase in sequelae. Yet the reply to this question is of crucial importance.

A particularly important problem in childhood

Accidents are important first of all in terms of *morbidity*; for various reasons (e.g. exposure, inexperience, immaturity, behaviour) they take a heavy toll of young people. Each year, 1 child in 10 suffers an accident for which it is necessary to call upon the health services at some level. This is a source of considerable expenditure.

Accidental injuries are just as worrying in terms of *mortality*; from the age of one year up to adulthood, accidents are the leading cause of death in all the industrialized countries and in a growing number of developing countries. Their importance becomes clear if we look at the indicator, number of potential years of life lost: this is over 665 000 annually in the United States of America as a result of traffic accidents to children and adolescents (*13*).

However, the choice of an indicator is not neutral. This indicator can be made positive by converting it into number of potential years of life gained as a result, for example, of preventive activities; alternatively, it could be extended into expectation of life free of disabilities to take into account the risk of sequelae and the successes in restoration.

A neglected area

The facts

Although a priority problem, accidents remain a neglected area in health policies. They occupy only a small place in national and international programmes, regardless of whether the programmes concern health activities proper or research. WHO itself only recently took an interest in accident prevention and management, while at INSERM there is very little research on this crucial problem. Many other similar examples could be given.

The same comment applies to training. According to an unpublished survey by the International Paediatric Association, there is scarcely any teaching on accidents in medical faculties and schools for allied health personnel, and what teaching there is practically always concentrates on the nature of the consequences of an accident (traumatology) and rarely on the epidemiological and preventive aspects.

Why is this?

There are many reasons for this:

- Many factors are involved in accidents and it is difficult to master all the aspects.
- There is widespread confusion in people's minds between the accident (event) and the injuries that result from it (consequence).

3

The people who observe the event and its circumstances are not the people who observe the consequences (injuries). There is a lack of tie-ups and coordination between people, services, record systems, etc.

- Follow-up studies are difficult to conduct. As a result there is a lack of reliable data on the medium-term and long-term consequences of accidents.
- There may also be psychological reasons arising out of a genuine ambivalence that is undoubtedly very widespread. Faced with the risk of accident everyone feels threatened and vulnerable; so it is better not to think about it and not to talk about it, so as not to tempt fate. Does the well-known individual reflex "accidents only happen to other people" exist at the collective level? At all events, conflicting interests operate at this level (the cost of safety, the motives of motor car manufacturers and advertisers). This may account for a kind of "law of silence" regarding this scourge of modern times.

Pointers to solutions

General

Better information—objective and not giving rise to anxiety—concerning accident risks and the available preventive measures is a prerequisite for creating the individual and collective awareness essential for any action.

Research on accident epidemiology, on the factors—environmental and psychosocial—involved, and on the means of prevention should make it easier to decide what measures need to be taken. These measures include preventive programmes that combine education, safety techniques and regulations, and which need to be evaluated. Just as important, however, is the formulation of a policy that combines all these activities in an integrated approach (including primary health care).

In a word, everything that can advance knowledge of the danger of accidents and help to develop attitudes and behaviour that will bring the risk under control should be encouraged from early childhood.

This is the context in which this book has been written, the outcome of several years' work by the WHO Global Programme for Accident Prevention (later the Injury Prevention Programme) and by a number of experts from France (particularly INSERM) and other countries.

This publication is concerned with the age group 1–19 years. These arbitrarily selected limits make it possible to eliminate:

– at the lower end of the age range, incorrect diagnoses of non-accidental injuries and cot deaths;
– at the upper end of the range, occupational accidents which raise different problems, though there are confounding factors, particularly some overlapping of age. However, the problem of suicides remains unsolved, especially in adolescence, and the borderline between suicide and accident is not always clear.

The book deals with three different but complementary approaches:

– the epidemiological approach, which specifies the available data in terms of mortality, morbidity, sequelae of accidental injuries and the methodological problems presented by collection and processing of the data;
– the psychosociological approach, which attempts to catalogue the psychological and social factors, whether endogenous or exogenous, conducive or decisive, that play a role in the origin of accidental injuries. The relationship of these factors with the child's level of development is a particularly interesting topic for study and can be used to guide preventive measures;
– the technological approach, obviously with different considerations for industrialized countries and developing countries.

In Part IV these sectoral approaches are integrated into activities for prevention (planning and evaluation), teaching and research.
An attempt is made in the conclusion to point to possible future directions for the policies of countries that wish to take steps to counter the dangers and consequences of accidents.

References

1. Accidents in children and young people. *World health statistics quarterly*, **39**(3): 226–284 (1986).
2. BAKER, S. P. *The injury control fact book*. Lexington, MA, Lexington Books, 1984.
3. BERGER, L. R. Childhood injuries: recognition and prevention. *Current problems of pediatrics*, **12**: 1–59 (1981).
4. CENTER FOR ENVIRONMENTAL HEALTH. *Injury control surveys*. Atlanta, GA, Centers for Disease Control, 1983.
5. MANCIAUX, M. & ROMER, C. J. Prevention of accidental injuries in childhood and adolescence. *Bulletin of the International Pediatric Association*, **6**: 243–249 (1985).
6. ROBERTSON, L. S. *Injuries: causes, control strategies, and public policy*. Lexington, MA, Lexington Books, 1983.

7. WALLER, J. A. *Injury control: a guide to the causes and prevention of trauma.* Lexington, MA, Lexington Books, 1985.
8. *Principles for injury prevention in developing countries.* WHO unpublished document, IPR/ADR 217–40.[a]
9. *Study group on assessment of country surveys on accidents in childhood, Ankara, 1982.* Unpublished WHO document, IPR/APR 216–21.[a]
10. *Symposium on accident prevention in childhood, Manila, 1983.* Unpublished WHO document, IPR/APR 218–22.[a]
11. *Programme development in child and adolescent safety.* Unpublished WHO document, IRP/APR 21 m 24H.[a]
12. *Report on accident and injury prevention at the primary health care level, Pattaya, Thailand, 1987.* Unpublished WHO document, IRP/APR 218 H.[a]
13. CHRISTOPHERSEN, E. R. Automobile accidents—potential years of life lost. *Pediatrics,* **71**: 855–856 (1983).

---

[a] A limited number of copies of this document are available from: Injury Prevention Programme, World Health Organization, 1211 Geneva 27, Switzerland.

PART I
THE EPIDEMIOLOGICAL APPROACH

Chapter 1
Mortality and morbidity: the available data and their limitations

A. R. TAKET, M. MANCIAUX & C. J. ROMER

Introduction

The purpose of this chapter is to review the available international data on accident mortality and morbidity with regard to the current situation and trends for young people. The emphasis will be on what can be learnt from the existing sources of data and statistics about the size of the problem posed by death and injury resulting from accidents to young people internationally. This will be illustrated by an examination of figures relating to the current situation and past trends for the countries in Europe and the Organisation for Economic Co-operation and Development (OECD); where possible these will be compared with those available for countries outside Europe and the OECD (1–3). No attempt will be made to address in detail the problems associated with the different stages of data collection and their use; these are the subject of Chapter 3. However, the various limitations on the reliability of data and the difficulty of interpreting statistics will be discussed as and when necessary to illustrate the potential problems.

First, the major sources of data on mortality and morbidity will be briefly reviewed and some of the main deficiencies and shortcomings in them outlined. Some general questions related to the need for better information on morbidity and its importance, particularly in developed countries, will also be discussed, and the major problems encountered in using and interpreting the data reviewed.

Then, the available data on mortality resulting from accidents are used to describe the current situation and historical trends. This section illustrates the importance of accidents as a major cause of mortality in young people in both developed and developing countries. The major causes of accidents are discussed, and trends in the absolute level of mortality from each cause and their relative contribution to the total accident mortality rates explored for countries in different regions. The use of mortality data to calculate indicators such as "potential years of life lost" is also illustrated, use being made of data for several countries.

The problems associated with the non-availability of adequate morbidity data are well illustrated in the third section, where the use of some morbidity data is considered and the need to take into account the links between mortality and morbidity is demonstrated.

The final section highlights some major conclusions and summarizes the needs for priority action in relation to the availability and use of data on accident mortality and morbidity.

Data sources and methodological problems

Mortality

Statistics on mortality resulting from accidents are available in detail (by different age groups and sex) for most causes of accidents in most of the developed countries and an increasing number of the developing countries, based on information collected by WHO. This is the source of the mortality information used in this chapter. The data are provided under the E code (external cause of injury) of the ninth revision of the *International Classification of Diseases* (ICD-9) (*1*); only a very few countries also provide information under Chapter XVII of the ICD ("Injury and poisoning"). This is unfortunate and limits severely the use that can be made of the data, as the distinction between the accident and the resulting injury is important and would yield useful information in both a research and a programme planning context (*2*).

When international comparisons are being made, however, it is important to bear in mind the variation in coverage, accuracy and coding practice from one place to another. This can cause particular problems with the interpretation of time trends, as all these factors may vary with time. A problem worthy of specific mention is the overlap—of uncertain extent—between codings for accidents and those for violence or suicide, which is particularly relevant where international comparisons are being attempted. Other methodological problems include:

- the distinction between accidents and injuries;
- the distinction between accidental and non-accidental injuries;
- the necessity of using both Chapter XVII and the E code of the ICD when reporting accidental deaths; and
- the possible use of lay reporting systems in countries that are poorly equipped from a statistical point of view.

These have been dealt with in WHO reports (*2, 3*) and will not be dealt with in detail here. It should be noted that, although problems exist, they may be no more serious overall than for many other kinds of health-related statistics; furthermore, an increased use of such data can only be a stimulus to their improvement. As a result, although there are considerable differences in the quality of the registration and processing of accident data in the various countries, comparisons are nevertheless possible.

The statistical analysis of causes of death can provide only incomplete information. Unlike the analysis of morbidity it does not examine the most frequent and—judged by their weighting—most important diseases, but only those characterized by their fatal outcome. The consideration of fatal accidents is, none the less, a first and essential step in the analysis of the whole problem and may point the way to suitable preventive action.

Morbidity

As far as data on morbidity resulting from accidents are concerned, the situation is far less satisfactory. A permanent system for the registration of accidents is out of reach in most countries, even the industrialized ones. Another possibility, the registration of injuries, is a complicated process, which must remain highly questionable on grounds of cost-efficiency. However, it is possible that limited registration procedures might meet the needs of researchers and health planners. These could involve the use of retrospective household surveys, or be based on a sample of the population, or on a network of practitioners, health centres or hospitals. Routinely collected statistics related to spells in hospital provide a potential source of information in many countries, provided that it is possible to establish that the admission is related to an accident. However, most of the existing sources of information on morbidity are inadequate for assessing the long-term morbidity or disability (either temporary or permanent) resulting from accidents. The exceptions to this are the very few specially designed studies; however, these tend to be very limited in terms of the population covered. Further discussion of the relevant issues can be found in Chapters 3 and 4.

Some limited information is, however, available internationally, namely the data on numbers of injuries and deaths from traffic accidents collected by the Economic Commission for Europe (4). While the information on mortality is often not strictly comparable with that supplied to WHO, these data constitute one of the best international sources for examining trends in mortality and morbidity related to one of the most important causes of accidents in the industrialized countries.

In the consideration of data on morbidity, it is of course necessary to distinguish between incidence and prevalence. For most purposes, when considering morbidity, it is also desirable to have an indication of its scale. It is for this reason that many approaches have been adopted to the problem of severity scales for injuries; these are covered in greater depth in Chapter 16. In connection with morbidity, data on levels of exposure to relevant risks and changes in them are obviously desirable, but are even less frequently available in practice; this issue is also discussed in greater detail in Chapter 16.

It is not proposed here to review in detail the potential problems associated with the different sources of data and their use. It is useful, however, before examining the data, to summarize the major potential problems involved in making international comparisons and interpreting trends, of which the first is the question of the accuracy and coverage of the reporting system. This is likely to be a particular problem with information from developing countries, the associated dangers including the misinterpretation of increasing trends in accident mortality (or morbidity); these may, in fact, be the result of an increase in the accuracy or coverage of the reporting system. The interpretation of trends can also cause problems if reporting practices vary during the period under study. Care must also be taken to avoid drawing conclusions from trends in rates based on very small numbers of deaths.

Finally, and most importantly, there are the changes in external factors that have taken place over the period concerned. This is best illustrated by means of an example. In order to interpret trends in mortality from motor vehicle accidents, factors including the introduction of laws regarding speed limits and wearing of seat-belts, the growth and extent of motorization, in terms not only of the number of vehicles but also of the numbers of kilometres travelled, and the road and transport network, should all be considered.

In any consideration of data, the purpose for which the information was collected must be borne in mind in determining whether its use in a different context is justified. This purpose will influence both the mechanisms and the definitions that should be used. In this connection it is useful to think in terms of three different purposes for which data may be required; while these by no means cover all the purposes of data collection, they are the most relevant in this context. Thus data may be required: (1) to determine the nature and extent of a particular problem and how it is changing with time and place; (2) for surveillance purposes and the identification of new risks; and (3) for the evaluation of intervention or prevention programmes or actions carried out with the aim of affecting the problem. In the remainder of this chapter we shall be mainly concerned with using data collected for the first of these purposes so as to demonstrate the importance of accidents to young people as a priority problem for action in the health and other sectors.

Accident mortality

Introduction

Previous reviews of the situation with regard to mortality due to accidents include the reports by Marcusson & Oehmisch (5) and Havard (6). Of these, the first provided figures for 50 countries (including 17 developing ones), for periods between 1955 and 1971, for children aged up to 14; the second was concerned with motor vehicle accidents in the 15–24-year age group using data obtained between 1950 and 1976. The present chapter draws on a study which updates and expands these basic analyses (7, 8); mortality from accidents due to different causes is examined for age groups up to the age of 19 years.

The data presented relate to 59 countries, i.e., all the countries for which some reliable information was available. Of these, 27 are in Europe, 5 are OECD countries outside Europe, and most of the remaining 27 are Latin American. Owing to differences in the availability of data from different countries, some of the analyses shown are based on a subsample of these countries. The E classification of external causes of injury and poisoning of the ninth revision of the *International Classification of Diseases* (1) has been used.

In order to examine recent trends, figures for 1981, which are available for most countries, are examined and compared with the corresponding figures for 1971. Changes with time, as well as differences between countries and regions, are thus explored. The analysis is performed separately for eight different age/sex groups, the age groups used being 1–4, 5–9, 10–14 and 15–19 years; for some aspects, the age groups 5–9 and 10–14 years are combined in order to reduce the amount of detail given.

A further analysis of detailed time trends using the full information available for each country was also performed (8). This involved applying various regression models to the data. On the basis of the results obtained, countries were classified according to the pattern of development of mortality due to accidental injuries. For reasons of space, the full results of this analysis cannot be reported here; however, an outline of the results for two major causes of accidental death, namely motor vehicle accidents and drowning, is given.

Importance of accidents as a cause of death in young people

For each country and each age/sex group, the five leading causes of death were ranked and changes in this ranking over time examined. This way of presenting the figures is of particular interest for policy-makers, since it enables the priority problems and their evolution in a particular country or group of countries to be identified.

Table 1.1 presents information on the average ranking of accidents among the five leading causes of death over the period 1977–1981, while Table 1.2 shows trends in the ranking of accidents in the five leading causes of death. Details of rankings for particular countries are not shown here because of lack of space. When these are examined, however, it can be seen that, on average, the ranking of accidents is higher in developed than in developing countries.

From Table 1.2 it can be seen that accidents are among the five leading causes of death for every country in each of the age/sex groups considered. The number of countries where accidents are ranked first is higher than the number at any other ranking except in the case of females aged 1–4 and 10–14 years. Table 1.1 also shows that accidents rank higher as a cause of death for males than for females. Finally, it is interesting to note that, for males, the 15–19-year age group is the one for which the highest number of countries is ranked 1, while for females it is the 5–9-year age group.

In Table 1.2, the most noticeable feature is how few of the countries exhibited a decrease in the ranking of accidents over the periods considered; on average this occurs slightly more often for females than for males. Finally it can be observed that, for each age group except 1–4 years, the ranking for accidents as a leading cause of death increased in more countries for females than for males.

Accidental deaths as a percentage of total deaths

Another way of examining the importance of accidents as a cause of death in young people is to look at the percentage of all deaths due to accidents. Table 1.3 shows the percentage of all deaths due to accidents in different age ranges in 1971 and 1981 for various countries. From this it can be seen that, on average, the developed countries have a higher percentage of all deaths due to accidents than do the developing countries. The OECD countries outside Europe typically lie towards the upper end of the distribution in most age groups. The table also shows that, in the higher age groups, more countries have a high percentage of deaths due to accidents in most cases. Distributions for males and females are fairly similar for the 1–4-year age group, but not for the others. The distribution did not change much between 1971 and 1981, although large changes occurred in a few countries.

The figures for accidental deaths as a percentage of all deaths are higher for males than for females in each age group for a large majority of countries. With some exceptions, countries with low values for

Table 1.1. Ranking of accidents among the five leading causes of death in 58 countries, 1977–1981 (or latest period for which data are available)

Rank	Males					Females				
	1–4	5–9	10–14	15–19	20–24	1–4	5–9	10–14	15–19	20–24
1	29	41	41	48	43	12	35	22	31	24
2	12	9	14	7	9	21	13	26	16	19
3	2	4	2	2	5	8	5	8	5	8
4	15	3	1	1	1	17	4	2	5	3
5	0	1	0	0	0	0	1	0	1	3
Greater than 5	0	0	0	0	0	0	0	0	0	1

Source: 7.

Table 1.2. Trends in importance of accidents among the five leading causes of death in 58 countries, from 1957–1961 to 1977–1981

Trend	Males					Females				
	1–4	5–9	10–14	15–19	20–24	1–4	5–9	10–14	15–19	20–24
Increasing importance	26	15	11	11	8	22	26	28	25	32
Constant importance	28	37	39	41	39	27	24	19	24	18
Decreasing importance	1	3	4	3	7	6	5	7	6	4
Insufficient data to assess trend	3	3	4	3	4	3	3	4	3	4

Source: 7.

Table 1.3. Distribution of accidents as a percentage of all deaths for 1971 and 1981 (or nearest available years) by country, age and sex group

Age, sex, and country groups	1971 Number of countries with accidents as a percentage of all deaths in the range:				1981 Number of countries with accidents as a percentage of all deaths in the range:				Total number of countries
	0–20%	20–39%	40–59%	60–79%	0–20%	20–39%	40–59%	60–79%	
Males, 1–4 years									
Europe	2	14	3	0	0	17	2	0	19
Other developed and industrialized countries	0	2	3	0	0	0	5	0	5
Middle-income developing countries	13	1	0	0	11	3	0	0	14
Females, 1–4 years									
Europe	5	12	0	0	2	15	0	0	17
Other developed and industrialized countries	0	5	0	0	0	3	2	0	5
Middle-income developing countries	11	0	0	0	10	1	0	0	11
Males, 5–9 years									
Europe	0	2	19	2	0	4	18	1	23
Other developed and industrialized countries	0	0	4	1	0	0	4	1	5
Middle-income developing countries	9	3	0	0	8	4	0	0	12
Females, 5–9 years									
Europe	1	8	7	0	0	12	4	0	16
Other developed and industrialized countries	0	2	2	0	0	1	3	0	4
Middle-income developing countries	9	2	0	0	10	1	0	0	11
Males, 10–14 years									
Europe	0	5	16	1	0	4	17	1	22

Other developed and industrialized countries	0	1	3	1	0	2	2	1	5
Middle-income developing countries	5	7	3	0	6	4	5	0	15
Females, 10–14 years Europe	1	11	3	0	0	13	2	0	15
Other developed and industrialized countries	1	2	1	0	1	0	3	0	4
Middle-income developing countries	10	0	0	0	9	0	1	0	10
Males, 15–19 years Europe	0	0	9	15	0	0	16	8	24
Other developed and industrialized countries	0	0	1	4	0	0	1	4	5
Middle-income developing countries	4	10	4	0	4	8	5	1	18
Females, 15–19 years Europe	1	11	8	0	0	13	7	0	20
Other developed and industrialized countries	0	1	4	0	0	1	3	1	5
Middle-income developing countries	9	1	0	0	8	1	0	1	10
Males, 20–24 years Europe	0	0	17	7	0	1	20	3	24
Other developed and industrialized countries	0	0	2	3	0	0	3	2	5
Middle-income developing countries	2	9	7	1	3	8	6	2	19
Females, 20–24 years Europe	4	12	3	0	1	16	2	0	19
Other developed and industrialized countries	1	3	1	0	1	2	2	0	5
Middle-income developing countries	8	1	0	1	8	1	0	1	10

Note: For each age and sex group only those countries with more than 20 deaths in the relevant years were included in the analysis.

Source: 7.

deaths due to accidents as a percentage of all deaths also have low accident mortality rates and higher than average total mortality rates; they are generally developing countries. Conversely, many of the countries with the highest figures for deaths due to accidents as a percentage of all deaths are those with accident mortality rates above average and below average total mortality rates; these countries are mainly industrialized. These features were also found in an analysis carried out by Marcusson & Oehmisch for children aged under 14 (5).

Yet another way of examining the importance of accidents as a cause of death in young people, namely in terms of the potential years of life lost, is considered later in this chapter.

The results discussed above clearly demonstrate the importance of accidental injuries as a leading cause of death in children and young adults in most countries of the world. This shows the importance of this issue for health planning as well as for preventive programmes.

Accident mortality rates by cause of accident and region

In this section, accident mortality rates and trends are considered for six regions of the world. The regions chosen for the analysis are based on the WHO regions, subdivided where possible to take account of countries at very different stages of development. In order to reduce the bulk of information presented here, the number of age groups considered has been reduced from four to three by combining the 5–9

Fig.1.1. Accident mortality per 100 000 boys aged 1–4.

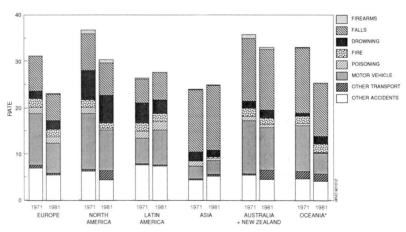

* Excluding Australia and New Zealand.

and 10–14 groups. Fig. 1.1–1.6 present this information graphically and also show for comparison the corresponding information for 1971. The following features may be noted in the information shown for 1981. Accident rates among males are higher than those for females for

Fig.1.2. Accident mortality per 100 000 boys aged 5–14.

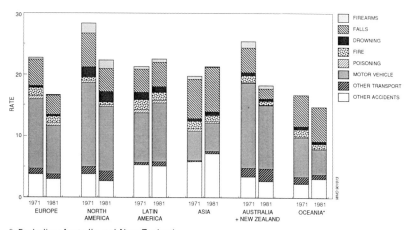

* Excluding Australia and New Zealand.

Fig.1.3. Accident mortality per 100 000 boys aged 15–19.

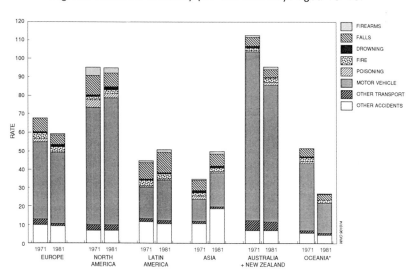

* Excluding Australia and New Zealand.

Fig.1.4. Accident mortality per 100 000 girls aged 1–4.

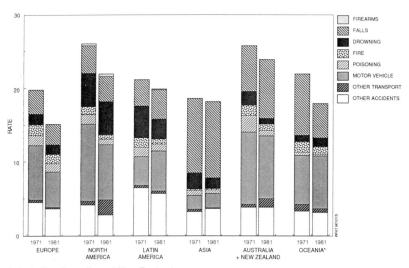

* Excluding Australia and New Zealand.

Fig.1.5. Accident mortality per 100 000 girls aged 5–14.

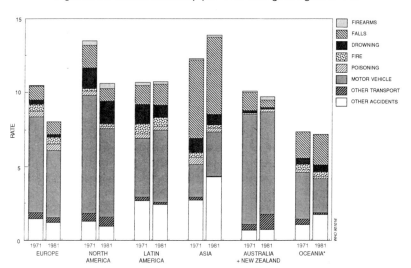

* Excluding Australia and New Zealand.

Fig.1.6. Accident mortality per 100 000 girls aged 15–19.

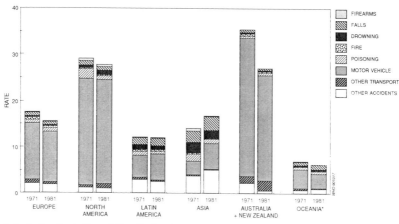

* Excluding Australia and New Zealand.

most regions and causes of death, the only striking exception to this being the rates for deaths caused by fire, where in Asia for the 5–14 and 15–19-year age groups the rates for females are noticeably higher than the corresponding figures for males. The major causes of accidental death are motor vehicle accidents, drowning and "other accidents". In the 15–19-year age group, motor vehicle accidents constitute the largest percentage of fatal accidents in both sexes and all regions, accounting for between 33.2% and 84.8% of all fatal accidents. For those aged 5–14, motor vehicle accidents are the main cause of accidental death, except in Asia and for males in Oceania (other than Australia and New Zealand), where drowning is the leading cause. For the age group 1–4 years, motor vehicle accidents are the leading cause of accidental death in Europe and North America for both sexes and in Australia and New Zealand for females (these are the regions with the highest concentration of highly industrialized countries); in the remaining regions, drowning is the leading cause (with the exception of Latin America, where the category "other accidents" is the largest).

For deaths due to motor vehicle accidents in all regions, the rate for those aged 15–19 is higher than that for any younger age group for both males and females. The differences between regions in which developed countries predominate and those in which developing ones are in the majority increase with increase in age.

Rates for deaths caused by fire are highest for the 1–4-year age group for males in all regions; for females, the rate is highest for the age group

1–4 in each region except Asia, where the rate for the 15–19 group is highest.

For accidental deaths due to drowning, the highest rates for females are found in the 1–4-year age group in all regions; for males, the highest rates are also in the 1–4-year age group, except in the two American regions, where the 15–19 year age group has the highest rate.

If the trends over the period 1971–1981 are considered, it can be seen that the total accident mortality rate for males decreased in four of the regions (Europe, North America, Australia and New Zealand, and Oceania) in each of the three age groups. Increases occurred among males for each age group in the other two regions (Latin America and Asia); both of these regions consist mainly of developing countries. For females, decreases occurred for each age group in five of the regions (Europe, North America, Latin America, Australia and New Zealand, and Oceania). In Asia, the rate decreased for females aged 1–4 but increased for the other two age groups. In the case of deaths due to motor vehicle accidents, rates decreased in the majority of cases, with the exception of most age/sex groups in Latin America and Asia and males aged 15–19 in North America. For deaths due to drowning, decreasing rates are observed in general, with the major exceptions of Asia and Latin America, where increasing trends are observed for most age groups.

Trends for individual countries

When figures for accident mortality rates in individual countries are examined, it is found that rates have fallen over the period 1971–1981 in the majority of countries in all age/sex groups (7). However, the range of rates observed is still very wide. In 1981, accident mortality rates for males lay between 6.9 per 100 000 (Japan, age group 10–14 years) and 104.5 per 100 000 (Austria, age group 15–19 years), while for females they lay between 2.2 (Japan, age group 10–14 years) and 67.7 per 100 000 (Cuba, age group 15–19 years). Most of the countries for which an increase in rates from 1971 to 1981 is observed are those with lower than average rates in both 1971 and 1981, the majority being developing countries; this observed increase may of course be due either entirely or in part to improvements in the registration of deaths in these countries. Examination of the ranking of countries in 1971 and 1981 showed that the relative position of countries with respect to their accident mortality rates did not change significantly during the intervening period. A strong association between male and female rates for the same age group was also found, the strength of the relationship decreasing with increasing age. For both sexes there is also a strong association between rates for age groups 1–4 and 5–14 years. No such relationship was found between the rates for the under-15 age groups and for those aged over 15.

For all age groups in all countries (except Guatemala, ages 1–4 and Egypt, ages 15–19), the total accident mortality rate for females is lower than the corresponding figure for males; the differences between the sexes become larger with increasing age. For both males and females, rates for the 1–4-year age group are greater than those for the 5–9-year age group in the large majority of countries. For females only, the rates for those aged 5–9 years are greater than the corresponding rates for those aged 10–14 in the majority of countries. Rates for males aged 10–14 are lower than those for males aged 15–19 in all countries; the same is true for females in every country except Chile. The percentage increases in rates in going from the 10–14 to the 15–19 age group are generally larger in the more highly developed countries.

Potential years of life lost due to accidents

Another way of emphasizing the importance of accidents as a cause of death in young people is through the use of the potential years of life lost (*8*, *9*, *10*) as an indicator. This is calculated for a broad age group, such as 1–19 years, by taking the total of the number of deaths in each of the constituent age bands (in this case, 1–4, 5–9, 10–14 and 15–19 years) multiplied by the difference between 65 years and the age at the midpoint of each age band. The choice of 65 is arbitrary to some extent, but has been chosen here because, in many countries, it is the age of retirement and the end of economically active life. It is, of course, possible to tailor the upper and lower limits used in the calculation to suit the situation and the purpose for which the figures produced are to be used.

Another related indicator which is of particular interest is the potential gain in life expectancy free of disability. This is a measure of the theoretical gain in life expectancy that could be obtained by eliminating deaths and disabilities from a given cause. Where it is wished to compare countries with very different mortality charac-teristics in the 0–4 age group, the indicator may be calculated as potential gain in life expectancy free of disability at 5 years of age. This indicator is of special interest when applied to accidents affecting young people. However, it is impossible to use it correctly where there is insufficient information; this must be obtained through long-term follow-up studies on the extent of disabilities resulting from accidental injuries.

Table 1.4 shows some illustrative figures for potential years of life lost for young people aged 1–24 in 1971 and 1981 for selected countries. Figures have been calculated both for accidental deaths and for all deaths; the percentage of the potential years of life lost from all causes of death attributable to deaths resulting from accidents is also shown. The countries shown in the table have been chosen to illustrate typical patterns found in Europe, other OECD countries and developing countries.

For young people aged 1–24, the potential years of life lost (PYLL) due to all causes decreased over the period 1971–1981 for all the countries shown in Table 1.4, except Cuba. The PYLL due to accidents declined in ten countries and increased in five (Costa Rica, Cuba, Mexico, Spain and Thailand) during this period. It is interesting to note that four of these five countries are outside the OECD. The PYLL due to accidents as a percentage of the PYLL due to all causes increased in 10 of the 15 countries during the period concerned, indicating that action to reduce mortality from accidents among young people should be given higher priority in those countries. In four countries, the PYLL due to accidents as a percentage of the PYLL due to all causes for young people aged 1–24 decreased. In two of these, Norway and Sweden, this decrease may well be the result of accident prevention programmes.

Also of interest is the relative size of the PYLL due to accidents for young people compared to that for all people aged under 65. This clearly shows the importance of action aimed at preventing accidents in young people. In 1981, for the countries shown in Table 1.4, the PYLL due to accidents for young people aged 1–24 as a percentage of that for people aged 1–65 lay between 32% (Sweden) and 66% (Egypt). This percentage is generally highest in countries outside Europe and the OECD. Significant decreases in the figure during the period 1971–1981 were observed in several countries, namely Canada, Cuba, Mexico, Norway, Sweden, Thailand and the United States of America.

Accident morbidity

An important question which is often raised in connection with the observed decreases in accident mortality rates in many countries, is whether they are accompanied by corresponding increases in morbidity resulting from accidents and, in particular, in morbidity resulting in long-term or permanent disability. If this were indeed so, it would have important and far-reaching consequences, both in general and for the provision of health services in particular. The most satisfactory way of examining this question is no doubt through detailed population

Table 1.4. Potential years of life lost (PYLL) 1971 and 1981 (or nearest available years) for selected countries due to accidents and to all deaths in young people aged 1–24 and to accidents in people aged 1–65

Country	PYLL due to accidents for people aged 1–24		PYLL due to all deaths for people aged 1–24		PYLL due to accidents as a percentage of total PYLL for people aged 1–24		PYLL due to accidents for people aged 1–65	
	1971	1981	1971	1981	1971	1981	1971	1981
Europe								
Austria	60 000	46 000	115 000	92 000	52	50	103 000	77 000
Belgium	61 000	53 000	127 000	104 000	48	51	104 000	90 000
Federal Republic of Germany	440 000	287 000	883 000	600 000	50	48	708 000	446 000
Norway	24 000	14 000	46 000	33 000	52	42	37 000	24 000
Spain	137 000	178 000	473 000	427 000	29	42	262 000	304 000
Sweden	30 000	18 000	72 000	48 000	42	39	54 000	37 000
Other developed countries								
Australia	119 000	108 000	223 000	184 000	53	59	173 000	163 000
Canada	212 000	175 000	382 000	315 000	55	56	318 000	274 000
Japan	637 000	336 000	1 535 000	881 000	41	38	1 037 000	576 000
United States of America	1 824 000	1 713 000	3 722 000	3 290 000	49	52	2 762 000	2 679 000
Middle-income developing countries								
Costa Rica	14 000	17 000	94 000	52 000	15	33	22 000	27 000
Cuba	62 000	93 000	176 000	197 000	35	47	85 000	156 000
Egypt	407 000	237 000	7 226 000	6 463 000	6	4	529 000	304 000
Mexico	248 000	507 000	5 727 000	4 654 000	4	11	340 000	742 000
Thailand	244 000	370 000	3 060 000	2 404 000	8	15	329 000	555 000

Note: All figures for PYLL given to nearest 1 000 years.

surveys, which would have to be specially organized; in the absence of such surveys in most countries, the possibility of using the aggregate data that are available in a wide range of countries can be considered. It has already been mentioned that the available data are, in general, inadequate for a detailed examination of this question. In this section, however, we attempt to illustrate the type of analysis that could, and indeed should, be carried out to examine this most important issue.

Table 1.5 presents a summary of trends in traffic accident mortality and morbidity in 17 countries during the period 1970–1982, taken from Council of Europe and Economic Commission for Europe sources. During this period, decreases in mortality were seen in 15 countries, of which ten (Austria, Belgium, Denmark, Federal Republic of Germany, Finland, Ireland, Italy, Netherlands, Sweden and Switzerland) also showed a decline in morbidity. The other five countries (Canada,

Table 1.5. Trends in traffic accident mortality and morbidity during the period 1970 to 1982 for selected countries

Country	Age group (years)	Period	% change over period in:	
			injuries	deaths
Austria	0–14	1970–82	−31.9	−60.4
Belgium	0–14	1970–82	−32.8	−8.9
Canada	0–19	1971–77	+12.3	−6.6
Denmark	0–14	1970–82	−52.5	−66.9
Finland	0–19	1971–78	−53.0	−35.2
France	0–19	1971–78	+11.0	−10.7
Federal Republic of Germany	0–14	1970–82	−26.8	−66.5
Greece	0–14	1970–82	+15.0	+34.5
Hungary	0–14	1970–82	+17.3	−25.6
Ireland	0–14	1970–82	−28.0	−6.8
Italy	0–14	1970–81	−17.4	−40.0
Netherlands	0–14	1970–82	−21.6	−62.1
Portugal	0–24	1971–78	+15.2	+32.3
Spain	0–14	1970–82	+12.2	−24.2
Sweden	0–14	1970–82	−22.3	−60.9
Switzerland	0–14	1970–82	−32.8	−61.1
United Kingdom	0–19	1971–78	+1.6	−5.8

Sources: *4, 12.*

France, Hungary, Spain and the United Kingdom) showed an increase in accident morbidity. In Greece and Portugal there were increases in both mortality and morbidity.

While the figures shown in the table are interesting, they do not conclusively prove or disprove an inverse association between mortality and morbidity. They do, however, illustrate the need for further examination of this issue. It would be possible to refine the analysis by examining data for males and females separately for smaller age groups and correcting for any change in the size of the population groups over time. This would be desirable, since the age groups used here are large and data for both sexes are combined, whereas it is widely accepted that patterns of, and trends in, accident mortality and morbidity vary considerably from one age/sex group to another (7, 11). It would also be advantageous to use a full time series of data rather than just the beginning and end points of a particular period.

Clearly a more sophisticated examination of the relationship between mortality and morbidity over time is required. One suitable starting point might be hospital admissions data. In some countries, these data identify admissions resulting from accidents (for example, the Hospital Inpatient Enquiry System in England and Wales), and most include information on outcome and, in particular, on whether the patient died in hospital or was discharged. This type of information would enable a more detailed analysis to be carried out for different age/sex groups and types of accident.

Discussion and conclusions

The analyses of accident mortality in children, adolescents and young adults reported here have clearly shown the importance of accident injuries as a leading cause of death in most countries in the world. As a basis for the discussion of health planning, the design of preventive programmes and the consideration of priorities for research, it is useful to consider here the major points to emerge from the analyses and to consider how the conclusions that can be drawn relate to those drawn from earlier studies.

The analysis of the rank of accidents as a cause of death showed very few countries where accidents were not among the leading five causes; this confirmed the results suggested by an earlier study (13), which was confined to only 15 countries. In addition, trends in the ranking of accidents as a cause of death were also examined, and very few cases found where accidents were declining in importance as a cause of death.

The decline in total accident mortality rates between 1971 and 1981 in the majority of countries for all the age/sex groups considered here is of considerable importance. With some exceptions, this pattern is also found for the different causes of accidental death. Motor vehicle accidents constitute one of the single most important causes of accidental death, and for this reason the picture that emerges from the current analysis is more encouraging than that found by previous studies. In a study of children aged up to 14 years, Marcusson & Oehmisch (5) reported an increase in mortality rates in most age/sex groups from motor vehicle and other traffic accidents over the period studied. For the 15–24-year age group, Havard (6) reported an increase in motor vehicle accident mortality rates for both sexes in all the countries studied. In the analysis reported here, which includes more recent data, decreasing mortality rates from motor vehicle accidents are apparent in just under half the series studied, whereas increases are found in only about one-fifth of all cases. However, no data are available that would allow the reliable estimation of the respective effects of preventive measures and of improvements in the care and treatment of the injured in the decline of mortality.

It is clear that, for health planners, neither the absolute number of accidental deaths nor their crude rate is sufficient as a measure of the importance of accident mortality or of changes over time. The relative figures, represented by accidental deaths as a percentage of all deaths, and by the ranking of accidental death as a cause of mortality, have also to be taken into consideration in establishing priorities. The evaluation of these variables over the years puts accidental deaths in the front line in almost all age/sex groups and in most of the countries studied in this report. Using the potential years of life lost as an indicator further emphasizes the importance of this cause of death and underlines its major socioeconomic consequences, since children, adolescents and young adults are particularly likely to die as a result of accidents.

However, in countries with constant or slightly decreasing rates, changes in mortality are no longer adequate to represent the situation and to permit the evaluation, for instance, of the effectiveness of specific countermeasures. Other indicators based on morbidity data have to be used and, as discussed earlier, the improvement of data on morbidity due to accidents remains a clear priority.

Some follow-up surveys are also needed in order to document the problem of long-term and permanent disabilities resulting from accidental injuries. For the time being, "no health system appears to be capable of calculating the impact of accidents . . . on overall disability figures in a given community" (11). This latter point should be taken into consideration in any attempt to estimate the socioeconomic cost of accidents, and the indicator "survival without sequelae" should be extensively used in accident statistics. Indicators that may prove useful in this context include measures of social disability, school absenteeism, duration of hospitalization, life expectancy, and life expectancy free of disability at appropriate ages. The calculation of many of these indicators will be possible only by the use of data from different sources, linked together for a common purpose. The integration of existing information systems in this way must be given a high priority. The calculation of other indicators will depend in many places on new, but important items of information being added to those collected by existing information systems.

Finally the relationship between mortality and morbidity should be studied further, starting from the basic question: "Is the decline in mortality, observed in most age groups, in many countries, counterbalanced by an increase in morbidity, especially in long-lasting or permanent disabilities?" If this were found to be the case, the positive aspects of the decline in mortality would be reduced by this displacement of the ill effects of accident injuries.

The different points raised here indicate a need for further research, and the following research studies and practical monitoring strategies are recommended:

1. *Mortality*:

   – better and more homogeneous registration, using the E code and Chapter XVII of the *International Classification of Diseases* (ninth revision);
   – the use of other indicators, such as the potential years of life lost;
   – the careful observation of ranking and trends over time;
   – surveys aimed at evaluating the respective role of various factors of a preventive or curative nature.

2. *Morbidity*:

   – the use of procedures for the registration of injuries on a limited, yet reliable and representative basis;
   – better recording of the severity of injuries, using uniform grading systems;
   – specific surveys, or the linkage of existing sources of information, in order to assess the important problem of resulting disability.

3. *Morbidity and mortality*:

- a systematic assessment of their socioeconomic cost;
- studies aimed at examining the interrelationship between trends in mortality and morbidity (the latter evaluated in terms of both its incidence and its severity).

References

1. *International Classification of Diseases.* Geneva, World Health Organization; Vol. 1, 1977; Vol. 2, 1978.
2. *Road traffic accident statistics: report on a WHO Ad Hoc Technical Group.* Copenhagen, WHO Regional Office for Europe, 1979 (EURO Reports and Studies, No. 19).
3. *Symposium on accident prevention in childhood: report of a symposium, Manila, 14–15 November 1983.* Unpublished WHO document WHO/IRP/ADR 218-22 2840E, 1984.[a]
4. ECONOMIC COMMISSION FOR EUROPE. *Statistics of road traffic accidents in Europe 1982.* New York, United Nations, 1983.
5. MARCUSSON, H. & OEHMISCH, W. Accident mortality in childhood in selected countries of different continents, 1950–1971. *World health statistics report*, **30**(1): 57–92 (1977).
6. HAVARD, J. D. J. Mortality from motor vehicle accidents in the 15–24 year age group. *World health statistics quarterly*, **32**(3): 225–241 (1979).
7. Accidents in children and young people. *World health statistics quarterly*, **39**(3): 216–284 (1986).
8. *Accident mortality in children, adolescents and young adults: analysis of current situation and current trends.* Unpublished WHO document IRP/APR 218, 1985.[a]
9. CHRISTOPHERSEN, E. R. Automobile accidents: potential years of life lost. *Pediatrics*, **71**(5): 855–856 (1983).
10. *Health field indicators: Canada and provinces.* Montreal, Department of Health and Welfare, 1979.
11. *The epidemiology of accident traumas and resulting disabilities: report on a WHO symposium.* Copenhagen, WHO Regional Office for Europe, 1982 (EURO Reports and Studies, No. 57).
12. MANCIAUX, M. ET AL. Epidemiology of children's traffic accidents in Europe. In: Kohler, L. & Jackson, H., ed., *Traffic and children's health.* Stockholm, The Nordic School of Public Health, 1987, pp. 37–55.
13. WHO Technical Report Series, No. 600, 1976 (*New trends and approaches in the delivery of maternal and child care in health services*: sixth report of the WHO Expert Committee on Maternal and Child Health).

---

[a] A limited number of copies are available from: Injury Prevention Programme, World Health Organization, 1211 Geneva 27, Switzerland.

Chapter 2
Accident mortality and morbidity in developing countries

D. MOHAN & C. J. ROMER

Introduction

In today's world there are dangers everywhere: not only on the roads but also in the home, at school, on playgrounds and sports grounds, in the factory and in the workshop, not only in the industrialized countries but also in the developing ones. In the world as a whole, accidents rank fifth among the leading causes of death; according to a WHO estimate, they were responsible in 1980 for 2 665 000 deaths, i.e., 5.2% of total mortality (Table 2.1). However, it is clear that this figure is only a mean, and much higher percentages are to be found in the developed countries which have eliminated or substantially reduced other causes of death, and among the more vulnerable age groups, i.e., young people and the elderly.

The first comprehensive worldwide study of accidents among children under 15 was published in 1977 by Marcusson & Oehmisch (1). It concerned accidental deaths in 1971 among three age groups—1–4 years, 5–9 years and 10–14 years—in 50 countries, including about ten developing countries, and the trends in accident mortality between 1950 and 1971. Since that time the situation has become better known: it is tending to improve in a number of countries (see Chapter 1). Nevertheless, accidents take an excessive toll of children and young people—including young adults—in the form of death, disability and suffering, a toll that is unacceptable in age groups that normally have the fewest health problems and the lowest death rates.

While accidents in the home are the most numerous, road accidents cause the most deaths. Havard (2) studied mortality from motor vehicle accidents in 15–24-year-olds. Between the two periods 1955–1959 and 1970–1974, mortality increased by over 600% in Mexico, 450% in Thailand, 250% in Venezuela and 210% in Chile. These increases were much greater than those seen in the developed countries. Two aspects of this alarming trend in road-accident mortality among young people are the growing number of girls affected by this "new morbidity" and the fact that the proportion of fatal accidents linked with use of alcohol seems to be increasing. A distinction needs to be made between the industrialized countries, where the adaptation to transport, industrial technologies and new drugs and chemicals has been gradual, extending over more than half a century, and the developing countries, where

Table 2.1. Estimated number of deaths by major causes, 1980, by WHO region (in thousands)

	Africa	America		South-East Asia	Europe		Eastern Mediterranean	Western Pacific		World		
		Developing countries	Developed countries		Developing countries	Developed countries		Developing countries	Developed countries	Developing countries	Developed countries	Total
Infectious and parasitic diseases (including certain respiratory diseases)[a]	3566	981	76	6777	310	661	1762	2623	68	16019	805	16824
Neoplasms	206	282	447	672	47	1397	165	829	197	2201	2041	4242
Diseases of the circulatory system and certain degenerative diseases[b]	836	773	1135	2407	149	4148	559	2890	425	7614	5708	13322
Certain conditions originating in the perinatal period	613	263	25	1282	70	137	386	466	7	3080	169	3249
Injury and poisoning	270	198	175	660	38	449	163	649	63	1978	687	2665
All other and unknown causes	1675	653	223	3634	185	920	927	2167	98	9241	1241	10482
Total	7166	3150	2081	15432	799	7712	3962	9624	858	40133	10651	50784

[a] Influenza, pneumonia, bronchitis, emphysema and asthma.
[b] Diabetes mellitus, ulcer of stomach and duodenum, chronic liver diseases and cirrhosis, nephritis, nephrotic syndrome and nephrosis.
Source: World health statistics annual, 1984.

these changes are taking place much more rapidly. In some developing countries, for example, motor vehicle ownership may double within five years without the corresponding necessary improvements in the environment. Likewise, all kinds of chemical substances and drugs are sold without any restrictions on the open market in most Third World countries; even the tiniest stores in the most remote villages sell chemicals, cleaning materials, pesticides, fertilizers and many other toxic substances. As a result, the risk of being involved in an accident has become so high in a short period of time that the per capita accident rates are higher than any rates ever recorded in the industrialized world. If this is taken in conjunction with the greater difficulty of obtaining high quality care, it will be understood why accident mortality is higher in developing countries than elsewhere. Accidents there are at least as numerous as in the industrialized countries, and their contribution to overall mortality is rapidly increasing in both absolute and relative terms. They represent an important problem by virtue of their actual numbers and their death rates. In Egypt, for example, in 1975–1979 accidental deaths accounted for 7.6% of all deaths among boys aged 5–14 years, compared with 44% in Sweden, but the death rate per 100 000 inhabitants for this age group was higher in Egypt than in Sweden: 14.7 and 13 respectively. A WHO report on maternal and child care published in 1975 drew attention to the mortality table for children in ten developing countries for which reliable statistics were available, and stressed the importance of accident injuries as one of the five leading causes of death in the different age groups (3). Ten years later the figures are even more disturbing, as can be seen from Table 2.2. Although accidents currently

Table 2.2. Accidents to children in ten developing countries[a]

Age group (years)	Year	Mortality rate (per 100 000)	Mortality ranking	
			Mean	No. 1 in:
1–4	1972	20	2.8	4 countries
	1982	25	1.8	5 countries
5–9	1972	14.7	2.7	6 countries
	1982	18.1	1.4	8 countries
10–14	1972	13.8	1.7	6 countries
	1982	17	1.3	8 countries

[a] Chile, Costa Rica, Cuba, Egypt, Guatemala, Mauritius, Panama, Singapore, Uruguay and Venezuela.
Source: 3.

account for only a small proportion of deaths, their role is liable to increase considerably in the years to come as improvements are brought about in the nutritional status of children and in communicable disease control.

In this chapter, we shall concentrate, not on the figures for accident mortality and morbidity in the developing countries (the value of which is often indicative only), but on the specific features of accidents in these countries, which vary considerably.

Accident pathology: incidence and causes

General

Most health care policies are heavily influenced by statistics based on mortality. This is largely true for health measures targeted at adults, but especially so for those aimed at children and young people. Mortality statistics are collected automatically in many countries because of death registration requirements, but often morbidity statistics are not, and it is necessary to rely on hospital-based data or on specially commissioned household surveys. For children and young people this poses a serious problem as death rates for those above the age of five years are low in all countries. Countermeasures based on mortality statistics alone may therefore tackle only a small, albeit serious, part of the problem. In this section both morbidity and mortality are considered to be of importance even though data on the former are difficult to obtain.

It is always difficult to select a straightforward method of classification when dealing with injuries. Very often, place of injury (home, school, etc.), type of injury (drowning, burns, etc.) and cause of injury (fall, car accident, machine, etc.) overlap with one another. Generally, those who carry out research work are experts in one or more of these areas, so that data are collected accordingly. In this chapter, a classification by type of injury has been attempted because countermeasures aimed at influencing product and environmental design will depend to a large extent on the type of energy exchange involved. The disadvantage of this approach is that the cause or place of injury may be repeated under different injury types, but a similar problem would arise if the classification were by cause of injury.

Mortality rates

It is difficult to compare injury mortality rates by geographical area, as details of accidents are not routinely recorded in all countries. This is particularly true for infant deaths in developing countries, and even for older children in the rural areas of many countries.

Data from Europe and North America, which may be considered to be reliable, show clear differences between young and older children, and sometimes between boys and girls. Injuries due to transport accidents seem to be the major accidental cause of death in all countries, the death rates being generally greater than 10 per 100 000 in the industrialized countries and lower in the developing ones. While a substantial number are killed inside vehicles in the former, most of those killed in the latter are unprotected road users, such as cyclists and pedestrians.

Deaths from drowning rank second in most countries and those due to fires third. In the industrialized countries, drowning occurs mainly during recreational activity, whereas elsewhere a large number of deaths are due to floods and water transport accidents.

Accidental falls and poisoning are generally more frequent in the developed countries; the causes of poisoning are very different in the two types of country. Pesticide and kerosene poisoning is a serious problem in many developing countries, but is generally uncommon in the developed ones.

Morbidity

Detailed statistics for morbidity rates are difficult to establish even under the best of circumstances. In the industrialized countries, the bulk of these data come from hospital-based statistics, so that minor injuries are neglected. In the developing countries even such data are hard to come by. However, it is important to understand the role of morbidity, as the relative importance of the various causal factors is different for mortality and morbidity. For example, factors responsible for falls, cuts, lacerations and minor burns can be different from those responsible for the main causes of accidental death. The number of children disabled or with restricted activity due to injuries may be an order of magnitude greater than the number of those killed. The similarities and differences in the products and environments associated with various injuries in developed and developing countries are summarized in Table 2.3.

Conclusions

A specific and comprehensive accident prevention programme must be based on better epidemiological knowledge of the problem. Some of this knowledge can be derived from the compilation and use of

Table 2.3. Products and environments associated with injuries in relation to level of development[a]

Type of accidental injury	Industrialized countries	Developing countries
Burns/scalds	Electrical appliances, cooking mishaps, radiators, home fires (cigarettes, matches, etc.), fireworks	Cooking mishaps, cooking stoves with open flame, coal and wood fires for heating and cooking, chemicals, fireworks
Cuts/lacerations	Toys, sports, playgrounds, furniture, household gadgets	Toys, sports, playgrounds, household gadgets, furniture, blades, occupational hazards (cottage industry, agriculture, construction, mines, etc.)
Drowning	Recreation: pools and beaches	Floods, falls into ponds and wells, recreation, water transport
Impact injury ;	Falls from rooftops and windows, recreation, sports, furniture; automobile occupants, cyclists, pedestrians, motorcyclists	Falls in the course of agricultural and construction work and from rooftops and windows, wells, sports; cyclists, pedestrians, motorcyclists, bus passengers
Amputation and mutilations	Motor vehicle accidents	Agricultural and other occupational hazards, transport accidents
Electric shock	Household gadgets, toys	Substandard and hazardous wiring, improper use of and substandard electrical gadgets
Poisoning	Medicines, household chemicals	Pesticides, cooking fuels, chemicals (household and occupational), medicines, seeds

Table 2.3 (*contd.*)

Type of accidental injury	Industrialized countries	Developing countries
Suffocation/ strangulation	Infant/toddler furniture, clothes and toys, plastic bags	Swallowing of seeds, toys
Injury due to firearms	Accidental use and crime	Enrolment of youth in militias
Insect and animal bites	Dogs	Dogs, snakes, scorpions, etc.

[a] Child abuse may be a cause in many of the above categories for both sets of countries, but has not been included.

mortality tables, but mortality is too global an indicator, subject to errors and in any case inadequate for measuring the extent of the problem, for evaluating the impact of a prevention programme, etc. Consequently, most data are obtained from the routine recording of accident figures, which is feasible in the developed countries, and from morbidity surveys. Even the least advanced countries are able to collect and assemble data, for example by using the system outlined by Kupka (5). This system has deliberately been kept as simple as possible so that it can be used with very little training, under limited supervision, by basic health personnel and even by professionals who do not belong to the health sector, such as teachers. It gives considerable scope for the recording of accidents under three headings: serious injuries, mild injuries, external causes of injuries. On the basis of this body of information, estimates of mortality and morbidity can be drawn up. Likewise, a document prepared by WHO, *Community prevention of accidental injuries in childhood: from knowledge to action* (6), provides the necessary basis for the preparation of training and prevention programmes that can readily be adapted to the specific problems of each country, or each region within a country. It is to be hoped that better knowledge of mortality and morbidity resulting from accidents to young people in the developing countries will create the necessary awareness among parents, teachers, health professionals, decision-makers and young people themselves, and that this will lead to the introduction of active and rational preventive measures.

References

1. MARCUSSON, H. & OEHMISCH, W. Accident mortality in childhood in selected countries of different continents, 1950–1971. *World health statistics report*, **30**(1): 57–92 (1977).

2. HAVARD, J. D. J. Mortality from motor vehicle accidents in the 15–24 year age group. *World health statistics quarterly*, **32**(3): 225–241 (1979).

3. WHO Technical Report Series, No. 600, 1976 (*New trends and approaches in the delivery of maternal and child care in health services:* sixth report of the WHO Expert Committee on Maternal and Child Health).

4. MANCIAUX, M. & ROMER, C. J. Accidents in children, adolescents and young adults: a major public health problem. *World health statistics quarterly*, **39**(3): 227–231 (1986).

5. KUPKA, K. Lay reporting of health information. *World health forum*, **2**(2): 211–217 (1981).

6. MANCIAUX, M. & ROMER, C. J. *Community prevention of accidental injuries in childhood: from knowledge to action.* Unpublished WHO document. Available on request from Injury Prevention Programme, World Health Organization, 1211 Geneva 27, Switzerland.

Chapter 3
Collection of data on accidents in childhood: problems of method

A. TURSZ

Introduction

Accident mortality statistics are routinely collected in all countries and give a fairly accurate picture of the number of deaths from accidents and their distribution by sex and age, in spite of imperfections in the registration of cases. However, it is difficult to analyse the circumstances in which accidents occur on the basis of these data, since the causes are often poorly specified. Moreover, only a small proportion of all accidents are fatal, accounting—according to several recent sources—for only one of every 1000 casualty consultations.

As mortality is not a sufficiently refined indicator on which to base the development of preventive measures, it is clear that reliable morbidity statistics are needed. Morbidity from accidents appears to be high, but is not well known or well quantified because of the difficulties of collecting the data. The first studies dealt with patients admitted to hospital after accidents, and their results suffered from selection bias in terms of the seriousness of the cases, the socioeconomic origins of the patients, and the type of health facility. Calculation of the frequency of accidents, estimation of the relative importance of each type of accident, and assessment of the overall seriousness of the problem require the collection of comprehensive data on accidents in a clearly identified population.

This type of study is difficult to design, especially in countries with complex health care systems. At the request of the Ministry of Health, a study of this kind has recently been undertaken in France by the National Institute of Health and Medical Research (INSERM) in collaboration with the International Children's Centre (ICC) in a health district near Paris. Its main original feature was that data collection was extended to include the private health sector, which is fairly widely developed in the country (1–3). The main objectives of the study were to estimate the frequency of accidents involving children, describe the characteristics of both the accidents and the children involved, and assess the feasibility of a permanent registration system. The study will be used here as an illustration of the difficulties likely to be encountered in the various stages of data collection, starting with the definition of an accident. A review of the advantages and disadvantages of comprehensive registration is needed, especially in the permanent systems of registration and surveillance that have been introduced in some countries to monitor fluctuations in the frequency of accidents, identify priority areas, detect new types of accident, and evaluate the impact of preventive measures. These systems are designed as adjuncts to preventive measures.

Definition

For the purpose of the study, an accident was considered to mean a potentially harmful, unexpected, unintended and abrupt occurrence affecting a child, which may or may not produce injuries, and which leads to medical consultation. This definition excludes premeditated violence—attempted suicide and battering—and sudden infant death. In young children it is not always easy to differentiate between accidental injury and maltreatment, and non-accidental pathology seems to be particularly common, as evidenced by an American study on fractures in the first year of life (4). This means that there must certainly be cases of battering among the data recorded in surveys on accidents.

The inclusion of accidents that do not produce injuries may be justified on the grounds that they arise out of the same circumstances as serious accidents. Moreover, even when there is no physical injury there may be some mental trauma which ought to be taken into consideration. However, it is harder to identify accidents that do not produce injury, especially in surveys carried out in health facilities.

It is also debatable whether accidents that do not lead to a medical consultation should be excluded from the study. In practice, consultation depends on accessibility, which varies from one country or area to another, on a wholly subjective view of the seriousness of the accident on the part of those responsible for the child, and on their level of anxiety, medical knowledge and social background. Accidents that do not lead to medical consultation can only be investigated by home surveys, which may be unreliable, since details of accidents may have been forgotten, especially when they did not involve recourse to medical care. In the health district in which the survey was conducted, care was considered sufficiently accessible to preclude the need for a home survey. In addition, the registration systems used in most of the industrialized countries are based on health facilities.

Survey method

Type of survey

We chose to carry out a cross-sectional survey, in which we collected data for one year in all preventive and health care facilities in one health district on all accidents to children resident in that district. Children admitted to hospital were also covered by a longitudinal study in which their records were re-examined 18 months after the accident to detect any sequelae. It is generally difficult to carry out longitudinal studies of an entire group of patients as many cases are lost to follow-up, especially after minor accidents.

The survey was carried out in 1981–82. A survey lasting one year can take account of seasonal factors (weather, school terms and holidays), but certain single events (e.g. introduction of regulations concerning certain substances) could only be covered by collection of data over a longer period.

Subjects included in the study

The survey was conducted in a health district in Yvelines, near Paris, comprising 40 communes of a semi-urban, semi-rural nature, with wide differences in their social characteristics. According to the 1982 national census, the population of this district was 450 454, with 98 764 children between the ages of 0 and 14 years.

Children were included in the study if they had the following characteristics:

- age 0 to 15 years 3 months at the time of the accident;
- permanently resident in the district;
- victims of accidents of all types, except those in which they were passengers in a four-wheeled vehicle (accidents of this type being registered by the police);
- presenting for consultation at a health facility in the district.

Children resident outside the district who attended a health facility in the district were excluded from the study. It was not possible to register accidents that occurred and were dealt with entirely outside the sector (those occurred particularly during the school holidays). Children who were referred to facilities outside the sector were included, however. Where one child sustained several accidents, each event was counted, but where a child attended more than one health facility for the same accident, duplicate registration forms were eliminated. In view of the many different places and types of accident that were registered, it was not possible to deal with the problem of exposure to risk.

Sources of information

The identification of all possible medical sources of information on accidents to children in the district was a major part of the survey.

Most of these sources were included in a one-year prospective study, while the remainder were covered by sample surveys or retrospective studies.

Two public hospitals, with their mobile emergency and resuscitation units, 11 private clinics and 28 maternal and child health centres participated in the one-year study. Medical practitioners were covered by a sample survey. A sample of general practitioners and specialists (paediatricians, ophthalmologists, ear, nose and throat specialists) in the district were invited to participate in the study, half of them for 7 days and half for 14 days.

On completion of the survey, a retrospective study was carried out of death certificates, data from the poison treatment centre, and public hospitals in the neighbouring districts. The poison treatment centre was included in order to register the accidents for which the only medical consultation was a telephone call to the centre.

The private health care sector (clinics, medical practitioners) was included in order to calculate the overall frequency of accidents. In countries where private and public health sectors co-exist, the number of accidents dealt with outside the public hospitals appears to be high. In the United States of America, for example, the casualty departments of public hospitals receive only 40% of the accident victims in need of medical treatment (5). When the organizers of the Massachusetts Statewide Childhood Injury Prevention Programme (SCIPP), involving 36 public hospitals, compared their data with those of the National Health Interview Survey (NHIS) for 1981, they found that the incidence of accidents to children established by the NHIS was twice that derived from their calculations; the difference was explained by the number of cases seen in the private health sector (6).

The role of medical practitioners appears to be especially important. In France, a survey of private practitioners throughout the country conducted in 1975 showed that accidents were the fifth most frequent reason for medical consultation for children under the age of 15 years (7). Davidson, in a study carried out in parallel with the present study at Lens and Montmédy, estimated that doctors were likely to know of 15% of accidents occurring annually (8), while in a study carried out in the same period at Bar-le-Duc, 22% of cases were seen by doctors (9). In a feasibility study for the Home Accident Surveillance System (HASS) in the United Kingdom in 1973–74, the importance of the role played by general practitioners and health visitors was clear (10), and in 1982 the organizers estimated that two-thirds of injuries due to accidents in the home in England and Wales were treated in hospital and one-third by general practitioners (11). The impossibility of securing the collaboration of these doctors in long-term data collection emerges from all these studies, and the organizers of the HASS no longer include them in their registration system, which is now based solely on public hospitals.

A data collection system based on health facilities does not ensure that all fatal accidents are included. This problem was also encountered by the organizers of the HASS, who abandoned the registration of fatal accidents and reported that analysis of death certificates in England in 1972 showed that 38% of deaths from domestic accidents occurred in the home (*12*). It was to identify these immediate deaths that we included death certificates among our sources of data. For the same reasons, the HASS system has been complemented since 1982 by the HADD (Home Accident Deaths Data Base) (*13*).

There are three major reasons for cases being dealt with outside the district: recourse to facilities near the child's place of residence but outside the survey district; transfer of cases with serious injuries to better equipped hospitals outside the district; and the occurrence and treatment of accidents away from the place of residence. The hospitals in the neighbouring districts were included in the survey to pick up the cases of the first type, and a thorough search was made for transferred cases, especially in the registers of the mobile emergency and resuscitation units. However, accidents that occurred outside the district, particularly during the school holidays, could not be included in the registration system, and were picked up only from other sources of information, such as the social security or insurance companies.

Method of data collection and personnel involved

In the public hospitals and their mobile emergency units, and in private clinics, responsibility for the collection of data was entrusted to the medical and paramedical personnel of the establishment. They were given the task of filling in a registration form for each child involved in an accident. The quality of these records was checked by members of the INSERM survey team from hospital registers and archives of medical records, and forms were filled in for cases that had been missed.

Dispensaries were covered by a postal survey. Since they keep no registers of consultations, their replies could not be checked. The medical practitioners were sent the forms by post and it was not possible to verify the data collected.

The retrospective study at the poison treatment centre and health facilities in the neighbouring districts, and the study of death certificates, were carried out by the INSERM survey team.

In national registration systems, such as the HASS in the United Kingdom or the National Electronic Injury Surveillance System (NEISS) in the United States (*14*), data collection is carried out by paid clerks. This task can nevertheless acceptably be entrusted to volunteers for a survey of limited duration.

Nature of the data collected and coding

The registration form completed for each accident victim contains the following information: sex, age, commune of residence, and nationality of origin of the child; date of the accident, day of the week, place of the accident, type of accident, circumstances and causative agent; nature and site of wounds; immediate sequelae; and treatment.

The questionnaire for those admitted to hospital includes further details concerning the composition of the family, socioeconomic status, the child's education, medical history (particularly accidents), the type of examination and treatment given, and the cost of hospitalization. This questionnaire was filled in by the INSERM survey team, who also coded the entire set of documents. A code was created for the circumstances and causative agents of the accidents.

The number and nature of the items recorded on the registration forms constitute a minimum and are not sufficient for the study of such factors as the child's social and psychological environment. In a survey of relatively long duration, in which a large number of cases are to be registered, it is important to make the work of data collection acceptable to the staff who will perform this routine task. We felt that a short, straightforward form, with boxes to be ticked and a minimum of text, was the best way to guard against under-reporting of cases. We nevertheless gave detailed explanations of the methods, aims and objectives of the study to the staff, impressing upon them that the circumstances of each accident must be described as accurately as possible. The questionnaires concerning the cases admitted to hospital, which were completed by the INSERM survey team, can be used as the basis for a more thorough analysis, particularly regarding psychosocial aspects and the cost of accidents.

Coding is one of the key factors in surveys and can greatly affect the usefulness of the analysis. In many studies, the circumstances of the accident and the causative objects or substances are coded with the E code of the International Classification of Diseases (ICD). This was created to describe causes of death, and is less appropriate for the often minor accidental injuries that are seen in outpatient practice, particularly as a result of domestic accidents to children. Moreover, this code was developed essentially for use in relation to traffic accidents and does not cater adequately for domestic, leisure and sports accidents. Thus sports injuries, which are seen with increasing frequency in children and young people, often have to be coded as falls. It also has the disadvantage of mixing the place of the accident with the activity of the victim and the causative agent. All these considerations have led certain authors to modify and complement the E code (6, 15), which, moreover, has no code for "no injury" or "psychological trauma". The HASS and NEISS systems have created *ad hoc* codes, which, however, are not suitable for children and which concentrate mainly on accidents in the home. It should be noted that the great advantage of the ICD code is that it is international and thus permits comparisons between studies from different countries.

Evaluation of registration

Reporting of cases

A total of 5483 cases were registered at the public hospitals and their mobile emergency units, comprising 4122 cases reported by the personnel and 1361 cases recorded in the course of verification by the INSERM survey team.

The quality of the registers and archives of medical records permitted a complete check of the data and exhaustive coverage. The rate of reporting by the personnel fell in the course of the study from 80% in the first six months to 66% in the second six months, giving an average of 75% for the survey period as a whole.

The inclusion of the mobile emergency units brought in three children who were not examined at hospitals in the district: two of these died at the time of the accident and one was transferred outside the district.

In the private clinics, 2579 cases were recorded, comprising 1826 cases reported by the staff and 753 cases recorded by the INSERM survey team. The absence of certain essential information (age, commune of residence) in some of the registers and the poor quality of the archives made these checks very difficult and the final results were incomplete. There were seven clinics for which complete data were not obtained, while the percentage of cases reported by staff could be calculated only in two establishments, in which it was possible to carry out the same checks as in the public hospitals. The rates of reporting in these two clinics were 50% and 54%.

Four of the dispensaries included in the survey returned forms, reporting 15 accidents. Of the 187 medical practitioners approached, 88 replied after two reminders, i.e. a response rate of 47%; 18 of these practitioners reported 32 accidents. The response rate was higher among specialists than among general practitioners, and better for a 7-day than 14-day period of recording. Seven days would nevertheless seem too short a period to record a sufficiently high number of accidents.

The study of death certificates by the INSERM unit revealed 13 fatal accidents in the survey district. Five cases escaped the registration system during the survey period, but the system did pick up one extra case, probably corresponding to a child temporarily resident in the district and therefore excluded from the survey.

The survey of the poison treatment centre covered seven months and picked up 323 cases of intoxication which had escaped the survey system based on the health facilities in the district.

In the public hospitals in the neighbouring districts (with the exception of one, where the data were unusable but which was the most distant from the survey district), 197 cases of accidents to children from the district were identified in the course of the survey year. There was no significant difference between these cases and those recorded at the public sector hospitals within the district with respect to the characteristics of the children and the accidents.

Table 3.1 shows the complete range of cases recorded. The base population was 98 764 children, and the total number of cases recorded in the district over a period of one year was 8048. Given the under-reporting (of the order of 50%) in private clinics, the sample

Table 3.1. Number of cases registered, by source and duration of survey

Source of cases	Duration of survey	No. of cases
Hospitals and mobile emergency units in the district	1 year	5 483
Private clinics in the district	1 year	2 550[a]
Dispensaries	1 year	15
Medical practitioners	7 or 14 days	32
Public sector hospitals in neighbouring districts	1 year (retrospective study)	197
Poison treatment centres in Paris	7 months (retrospective study)	323
Death certificates	1 year (retrospective study)	5[b]

[a] Excluding cases also recorded at public hospitals (29 cases).
[b] Excluding deaths already recorded.

survey response from practitioners, the impossibility of checking the data from dispensaries, and the incompleteness of the data received from the poison treatment centre and the hospitals in the neighbouring districts, it is not possible to advance an exact figure for the incidence of accidents. However, it may reasonably be estimated to be at least 10%, suggesting that each year one out of every 10 children in the district consults a medical practitioner as a result of an accident.

These data highlight both the problems of reporting by the staff responsible for data collection and the important role of the private sector in the treatment of child casualties. Although the registration in the public hospitals was complete, the rate of reporting was less than 75%. This was nevertheless better than the rate of reporting by staff in the Home Accident Surveillance System (HASS) in the United Kingdom, which was 59% in 1982 (11). The reasons for this under-reporting lie not so much in lack of motivation on the part of the staff, who were very responsive to the information they were given, but in the organization of work and the excessive load of consultations. The fall in the rate of reporting in the course of the survey suggests that, if the study had been continued, a routine would have developed with a rate similar to that found in permanent systems. The solution is thus to replace or rotate the survey staff at intervals or to "restimulate" them through training courses. It should be noted that, when changes were made to the training of the HASS staff and in relations with hospitals, the rate of reporting in the United Kingdom noticeably improved, reaching a level of 70% in 1986 (13).

Of all the cases recorded, 32% were identified through private clinics. In view of the considerable under-reporting of cases from these establishments, it seems likely that about 50% of all children involved in accidents in the district seek treatment at private clinics. The inclusion of such clinics in accident surveys would therefore appear to be fully justified in all countries with a well developed private health care system. In addition, the cases recorded at the private clinics differed significantly from those seen at the public hospitals; the accidents treated at these clinics were not always minor, as evidenced by the slightly higher rate of fractures seen in the private clinics (Table 3.2). Verification of data was nevertheless very difficult and sometimes impossible. In a survey carried out at Bar le Duc, the collection of data in the private clinics was found to be the least satisfactory (9). The problem of under-reporting was compounded by the poor quality of record-keeping.

The difficulties of collaboration with the private health care sector are also evident in the results of the sample survey of practitioners, who reported accidents only for very brief periods. Their role nevertheless

Table 3.2. Comparison of the cases registered at the public hospitals and private clinics

	Public hospitals (5483) (%)	Private clinics[a] (1700) (%)
Sex[b]		
Boy	63	62
Girl	37	38
Age[c]		
0–2 years	22	15
3–5 years	20	18
6–11 years	36	37
> 12 years	22	30
Place of accident[d]		
Home	34	28
School	16	11
Public highway	14	13
Sport	10	13
Other or not specified	26	35
Type of accident[d]		
Injury	86	95
Burn	2	2
Penetration of foreign body	4	2
Poisoning	5	0.5
Other or not specified	3	0.5
Nature of injuries[d]		
Head injury with sign	6	1
Contusion	39	37
Wound	32	36
Sprain	8	9
Fracture	15	17
Site of injuries[d]		
Head	36	32
Upper limb	28	34
Lower limb	18	22
Trunk	3	4
Multiple injuries	15	8
Hospital admissions[d]	16	6
Transfer or mobile unit[d]	2	0

[a] Four private clinics in which recording was complete.
[b] Difference between public hospitals and private clinics not statistically significant.
[c] Difference between public hospitals and private clinics statistically significant ($P < 0.001$).
[d] Difference between public hospitals and private clinics statistically significant, with and without adjustment for age ($P < 0.001$).

appears to be important. Of the general practitioners and paediatricians who replied, 27% had examined children who had been involved in accidents, notwithstanding the short period on which they were asked to report. A recent study in Belgium, in which home accidents were recorded for one year by a sentinel network of general practitioners, suggests that very reliable data can be obtained when practitioners volunteer to participate (16).

The importance of including dispensaries will depend on the country. In France it would not appear to be justified, in view of the preventive character of these establishments. However, they are a major source of care in the rural areas of certain countries, especially developing countries.

The results of this study underline the importance of including death certificates as a source of information. The role of the poison treatment centre, however, appears to have been minor, as the extra cases picked up through them were incidents rather than real accidents, e.g., the absorption of relatively harmless substances, with no medical consequences. It is open to question whether a telephone call to a poison treatment centre without presentation for treatment should be considered a medical consultation.

Finally, the frequency of accidents to children estimated from this study was close to, or slightly lower than, the frequencies found in several other studies carried out recently in public sector hospitals (6, 17) and in the combined public and private health care sectors (8, 9). It is difficult to make comparisons between different studies since they frequently differ in the sources of information used, age groups, or types of accident that have been selected.

Cases will inevitably be lost and there may be several reasons for incomplete registration in any given population, even when the collection of data is confined to health facilities:

- under-reporting by both public and private health establishments;
- the impossibility of including medical practitioners in a long-term study (one year or more);
- a poor rate of response on the part of medical practitioners to sample surveys;
- transfer of accident victims to hospitals outside the district under study;
- occurrence and treatment of accidents outside the district under study (e.g. during the school holidays).

Verification is essential if these losses are to be minimized, but this is not always easy, depending on the place of the survey, and may be impossible because essential documentation is not available. The problem of poorly maintained documentation and archives is a major obstacle in some developing countries.

Comparison of reported and unreported cases

As will be seen from Table 3.3 there are significant differences between the cases reported and the cases not reported. In the hospitals, the patients who were not included in reports tended to be older, with a higher percentage of intoxications; the injuries were different in

Table 3.3. Comparison of characteristics of reported cases and cases "overlooked" by the hospital personnel

	Accidents reported (4122) (%)	Accidents not reported (1361) (%)
Age[a]		
0–2 years	22	22
3–5 years	20	18
6–11 years	37	31
> 12 years	21	29
Type of accident[a]		
Injury	87	82
Burn	3	2
Penetration of foreign body	3	5
Poisoning	3	10
Other or not specified	4	1
Nature of injuries[a]		
Head injury with sign	5	8
Contusion	39	38
Wound	34	27
Sprain	7	11
Fracture	15	16
Site of injuries[a]		
Head	38	28
Upper limb	28	30
Lower limb	16	22
Trunk	3	3
Multiple injuries	15	17
Hospital admissions[a]	14	22

[a] Difference between cases reported and cases overlooked statistically significant, $P < 0.001$.

nature and site, and the patients were more often admitted to hospital. The same types of differences were found in the private clinics.

It is thus impossible fully to describe accident morbidity among children by extrapolating from the cases reported by the hospital staff, as is the usual practice in the analysis of the HASS results. The organizers of the HASS do nevertheless admit the existence of selection bias (11) and, particularly, the poor reporting of accidents that occur at night. Unfortunately, when verification and retrospective capture of data are impossible, the characteristics of accidents have to be studied from the cases that are reported. This was the case in certain private clinics, which underscores the problems associated with the participation of the private health care sector in such studies.

Quality of the data collected

The quality of the data was assessed on the basis of the percentage of items to which no reply was given on the report forms. As will be seen from Table 3.4, which relates to the data recorded at the two public hospitals, the age and sex of the children, the immediate sequelae, and the nature of treatment were noted in nearly every case. Clinical details of the type of accident and the nature and site of injuries were specified in 97–98% of cases. The data elicited by questioning are often missing, however, and the child's nationality, and the place and causative agent

Table 3.4. Items not specified by the personnel and the INSERM survey team for the two public sector hospitals

	Cases reported by personnel (4122) (%)	Forms completed by INSERM survey team (1361) (%)	Total (5483) (%)
Sex of child	0	0	0
Age of child	0	3	1
Nationality of child	2	27	8
Place of accident	12	44	20
Type of accident	4	0	3
Nature of injuries	4	3	3
Site of injuries	3	2	3
Causative agent	31	19	28
Sequelae and treatment	0	6	2

of the accident are poorly reported. The last two are particularly poorly specified in the forms filled in retrospectively from medical records by the INSERM survey team. While medical records abound in clinical data, they rarely contain information of a social nature or a detailed description of the circumstances of the accident.

Many authors have noted that medical records, and especially casualty records, contain few data useful for prevention, such as the place, circumstances and substances involved in accidents. The effectiveness of the verification process is therefore limited, since it is often impossible to obtain these data retrospectively. One of the most important roles of a national registration and surveillance system is to identify dangerous places and substances, which should therefore be noted by the clerks engaged in data collection. However, the same problems can be observed in connection with interview data. In 1982, in the results published by the HASS (*11*), the place of the accident was specified in only 39.4% of cases, whereas the type of injury was missing in only 0.5% of cases. It would seem that the very scope of these large registration systems means that they are rather superficial. It is questionable whether they fulfil their objective of aiding prevention activities, in view of the methods employed, since it is difficult in the context of routine hospital registration to obtain the complete description of circumstances which is essential to any consideration of safety standards.

Discussion and conclusions

The recording of data on accidents to children in a given population, which is the only method available for the investigation of incidence, is fraught with methodological difficulties, arising out of the high frequency of accidents, the multifactorial nature of their causes, and the multiplicity of sources of information.

Since there is no agreement on a single definition of an accident, it is important for any study to define clearly what is meant by an accident and to ensure that all criteria for inclusion and exclusion are clear and are communicated both to the personnel who will collect and code the data, and subsequently to those who read the published results.

Registration of accidents in a limited geographical area cannot claim to be representative of the national situation. In the study presented here, the health district selected was very close to Paris, communications were easy and health facilities numerous, which probably explains why few cases were lost to facilities in neighbouring districts. In other parts of France with a less developed infrastructure, the problem would be different, and if a permanent system of accident registration were to be established, a map of hospital catchment areas would be needed.

This problem is more acute in the developing countries. Several areas need to be involved in the study, and the creation of a national system could be based on a rotating system of sampling, in which each area in turn participates in the survey, say for one year. This approach, which has been adopted by the HASS (*10*) and the NEISS (*14*), also has the advantage that it alleviates the problem of the fall-off in reporting by staff after a certain length of time.

Public sector hospitals are the most reliable source of information, because of the accessibility of documents of good quality which ensure that registration is complete. There is also the assurance that the most serious cases will be picked up. It should nevertheless be noted that the quality of records varies from country to country and may be problematic in some developing countries. If the objective is to calculate accident frequency, it is important to use other sources as well as public sector hospitals. While in some countries the private sector does not appear to be very highly developed or much concerned with the problem of accidents (*17*), in others it is a major source of cases. However there are difficult problems in collaboration and the utilization of documents, which are often of doubtful quality. There are other sources of information, particularly insurance claims, which also deserve consideration. It should be noted that facilities other than public sector hospitals are not usually included in large national systems for the registration and surveillance of accidents, which are based on hospital casualty records. Death certificates, for example, are not included in the HASS.

In some cases, families may be a not inconsiderable source of cases, including severe cases, especially in countries where access to care is difficult.

In all the places in which studies have been conducted, the main problem has been under-reporting, particularly in the private health care sector (very low rate of reporting by clinics, low response rate by practitioners to sample surveys, shortness of the survey periods accepted by practitioners). Verification is therefore essential, especially as there may be some selection bias in the reporting of cases. Nevertheless, verification does not correct the problem of lack of precision. This lack of precision applies particularly to the information needed for the development of preventive measures (the place, circumstances and causative agents of accidents), and is particularly common in large national registration systems. The remuneration of the staff responsible for data collection does not seem to improve the quality of the data. The coding of data on circumstances is difficult in the absence of a universally acceptable code that is suitable for childhood accidents. The E code of the ICD could be used as a routine instrument, and might be complemented by specific *ad hoc* codes developed in the context of research.

National registration systems ultimately present certain advantages: they provide a fairly good measurement of frequency, they pick up rare cases or new types of accident, and can be used to evaluate the impact of preventive measures or health education campaigns, to pinpoint priority areas and to identify the differences between regions. However, they also have many disadvantages: they are extremely expensive and complex, on account of the many sources of information involved and the need for verification, and they are often superficial, unable to provide information on the psychosocial context or the physical environment of accidents. In fact their principal defect lies in the multiplicity of their objectives. The calculation of frequency and the evaluation of the conditions in which accidents occur require different epidemiological approaches. These registration systems provide a sort of overview of the situation, which can be used as a starting-point for more in-depth studies.

There are certain particular problems to which other methods of study can be applied. The role of the psychosocial background in the occurrence of accidents can be approached through case-control studies, and the harmfulness of certain substances can be assessed by in-depth surveys of the substance in question, covering a limited number of cases. Some solutions may also be found to the extremely cumbersome workings of large registration systems. The number of cases recorded might be reduced by random sampling of facilities and accidents, but there are limitations to this approach, in that the frequency of certain types of accident is low. The computerization of casualty records would no doubt make it possible to obtain a complete count from the hospitals and a good description of clinical injuries. However, such systems would probably provide little information on the circumstances of the accidents and would not be applicable in all countries.

There is, in fact, no single system that is applicable in all countries and the goal of exhaustive registration can only be regarded as unrealistic for the time being. In some developing countries, where the number of health care facilities is inadequate or access is difficult, incomplete data are better than none.

Finally, while good quality epidemiological surveys provide the best support for education and prevention activities and for their evaluation, and however much epidemiologists may wish to carry out studies in ideal conditions (survey of a quantified population, elimination of bias, recalling of all cases), they have to accept that politicians and decision-makers are often responsive to arguments other than the scientific soundness of the studies.

References

1. TURSZ, A. ET AL. Enregistrement des accidents de l'enfant dans les structures de soins et de prévention d'un secteur sanitaire. *Revue d'épidémiologie et de santé publique*, **32**: 286–294 (1984).
2. FÉLIX, M. & TURSZ, A. *Les accidents domestiques de l'enfant*. Paris, International Children's Centre.
3. TURSZ, A. ET AL. Childhood accidents: a registration in public and private medical facilities of a French health care area. *Public health*, **99**: 154–164 (1985).
4. MCCLELLAND, C. Q. & HEIPLE, K. G. Fractures in the first year of life. A diagnostic dilemma . *American journal of diseases of children*, **136**(1): 2629 (1982).
5. RIVARA, F. P. & BERGER, L. R. Consumer product hazards: setting priorities for research and regulatory action. *American journal of public health*, **7**: 701–704 (1980).
6. GALLAGHER, S. S. ET AL. The incidence of injuries among 87 000 Massachusetts children and adolescents: results of the 1980–81 statewide childhood injury prevention program surveillance system. *American journal of public health*, **74**: 1340–1347 (1984).
7. BAROIS, A. La morbidité par accidents chez l'enfant (0–15 ans) à partir de 4 enquêtes différentes portant chacune sur une année. In: *Journées parisiennes de pédiatrie 1981*. Paris, Flammarion Médecine Sciences, 1981, pp. 367–376.
8. DAVIDSON, F. & MAGUIN, P. Les accidents chez les enfants. Etude épidémiologique d'une zone rurale et d'une zone urbaine. *Archives françaises de pédiatrie*, **41**: 67–72 (1984).
9. SPYCKERELLE, Y. ET AL. Etude de l'incidence et des caractéristiques des accidents de l'enfant dans une ville de 20 000 habitants. *Revue de pédiatrie*, **20**: 159–166 (1984).
10. *Collection of information on accidents in the home. Proposals for an accident surveillance system*. London, Department of Prices and Consumer Protection, 1976.
11. *The home accident surveillance system, 1982. Presentation of twelve months' data*. London, Department of Trade and Industry, 1983.
12. *The home accident surveillance system. Analysis of domestic accidents to children*. London, Department of Prices and Consumer Protection, 1979.
13. *The home accident surveillance system, 1986. Tenth annual report*. London, Department of Trade and Industry, 1987.
14. *National electronic injury surveillance system*. Washington, DC, US Consumer Product Safety Commission, 1973.

15. HONKANEN, R. & MICHELSSON, J. E. Construction of the computerized accident registration system in a casualty department. *Scandinavian journal of social medicine*, **8**: 33–38 (1980).

16. *Les accidents domestiques en Belgique, 1984.* Brussels, Institute of Hygiene and Epidemiology, 1986.

17. NATHORST WESTFELT, J. A. R. Environmental factors in childhood accidents. A prospective study in Göteborg, Sweden. *Acta paediatrica Scandinavica*, suppl. 291 (1982).

Chapter 4

Incapacity of accidental origin in young people

L. TIRET, V. NICAUD, P. MAGUIN & F. HATTON

Definition

In the context of this discussion, the term incapacity is taken as covering several different aspects of the consequences of accidents. WHO has defined three components within the overall concept of incapacity:

- *impairments*, defined as any loss or abnormality of psychological, physiological, or anatomical structure or function;
- *disabilities*, i.e. any restriction or lack (resulting from an impairment) of ability to perform an activity in the manner or within the range considered normal for a human being;
- *handicaps*, which are the disadvantages, resulting from an impairment or disability, that limit or prevent the fulfilment of a role that is normal, in the light of age, sex and social and cultural factors, for the individual.

These three levels—the exteriorized, objectified and socialized aspects of an intrinsic disorder—can be used to describe the consequences of accidents in all their dimensions. Although this sequence suggests a logical progression between the three levels—impairment to disability to handicap—the situation is sometimes more complex. All the links in the chain are not necessarily present in a given case: someone may be impaired without having a disability, or may have a disability without it being a handicap. Moreover, each of the components is liable to act upon the others and alter the sequence.

Methodological problems in assessing incapacity

Sources of data

Data on incapacities can be obtained either from routine statistics or from special surveys. The routine statistics in this field are very limited and provide only a partial view of the situation: they are generally produced by health insurance systems or by committees set up to determine disability rates. In France there is no register of incapacitated people, except for incapacities of congenital origin.

Surveys provide fuller information. Two types of survey can be distinguished, according to the observation period:

- *Cross-sectional* surveys are conducted during a specified period of time, often very short (one day, one week) and show the characteristics of the population at a given moment. They thus indicate the prevalence of incapacity at the time of the survey. Some are one-off surveys, some are regular surveys, such as the studies of the health status of the population which are conducted in most industrialized countries.
- *Longitudinal* surveys follow up accident victims over a long period. These surveys can be used to measure the incidence of incapacity, but they are rarely carried out because they require expensive and complex techniques.

Study population

The population chosen will depend on the objectives of the study. If the aim is to estimate the overall frequency of incapacity it will be necessary to conduct a survey among the general population (or among specific subgroups if information is sought on specific risks). It should be noted that the origin of an incapacity is not always known, and it is therefore sometimes impossible to distinguish between incapacity due to accident and incapacity due to a disease or a malformation.

If information is sought on the occurrence of incapacity after accidents, the study population will consist of accident victims, whereas if the research topic is the severity of incapacity, the study will need to be conducted on a population of incapacitated people.

Assessment of incapacity

The International Classification of Impairments, Disabilities and Handicaps (ICIDH) (*1*) can be used to code the incapacity in terms of the three components defined above. Such coding is currently at the trial stage. Specialists in rehabilitation have coded a number of their case files in order to see whether the classification gives a satisfactory description of the characteristics of incapacitated people.

Of the 493 files completed, 38 were for people under 20 years of age who had suffered an accident (a traffic accident in 34 cases). Of these 38 subjects, 33 had at least one impairment, leading in 14 cases to one or more disabilities. Eight of these 14 subjects were handicapped by their disabilities. The nature of the impairments, disabilities and handicaps is shown in Table 4.1. This information must be interpreted with caution, however, since the sample tested was not necessarily representative of the handicapped population.

Table 4.1. Impairments, disabilities and handicaps observed in 38 subjects under 20 years of age included in the ICIDH trial

Impairments[a]		Disabilities[b]		Handicaps[c]	
Type	No.	Type	No.	Type	No.
Intellectual	2	Communication	4	Orientation	1
Psychological	7	Personal care	18	Physical	
Aural	1	Locomotor	17	independence	5
Ocular	4	Domestic activities	4	Mobility	4
Visceral	11	Dexterity	10	Occupation	6
Skeletal	39	Endurance	5	Social integration	3
Disfiguring	5	Other	9		
Other	18				
Total	87[d]	Total	67[d]	Total	19[d]

[a] 5 subjects had no impairment.
[b] 24 subjects had no disability.
[c] 30 subjects had no handicap.
[d] An individual subject may have several impairments, disabilities or handicaps.

This experiment brought a certain number of problems to light. The major difficulty was that the impairments and disabilities could be assessed only by specialized teams made up of physicians and allied health personnel (physiotherapists, psychologists, speech therapists, ergotherapists, etc.). As far as the evaluation of social handicap is concerned, it is often difficult to determine how individuals cope in their living environment. Moreover, the concept of handicap refers more or less implicitly to a standard that is not always easy to define. Children present a specific problem inasmuch as the description of disabilities and handicaps is not always well adapted to the child's activities.

Data available in France

Statistics of the National Health Insurance Fund for Wage-earners (CNAMTS)

Statistics on occupational accidents that led to absence from work or to permanent disability in wage-earners under 20 years of age are shown in Table 4.2 (2). In 1983 over 3000 accidents to young people were followed by permanent disability, which represents almost one such

Table 4.2. Occupational accidents leading to absence from work or permanent disability among young wage-earners (France)

Age	No. of wage-earners	Accidents leading to absence from work		Accidents leading to permanent disability	
		No.	Frequency[a] (%)	No.	Frequency[a] (%)
< 16 years	13 816	838	6.1	89	0.6
16–17 years	82 900	22 620	27.3	1 070	1.3
18–19 years	331 598	49 590	15.0	2 229	0.7
Total	428 314	73 048	17.0	3 388	0.8

[a] As percentage of number of wage-earners in the age group.

accident per 100 wage-earners. It is among people aged 16–17 years that the incidence of disability is highest.

Epidemiological surveys

Cross-sectional population survey.

A survey of health and medical care was conducted in 1980 on a representative sample of households in France (3): 7323 households or 21 007 subjects, 23% of whom were aged under 15 years and 22% from 15 to 29 years. This survey can be used to estimate, for the country as a whole, the number and percentage of young people living at home who have an incapacity of accidental origin for which they receive financial assistance. Incapacitated persons living in institutions are not included. Almost 25 000 young people suffer incapacity of accidental origin, i.e. a prevalence of 1 per 1000. The prevalence in the 15–29-year age group is twice that observed in those under 15 years of age (Table 4.3). In this survey incapacity of accidental origin accounted for a greater proportion of all incapacity (15%) than has been found in other countries: in England and Wales, for example, a study of 90 000 people with incapacity revealed an accidental origin in 2% of cases, and the same proportion was found in a sample of 5090 children in Switzerland (4). This difference is no doubt linked to the fact that in the French survey only incapacity recognized by financial assistance, i.e. severe incapacity, was taken into account.

Table 4.3. Estimated number of young people living at home
who have an incapacity of accidental origin for which they
receive financial assistance (France)

Age	Total population	Incapacity of accidental origin	
		No.[a]	Frequency[a] (per 10 000)
0–14 years	11 934 153	8 014	6.7
15–29 years	11 929 209	16 753	14.0
Total	23 863 362	24 767	10.4

[a] Estimate for France as a whole.

Cross-sectional survey of outpatients

A survey was carried out of accident morbidity diagnosed in the
Nord/Pas-de-Calais region in one year (1982–1983) (5). It covered all
outpatients seen by physicians, whether in private practice or at
a hospital (one day was selected at random for each physician). The
sample comprised 41 333 patients, of whom 30% were under 25 years
of age. These patients were divided into two groups, one to provide
information on the incidence of incapacity following an accident, the
other information on the prevalence of incapacity among the
population consulting private practitioners. It was found that an
accident was the reason for consultation in 6% of cases, and this figure
increased with age (Table 4.4). The physician assessed the foreseeable
severity of the sequelae on the day the patient was seen; these were
generally minor, but the incidence of major sequelae increased with age
(Table 4.5). In 0.3% of cases, the patients consulted the physician for
reasons other than accident injuries, but also presented incapacity of
accidental origin. This proportion increased sharply with age, from
0.05% in those under 5 years of age, to 0.6% for those between 15 and
24 years. Most of the incapacities affected the motor apparatus. Of the
42 incapacitated subjects, 13 had to work less and nine had stopped
work altogether.

Table 4.4. Proportion of outpatients consulting following an accident,
Nord/Pas-de-Calais, 1982–83

Age	Total no. of outpatient consultations	Consultations following accident	
		No.	Frequency (%)
< 5 years	3 724	82	2.2
5–14 years	3 656	205	5.6
15–24 years	5 028	436	8.7
Total	12 408	723	5.8

Table 4.5. Predicted severity of accident sequelae[a] in young people
presenting as outpatients, Nord/Pas-de-Calais, 1982–83

Prognosis	Age group		
	< 5 years (N=82)	5–14 years (N=205)	15–24 years (N=436)
Complete recovery	62.2%	70.7%	60.9%
Minor sequelae	19.5%	7.3%	18.3%
Major sequelae	–	1.5%	3.4%
Unpredictable	18.3%	20.5%	17.4%

[a] Prognosis made on day of consultation.

Longitudinal survey on children admitted to hospital after an accident

A survey conducted in Yvelines, France (6), in a health district
containing 98 764 children under 15 years of age recorded accidents
requiring medical assistance in a public or private hospital for a period
of one year (1981–1982), excluding accidents to passengers in four-
wheeled vehicles, suicides and proven cruelty (see Chapter 3). The
medical records of 785 hospitalized children were examined for
sequelae one to two years after the accident. Of these children, 4% had
minor sequelae and 6% major sequelae. The frequency of major
sequelae was higher than in the outpatient survey cited above, probably
because the initial injuries, by virtue of the fact that they required
admission to hospital, were more severe. Here again the sequelae

Table 4.6. Incidence of moderate or severe sequelae
in children admitted to hospital after an accident,
Yvelines, 1981–82

Age	No. of children	Sequelae	
		No.	Frequency (%)
0–5 years	313	10	3.2
6–11 years	293	18	6.1
12–14 years	179	16	8.9
Total	785	44	5.6

increased with age (Table 4.6). They were more frequent following
sports accidents than other accidents. Eye injuries had particularly
severe consequences: of 27 children admitted to hospital with eye
injuries, 11 had major sequelae.

Studies of specific types of injury

Interesting additional information can be obtained from the
longitudinal study of children with specific injuries. One such study,
conducted at Lille General Hospital, monitored 63 young people with
spine injuries (7). Initially 21 of them had neurological signs. Eleven
recovered completely; 10 have sequelae, and six of these are paraplegic.
The special risks incurred by children in the event of fracture or
dislocation of the spine must also be mentioned, for at this period of
growth there is a risk of severe secondary deformity. This was confirmed by a study of 42 children in the hospitals at Garches and Poissy
and at the Roscoff Heliotherapy and Thalassotherapy Centre (8).

A study in the United States of America of 344 young people under
18 years of age who had suffered a head injury followed by coma
lasting over 24 hours showed the severity of this type of injury. One
year later 10% were severely disabled, 9% were totally dependent and
8% were still in coma. Likewise, a study conducted at Garches (10), on
100 young people who suffered head injuries with initial coma lasting
15 days, found that only 22% were able to resume fully their educational or occupational activities. Half of these young people were
unable to resume their previous activities at all; in particular, none of
them was able to enter university.

Psychosocial consequences of accidents in childhood

An often neglected aspect of the consequences of accidents to children is the repercussions on family life. This aspect was tackled in a study conducted in three centres and covering 82 severe accidents to children (*11*). Three interviews were conducted with the family: the first soon after the accident, the second 3–6 months later, and the third one year later. This study showed that the disruptions to the family produced by an accident can be considerable, both in terms of the relations between mother and father and those between the parents and other children. In addition to the efforts made by the health care teams to accept, welcome, and inform the parents, thought needs to be given to the support that should be provided for families facing such a situation.

Looking to the future: longitudinal survey of accident victims

In order to provide fuller information on the consequences of accidents, an epidemiological survey is currently being conducted in the Aquitaine region of France. Its objectives are as follows:

– to assess the number and frequency of severe accidents and poisonings, i.e. those producing immediate death or requiring hospitalization of the victim;
– to determine the consequences of these accidents for the hospital (in terms of workload) and for the individual (in terms of resultant incapacity).

The survey protocol is set out in detail in Annex 1. Some results pertaining to the first objective of the study are already available. Of the subjects admitted to hospital for treatment of injury or poisoning, 34% were under 24 years of age. The types of accident and the nature of the injuries are presented in Tables 4.7 and 4.8. Falls and traffic accidents were the two predominant causes, but with different distributions according to age. There is a high proportion of burn injuries among young children. Poisonings are common in those under 5 or over 15 years of age, but in the latter group they are mainly accounted for by suicide attempts. The high frequency of head injuries can no doubt be explained by the fact that children are often admitted to hospital simply for observation. Most head injuries are in fact mild, only 17% of them being considered severe.

The consequences of the accidents have not yet been evaluated, since the longitudinal study is still in progress. However, an initial assessment of the immediate consequences has been made with the aid

Table 4.7. Types of accident leading to hospitalization of young people, by age, Aquitaine, 1986

Type of accident	Age group		
	0–4 years (N=404) (%)	5–14 years (N=815) (%)	15–24 years (N=1793) (%)
Road accident	10.8	25.0	44.8
Fall	22.4	34.8	11.9
Fall from height	24.9	17.4	5.3
Injury by blunt or sharp instrument	8.8	12.4	15.1
Drowning	1.3	0.4	0.2
Burn	5.3	1.1	1.4
Poisoning	21.4	4.2	17.9
Foreign body	1.8	1.0	0.2
Other	3.3	3.7	3.2

Table 4.8. Nature of injuries sustained in accidents to young people, by age, Aquitaine, 1986

Nature of Injury	Age group[a]		
	0–4 years (%)	5–14 years (%)	15–24 years (%)
Head injury	33.4	29.1	29.0
Eye injury	1.2	2.5	3.6
Fracture of spine	1.2	5.4	8.7
Fracture of upper limb	8.9	27.7	11.9
Fracture of lower limb	3.7	8.5	9.7
Dislocation, sprain	2.2	10.4	15.6
Wound[b]	23.0	27.6	35.5

[a] Column totals may exceed 100% since one subject may sustain more than one injury.
[b] Excluding burns.

of the "injury severity score" proposed by the American Association for Automotive Medicine, using a scale from 1 to 75 (*12*). The severity of injuries increases with age (Table 4.9). One of the interesting aspects of this study will be the comparison of the initial severity of the injury with the resulting incapacity.

Table 4.9. Severity of injuries sustained by young people (injury severity score), by age, Aquitaine, 1986

Injury severity score	Age group		
	0–4 years (%)	5–14 years (%)	15–24 years (%)
1–4	71.6	53.4	48.0
5–9	24.0	39.4	38.6
10–14	2.0	3.6	6.3
15–19	2.4	1.7	3.1
> 20	–	1.9	4.0

References

1. *International Classification of Impairments, Disabilities, and Handicaps: a manual of classification relating to the consequences of disease.* World Health Organization, Geneva, 1980.
2. *Statistiques technologiques d'accidents du travail* - Année 1983. Paris, Caisse Nationale de l'Assurance Maladie des Travailleurs Salariés.
3. COLVEZ, A. & ROBINE, J. M. Incapacités et handicaps dans la population vivant à domicile. *Solidarité santé - études statistiques*, **3**: 7–20 (1984).
4. JACKSON, R. H. Accidents and handicap. *Developmental medicine and child neurology*, **25**: 656–659 (1983).
5. HATTON, F. ET AL. Motifs de soins et diagnostics en médecine ambulatoire dans la région Nord-Pas de Calais. *Solidarité santé - études statistiques*, **5**: 61–88 (1986).
6. FÉLIX, M. & TURSZ, A. *Les accidents domestiques de l'enfant.* Paris, International Children's Centre.
7. BOURLOIS, R. *Les traumatismes du rachis chez l'enfant (à propos de 63 observations).* Doctoral thesis, University of Lille, 1983.
8. POULIQUEN, J. C. ET AL. Le risque de déviation rachidienne évolutive dans les fractures et luxations du rachis chez l'enfant. *Revue de chirurgie orthopédique et réparatrice de l'appareil moteur*, **64**: 487–498 (1978).
9. BRINK, J. D. ET AL. Physical recovery after severe closed head trauma in children and adolescents. *Journal of pediatrics*, **97**: 721–727 (1980).
10. BARRAL, C. La réinsertion scolaire des enfants et adolescents traumatisés crâniens après la période d'éveil. *Les cahiers du Centre technique national d'Études et de Recherches sur les Handicaps et les Inadaptations* (CTNERHI), **26**: 91–92 (1984).
11. MAGUIN, P. & DAVIDSON, F. Conséquences psycho-sociales des accidents graves de l'enfant. In: *Journées parisiennes de pédiatrie*, Paris, Flammarion Médecine-Sciences, 1981, pp. 416–424.
12. AMERICAN ASSOCIATION FOR AUTOMOTIVE MEDICINE. *Abbreviated injury severity score (AISS).* Illinois, 1980.

Chapter 5

Evaluating the economic consequences of accidents to young people

A. TRIOMPHE

Introduction

The study of the economic consequences of a pathological condition and, in particular, of its cost is an essential part of health economics. Such studies may be carried out for various reasons:

- The aim may be to measure the total resources devoted to protecting the health of a given population over a given period. This is the purpose of national health accounts, considered as "satellite" accounts orbiting around the central nucleus of national accounts. The aim is then to achieve a better understanding in quantitative terms of the functioning of the national economy, in the same way as for other specific non-commercial activities or fields (education, housing, etc.).
- The aim may be to improve these accounts by breaking down the cost according to the main pathological conditions, so as to determine the distribution of the total allocated to health protection. However, because of the extremely difficult problems associated with allocating costs in this way, such a study has not yet been attempted in France in relation to accidents to children.
- If the aim is to determine the total economic impact of accidents to children, further considerations are necessary. These include the difficult business of evaluating the losses of production associated with such accidents or with premature death, as well as the losses of or decreases in "well-being" resulting from morbidity and mortality (1). The cost of accidents is then seen to be an aggregate of two components, one measuring the efforts made by society to prevent them, and the other the results that, in spite of these efforts, adversely affect national production or the well-being of individuals.

In practice, the cost of accidents is expressed in monetary terms in order to show how deplorable it is that there are so many of them and as an argument for reducing their number. On this basis, discussion then centres on the action to be taken, and in particular on accident prevention and the cost of medical care. In fact, the resources consumed as a result of accidents to children (2) are linked to the structure of the health services and the medical procedures recommended, and, to a large extent, to the way that the guardians of the child concerned seek help.

A study carried out in 1982 by the *Centre de Recherche, d'Étude et de Documentation en Économie de la Santé* (CREDES) (*3*) of 1350 general practitioners showed that most children involved in accidents are taken to a general practitioner. In the United States of America also, a visit to a general practitioner is the most common method of seeking care for relatively minor accidents (*4*) (see Table 5.1). Thus, in 1980–81, of 78 151 children under 6 years of age who had been involved in an accident, 38.7% were taken to the surgery of a general practitioner; other methods of seeking help include a telephone call to ask for preliminary medical advice (21.8% of cases), transport to a hospital emergency unit (29.9% of cases), and a visit to a hospital (5.8% of cases). The proportion taken to a general practitioner increases with the age of the child. Hospitals play the predominant role in dealing with serious accidents.

Role of hospitals

Hospitals are open at all times of the day and often possess major items of equipment. Their role in dealing with child victims of accidents is threefold. In the first place, they provide an emergency service where the child can be examined. In many cases, such examinations reveal that only simple forms of treatment are needed, and these are carried out on the spot. As a recent French study has shown, this occurrs in 85% of cases (*5*). The hospital can also act as a referral centre from which the child can be directed to another, more specialized establishment possessing, for instance, a neurosurgical unit or a

Table 5.1. Methods of seeking help following a relatively minor accident to a child (USA, 1980–81)

Age group (years)	Telephone call (%)	General practitioner (%)	Emergency unit (hospital or clinic) (%)	Visit to hospital or clinic (%)	Other (%)
< 6	21.8	38.7	29.9	5.8	3.7
6–16	6.7	53.2	25.3	8.1	6.7
17–24	6.6	52.6	26.3	6.2	8.3

Source: *4*.

paediatric emergency unit. Finally, and above all, it is a treatment centre in which the child can be hospitalized for treatment of the injury.

Because of this triple role, hospitals play an important part in the treatment of children involved in serious accidents. In the *Assistance publique de Paris*, which comprises 39 hospitals or groups of hospitals, the consequences of accidents occupy an important place. In fact, accidents constitute the third most common cause of hospitalization (Table 5.2). In 1984, in the *Assistance publique*, 8949 children were hospitalized as a result of accidents (6), accounting for 11.5% of the total number of children hospitalized (for a short stay) during the year. Most of those hospitalized as a result of an accident had suffered an injury, but the proportion decreased between 1980 and 1984 (Table 5.3). Thus injuries accounted for 85.6% of admissions in 1980 but

Table 5.2. Admissions of children to hospitals belonging to the *Assistance publique de Paris* by cause (short-stay patients), 1984

Cause	No. of admissions	%
Infection	12 955	16.58
Congenital disorder	11 394	14.58
Accident	8 949	11.46
Tumour	3 043	3.90
Other	41 784	53.48
Total	78 125	100.00

Source: 6.

Table 5.3. Admissions of children involved in accidents to hospitals belonging to the *Assistance publique de Paris*, by type of accident, 1980 to 1984

Type of accident	1980		1982		1984	
	No.	%	No.	%	No.	%
Injury	7909	85.6	7447	83.2	7153	79.9
Poisoning	1328	14.4	1509	16.8	1796	20.1
Total	9237	100	8956	100	8949	100

Source: 6.

79.9% in 1984. Furthermore, the average duration of hospitalization for injury decreased steadily, falling from 6.3 days in 1979 to 4.8 days in 1982. Cases of poisoning, as a proportion of all accidents requiring hospitalization, increased; they accounted for 14.4% of admissions in 1980 and 20.1% in 1984.[a]

As regards costs, the average cost of a day in hospital in a toxicological emergency unit in the Paris region in 1984 was 3829 francs; the average cost per stay in the same year in a department of the same type was 10 580 francs (Table 5.4). The average cost per day in a paediatrics department in 1984 was 1693 francs, but individual hospitals could charge up to three times as much. Hospitalization is necessary only in a few cases, in particular, in cases of poisoning; however, it is often ordered as a precaution, at high cost to society.

Table 5.4. Average costs in hospitals belonging to the *Assistance publique de Paris*, according to department

	Cost per day (francs)	Average cost per stay (francs)
Emergencies, all types	3574.91	30 672
Toxicological emergencies	3828.99	14 052
Paediatrics	1692.94	15 580
Highly specialized treatment	2736.76	25 533
Emergencies in child surgery	3401.59	55 310
Burns	4727.68	108 122

Cost of accidents

Poisoning

Of 13 466 cases of child poisoning studied by the poison treatment centre of Paris in 1978, two-thirds of the children remained at home, where they were examined by a general practitioner; the poisoning was found not to be serious in 46% of the cases, and the doctors concerned did not recommend any form of medical treatment (7).

Hospitalization was therefore necessary in only one-third of the cases of poisoning studied by the centre, and only 4.6% of victims were

---

[a] I am grateful to Mme Grasset and Professor Chevallier (*Service d'épidémiologie, Assistance publique de Paris*) for these figures.

Table 5.5. Types of care provided at the poison treatment centre, Paris, 1978, after child poisoning

Type of care	Percentage of cases
No medical treatment	46
Treatment by general practitioner	18
Hospitalization:	
– in departments of paediatrics or general medicine	31.4
– in emergency units	4.6

Source: 7.

admitted to hospital emergency units (Table 5.5). According to the poison treatment centre of Paris, 27 000 cases of child poisoning were recorded in the various poison centres in France in 1984, but there are almost certainly twice this number of cases of poisoning altogether each year. On this basis, the cost of child poisoning in 1984 can be estimated at 500 million francs, taking into account all the visits to and examinations by general practitioners, admissions to emergency units, and hospitalization in departments of general medicine and paediatrics.

Injuries

The estimate given above, although approximate, does provide an order of magnitude reflecting the heavy burden for society that child poisoning constitutes. However, the cost of injuries caused by accidents is much higher, partly because they are responsible for five times the number of admissions to hospital, and partly because they are often followed by permanent disability. In 1982, Huault reported that one-third of all children admitted to a general paediatric emergency unit following an accident died or suffered from long-term sequelae (5). In addition to the cost of the treatment required by child victims of accidents, there is thus the cost of the handicaps of those who do not fully recover. It is difficult to give a figure for this, since information is not available for the country as a whole on the number of child accident victims who suffer from long-term sequelae.

Nevertheless, methods for calculating the cost of accidents do exist. Thus, if the direct costs (essentially the costs of transport, of hospitalization and of outpatient treatment) are added to the production lost as a result of absences from work, disabilities and premature deaths, it is possible to calculate the social cost of accidents. This has been done for road accidents in Sweden (8) (Table 5.6) and in the United States of America (9) (Table 5.7). However, the results obtained should not be considered as giving a figure for the value of a life (10), for the total cost of a handicap or a fatal accident (11), or for the harm done to society. It may be asked whether the total cost obtained can be considered as an indicator of the economic and social consequences of accidents for society. In reality, this figure—the cost of

Table 5.6. Cost to society of road accidents in Sweden, 1982 (millions of Swedish kronor)

Component	Cost
Transport	34.7
Hospitalization	363.2
Outpatient treatment	364.8
Total medical costs	762.7 (30.4%)
Absences from work	141.2
Disability	689.1
Premature deaths	916.8
Total lost production	1747.1 (69.6%)
Total	2509.8

Source: 8.

Table 5.7. Cost to society of road accidents in the United States of America, 1980 (millions of US dollars)

Component	Cost
Medical costs	3 326 (5.8%)
Production lost	14 237 (24.9%)
Other losses	39 636 (69.3%)
Total	57 199

Source: 9.

accidents—is simply the result, expressed in monetary terms, of adding up a list of potential losses corresponding to the "expected future production lost" of the child accident victims, and the medical costs. In all cost-benefit studies, the medical costs account on average for only 10–20% of the total (*1, 5*), the potential production losses accounting for by far the greater part of the total cost. In this discussion, the problem that is being faced is one of defining social goals: should child accident victims be protected and cared for by society essentially because of their role as producers or are they entitled to such care and protection on other grounds?

"Invisible" economic consequences of accidents to children

While it is impossible to define precisely an indicator of the severity of the psychosocial consequences of a pathological condition that can be measured continuously, it is nevertheless clear that the ability of child accident victims to study may be affected and that they may therefore have to interrupt their education, either temporarily or permanently. Thus, in the United States, the average annual number of days spent in bed by children aged under 17 years following an accident was 27.7 days per 100 children in 1981–82 (*4*). This figure is an average, and the actual time varies with the income of the family concerned, which is itself related to the form of medical care provided (Table 5.8). In addition, the number of days of "limited activity" varies with age and sex, as do the number and severity of the accidents themselves (Fig. 5.1).

Table 5.8. Annual number of days spent in bed by children aged less than 17 years as a result of accidents, by family income, United States, 1981–82

Family income (US $)	Number of days spent in bed (per 100 children aged less than 17 years)
< 10 000	39.5
10 000–14 999	20.9
15 000–24 999	27.4
> 25 000	23.2
All incomes	27.7

Source: *4*.

Fig. 5.1. Number of days of limited activity (*4*)

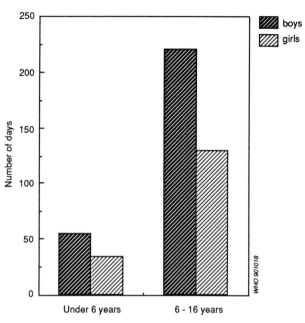

As part of a study carried out by the National Center for Health Statistics in the USA (*12*), absences from school as a result of accidents were calculated for children from 6 to 16 years of age, in 1980–81; the figures found were 43.6 days per 100 boys and 28.5 days per 100 girls (Fig 5.2). There is a clear relationship between family income and the number of days of absence from school, the latter being highest, at 66.3 days, for children from families with an income of less than US$ 10 000 per year.

Cost of prevention

The magnitude and diversity of the economic and social consequences of accidents to children are in marked contrast to the small amount of money spent on preventing them. Thus, since 1982, the *Comité français d'éducation pour la santé* (CFES) has for the first time begun to study accidents to children in the home. This study has been based on epidemiological and psychosociological data, and on experience in other countries, in particular, in Scandinavia and the United Kingdom.

Fig. 5.2. Number of school days lost as a result of accidents or of
impairments connected with an accident
(per 100 children aged from 6 to 16 in 1980–1981)
United States, 1981 (*4, 12*)

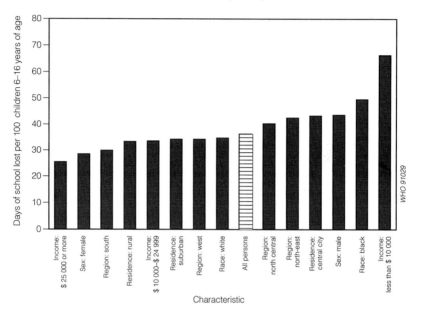

On this basis, CFES has set itself the task of:

– improving parents' knowledge of the psychomotor development
  of their children;
– improving parent–child relationships by encouraging families to
  adopt an educational attitude towards risk;
– providing information on the various risk factors.

Before turning its attention to the public as a whole, CFES has
attempted to increase the awareness of opinion-makers (architects,
town planners, health professionals, teachers, etc.). Meetings have been
organized and methods of presenting information developed (slide
shows, films, exhibition panels). For the general public, a television
series was made. A total of 1 800 000 copies of a brochure were printed,
and educational kits distributed to the pupils of primary schools. The
number of children covered since 1983 is estimated at 800 000. The cost
of all these preventive activities amounted to 9 750 000 francs over the

period 1982–84. In addition, the efforts made by CFES were supported by activities in the field, financed by local authorities.[a]

It is difficult to determine how effective such activities are. This would require a study of the changes in morbidity due to accidents in a target population for which such activities had been carried out, in comparison with a reference population. An estimate of the expenditure thus avoided could then be compared with the funds invested in prevention. The difficulty of such a calculation can readily be appreciated, and it is in any case open to criticism both from the point of view of the principles on which it is based and from that of the results obtained. It would undoubtedly gain from being restricted to a precisely defined category of accidents for which specific preventive measures are available (of a technological character, for example) that are comparatively easy to cost.

In fact, accidents to children and, in particular, serious accidents are the consequence of inadequacies in the environment; this is often true, for example, in the case of the architecture of schools (13). In addition, a study of the mechanisms responsible for accidents shows the major role played by various economic factors. One example is that of the time that the mother can give to making sure that the child is safe, which in turn depends on her job and on the arrangements made for looking after the child in her absence; these affect the precautions that she takes (14) and help or hinder the education that she gives to her child with regard to the risks of daily life (15).

Conclusions

The economic consequences of accidents to children and, in particular, their cost, is a subject that has been little studied in France. While there are simply methodological problems in evaluating the medical resources required to care for child accident victims and to reduce the seriousness of their consequences, cost-benefit studies aimed at assessing the financial consequences of accidents to children in terms of loss of production raise important ethical problems.

In fact, the real importance of economic studies of accidents to children lies in improving our knowledge of the costs associated with the care of child victims of accidents and the prevention of handicaps. In this connection, the diversity of the medical facilities capable of dealing with child accident victims constitutes a partial response by society to the consequences, for the persons concerned, of the accidents

---

[a] I thank the *Comité français d'Education pour la Santé* (CFES) for providing these data.

that it causes. When a child suffers a serious accident, it gives rise to a whole series of problems affecting all organizational levels, from the health care facility responsible for the initial care, the family, which has to take extra responsibility for various activities (transport, education), and society, which may have to take over or replace the family structure ensuring that an appropriate place is found for the child. The so-called social cost for society is thus the series of problems following the accident that are not solved socially or institutionally. Whatever social arrangements may be made, it will be impossible to avoid or to compensate completely for the loss of autonomy, the dependence and the dislocation that result from a serious accident to a child. The greater the effort made to integrate a child who has had an accident, the higher the corresponding economic cost but also the lower the social cost. It is therefore necessary to broaden the area covered by the study of the consequences of an accident, and to differentiate between its various aspects, since its manifestations involve a whole network of social or personal factors apart from the accident itself. The validity of any assignment of the economic consequences and of the costs of an accident to any particular cause is far more complex than might appear at first sight and may lead us to question the entire social system, because of the place and the role assigned to handicaps.

References

1. LE NET, M. *Le prix de la vie humaine, le coût des maux sociaux*, 3rd ed. Paris, La Documentation francaise, 1980.
2. LEVY, E. ET AL. *Evaluer le coût de la maladie*, Vol. I. Paris, Dunod, 1977.
3. LEFUR, P. & SERMET, C. *Clientèle, morbidité, prescriptions en médecine libérale, échantillon national 1982–83*. Paris, CREDES, 1985.
4. NATIONAL CENTER FOR HEALTH STATISTICS (NCHS). *National Health Interview Survey* (NHIS). Washington, DC, 1981.
5. HUAULT, G. L'accident vu par l'hôpital. *Praticien*, **449**: 31–40 (1982).
6. *Morbidité par accident chez l'enfant hospitalisé à l'Assistance Publique des Hôpitaux de Paris*. Paris, Assistance publique des Hôpitaux de Paris, Service d'Épidémiologie, Direction du Plan, 1984.
7. COÑSA, F. Travail du centre anti-poison et du service de réanimation toxicologique, Hôpital Fernand Widal, Paris. *Santé sécurité sociale. Statistiques et commentaires*, **1**: 67–74 (1978).
8. HARTUNIAN, N. S. ET AL. The incidence and cost of cancer, motor vehicle injuries, coronary heart disease and stroke: a comparative analysis. *American journal of public health*, **70** (12): 1249–1260 (1980).
9. CONN, J. M. *Death from motor vehicle-related injuries, 1978, 1984*. MMWRCDC Surveillance Summaries 1983–1985, pp. 41–45.
10. ANISIMOV, V. S. Calculation of the economic loss to society as a result of a child's death from injuries. *Medical care*, **23** (1): 14–19 (1985).

11. FISCHER, R. P. ET AL. The economics of fatal injury: dollars and sense. *Journal of trauma*, **25** (8): 746–750 (1985).

12. Persons injured and disability days due to injuries, United States 1980–81. *Vital and health statistics*, Series 10, No. 149. Hyattsville, National Center for Health Statistics, 1985 (DHHS Publication No. (PHS) 85-1577).

13. PARISOT, D. Accidents d'enfants en milieu scolaire. Situations accidentelles et prévention. *Prévenir*, **10**: 97–104 (1984).

14. LARDE, P. Les effets sanitaires des choix de politique économique et sociale. In: *Colloque de l'Association économique et sociale, Paris, 27–28 September 1984*. Paris, Commissariat général au Plan, 1984.

15. ALIES-PATIN, J. M. & HOLLA, H. *Les accidents de la vie domestique chez l'enfant*. Paris, Départment statistique de la CNAMTS, 1987 (Dossiers Études et Statistiques No. 7).

PART II
THE PSYCHOSOCIOLOGICAL APPROACH

Chapter 6
Psychosocial factors in childhood and adolescence

E. A. SAND

This chapter considers in detail the information available on the associations between psychosocial factors and the occurrence of accidents, particularly in childhood and adolescence.[a]

Definitions

The definition of the term "accident" has been considered in Chapter 3, and will therefore not be discussed in detail here. It can be defined as an unpremeditated event resulting in recognizable or visible injury or damage (2, 3).

For the purposes of this discussion, childhood, which is defined by both biological and social criteria, is taken as the period from birth to puberty; at this point, adolescence begins, continuing until occupational and psychosocial independence is attained (through the establishment of a lasting relationship, for example) (4). The subdivisions of these periods of life (e.g., early childhood versus late childhood) are less clearly defined and differ from one study to another. In spite of the variations between different countries, the age at which schooling begins is of particular interest in view of the numerous opportunities for education and prevention that school provides.

Psychosocial factors can be defined in many ways. At the Twenty-ninth World Health Assembly, the Director-General of WHO defined them as factors stemming from the behavioural and psychological characteristics of the individual and the structure and function of social groups (5). The most important are (1):

- family kinship patterns, links and structures;
- life-styles;
- the social system's institutionalized ways of coping with threats and solving conflicts;
- cultural characteristics, such as the values and beliefs governing the socialization of children and, in particular, child-rearing practices;
- psychological characteristics, such as attitudes and personality.

---

[a] In January 1980, a WHO Technical Group on psychosocial factors related to accidents in childhood and adolescence met in Brussels under the aegis of the WHO Regional Office for Europe and in cooperation with the Belgian Government (1). The report on this meeting, published in 1981, contains a useful discussion of psychosocial factors, and was a source of essential information in the writing of this chapter.

These factors rarely act in isolation, but must be considered in association with other variables, in particular those of a biological and ecological nature. Thus, the living conditions of individuals and groups are affected by, on the one hand, the intelligence, neurological maturity and circadian rhythms of the individuals and on the other, the natural and social environment, meteorological and climatic conditions, etc. All these factors act together in determining the probability of the occurrence of an accident.

In reality, this vast collection of factors must be considered as a whole, in view of the fact that they are constantly interacting with one another through a variety of mechanisms. For the sake of clarity, however, it is essential, before any overall model is put forward, to pick out the main components. Certain factors can act independently or have a decisive effect in the series of events leading to accidents.

It must be emphasized, finally, that psychosocial factors play a major role in the series of events leading to an accident, in particular in childhood and adolescence, although one that it is impossible to measure precisely, in view of the enormous number and variety of events that have to be considered. However, this share in the responsibility for accidents would appear to be well over 50%.

Personal factors

Most of these factors develop and make themselves apparent as a function of, and in relation to, the child's social environment. The personality of the child, and in particular his or her intelligence, level of emotional or affective development, and psychomotor skills, play a pivotal role in any predisposition to accidents. To these must be added factors that act for shorter periods or are transitory in character, such as fatigue, overwork, etc.

The importance of intelligence has long been emphasized (6, 7) and has again been found to be a contributory factor in several recent studies. It is clear that the correct assessment of a particular situation, whether on the road, on the playing field or at home, the integration of the various sense data and, finally, the choice of appropriate behaviour and the taking of a decision are facilitated by a high level of intelligence (8). A longitudinal study carried out in Newcastle upon Tyne, England, showed that children having a below average score for initiative, concentration and reliability had a higher incidence of accidents (1).

The motor coordination, skill, and physical strength of the child have also been associated with the probability of the occurrence of accidents, in particular by Manheimer & Mellinger (9), but this had already been suggested by Fuller (10). The highest probability of accidents is found among the most athletic, daring and active children and especially boys. This suggests that it may be worth reconsidering the concept of "proneness", which goes back to Dunbar (*11*) and which, since 1947, has been strongly criticized from time to time before reappearing in a less clear-cut form. The term "liability" has been used in the literature; this suggests both a certain degree of probability and of proneness to accidents connected with the personality; it is not an "all or none" situation but a continuous evolution (*9*).

In the light of the contributions made by Manheimer & Mellinger (*9*) and more recently by Padilla et al. (*12*), and accepting that "accident-proneness" is affected by factors in the environment, it is difficult to deny that certain individuals, whether adults or children, have a higher probability of being involved in accidents of different types under comparable external conditions. This "liability" is apparently associated with the personality of these individuals as a whole and cannot be fully explained by factors, such as retarded physical or mental development or neurotic tendencies, which would expose the child more frequently to high-risk situations and, in addition, reduce his or her ability to cope ("coping mechanisms"). In the main, a reduction in the ability to cope with dangerous situations might perhaps be the consequence of aggressiveness towards other children together with status- and attention-seeking behaviour (*9*).

The other characteristics described are as follows:

- activity (rapidity of movement);
- extrovert personality;
- exploration drive and independence-seeking behaviour;
- tendency to take risks;
- tendency to fight;
- above-average athletic ability.

These characteristics bring to mind the concept of "unbalanced personality" mentioned in the report on the Brussels meeting (*1*).

However, even though some children at certain stages of their development appear to have a higher risk than others of being involved in an accident, the concept or, worse, a "label" of a stable high-risk personality ("accident proneness") can only be applied to a very small number of children (*9*).

Another aspect of the child's capacity to cope with risks, namely that of learning about social life and the physical environment, and in particular about the risk of accidents, must be incorporated in the scenario described above. As the central nervous system gradually matures and the sense organs more fully and more precisely detect the signals received from the environment, the child, and subsequently the adolescent, become increasingly independent. In early life, safety is ensured solely by the "passive" protection provided by adults, e.g., parents and teachers, and by the physical environment. It is the task of architects and town planners, furniture designers, packagers of pharmaceutical products, etc. to ensure that their products are designed to provide a safe environment. Nevertheless, it is clear that the choice of objects made available to children and their appropriate use will depend largely on teachers and parents.

Children thus gradually learn to assess the dangers that confront then and to choose appropriate behaviour for dealing with them. However, as Platt has shown (13), in the majority of cases the choice of behaviour, for example in a road traffic situation, is liable to random error as a result simply of the imperfect nature of the human organism, the fact that estimates are frequently inaccurate, and the vagueness of the signals received from the environment. To these must be added, in the case of children and adolescents, the fact that they are still in a learning situation, which in itself means that the probability of error will be higher. Nevertheless, errors will tend to become less frequent as the learning process continues, allowing the person to choose behavioural responses more judiciously and more quickly.

Thus, parents and teachers need to give their children new responsibilities at the right time, to help them to achieve a higher degree of independence. Their knowledge of the children, of the skills that they have already acquired and of their rate of development provides the basis for this process of learning to become independent. Trudewind, in Germany, has shown that mechanisms of the same kind determine the development of the motivation to achieve, in particular in education (14).

Among the personal factors, the abuse of psychotropic substances and, above all, of alcohol is extremely important, whether they are abused by the parents or the child or adolescent. This problem has been dealt with in a very large number of studies and by a WHO Technical Group in 1981 (15), as well as in a more recent publication specifically concerned with young people (16).

This emphasizes, once again, the need to avoid a compartmentalized approach to the causation of accidents and to see the child in the context of the social setting, of which the family is a particularly important component.

Social factors

A large number of social variables—cultural, socioeconomic and psychofamilial—must be taken into account. A WHO Technical

Group (*1*) considered that social factors had primarily a mediating influence, operating "indirectly" on the child's development and social environment. This mediating influence is only one aspect of the complexity of this environment, in which it is often impossible to determine the order of events that are subtly interrelated.

The influence of the cultural background in the broader sense must be emphasized. Thus Levy (*17*) considers that the educational environment, e.g., its "orthodoxy" and the degree of strictness with which the child is supervised, is linked to the possibility of being involved in accidents. Supervision is strict in France, Italy and Spain, less so in Canada and Japan, where children are more frequently on their own and thus exposed to risks. In these latter countries, the incidence of accidents is higher (cf. Chapter 1). Such data should be taken into account in prevention programmes, even if their direct impact on these programmes does not seem to be very clear.

Socioeconomic status, which is relatively difficult to influence through accident prevention programmes, nevertheless merits the attention of those responsible for prevention. The immediate environment of the child, the home and surroundings are closely correlated with the socioeconomic status of the family. Certain practical risks, for example, associated with electrical equipment, might attract the attention of health personnel; this might lead, sometimes at little cost, to useful changes. In addition, this could provide an opportunity for exchanges of views, whether informative or educational, with a family.

The WHO Technical Group also emphasized that values and attitudes favouring competitiveness and individual achievement could adversely affect the maintenance of a healthy social environment; in contrast, efforts directed towards social solidarity and responsibility to group goals can have positive preventive and therapeutic effects (*1*).

In addition, tendencies towards deviance are associated, as mediating influences, with higher risks. This applies, in particular, to certain adolescent and young adult drivers who are socially maladjusted, i.e., delinquent or criminal (*1*). This appears to be a case in which psycho- and sociopathological symptoms are associated with one another, although the chain of possible causes and effects can only rarely be identified. Here, it is essential to avoid personality stereotypes and any tendency to labelling.

These psychological or psychiatric mechanisms are well known to clinicians and psychologists. In a study of a large sample of women in a district of London, England, Brown & Davidson found a significant correlation between the presence of depression in mothers and a high incidence of accidents in their children. The authors believed that the association could not be explained simply by the fact that those mothers supervised their children less well. It is possible that these children were disturbed or anxious because of their mothers' illness, and externalized their anxiety in the form of greater physical activity and of impulsive acts that were poorly adapted to the circumstances (*18*). Other striking sociological and psychological factors have been described by various authors, relating essentially to the configuration or stability of the family unit, the stress to which the family is subjected at certain times, and that imposed on the child as a consequence (*19–22*).

Whether or not education is successful, as mentioned previously, will depend on the correct assessment by parents and teachers of the child's stage of neurological, intellectual, emotional and psychosocial maturation. The relationship of these people with the child enables them to appreciate his or her abilities and to take appropriate educational decisions, although the risk of error is always present (*23*). Tendencies to overprotection may arise, often linked to excessive or even neurotic fears of exposing the child to risks with which he or she cannot cope alone.

The integrity of the family and the social support networks appears to influence the probability of the occurrence of accidents. Psychosocial studies suggest that accidents and diseases in childhood, particularly if repeated, are symptoms of a disturbance in the network of social relations, both within the family and between it and other networks (*24*). The term "family conflict" is used by Sobel in connection with the risk of accidental poisoning in children (*25*).

In addition, a family move may also precipitate the occurrence of accidental burns: Knudson-Cooper & Leuchtag found that 63% of a sample of children with accidental burns had moved home in the previous twelve months (*24*). The measurement of family stress by means of a questionnaire developed by Holmes & Rahe (*26*) indicated a significantly high level of stress in families moving home.

There can be no doubt that, among the factors associated with the psychosocial environment, the characteristics of the family have a decisive influence because of their early and prolonged effect on the overall development of the child. Thus, Wadsworth, after a detailed study of more than 17 000 children followed from birth to the age of five years, found that the accident incidence rate varied with the family structure. It was low in children living with both parents, higher in one-parent families, and higher still among children brought up by their mother and a stepfather (*19*).

Thanks to the work, in particular, of Bandura (*20*), Eron (*21*) and Lefkowitz (*22*), the considerable influence of the model provided by parents and teachers on the behaviour of children is well known. This applies, more particularly, to aggressive behaviour as well as to certain more general attitudes towards society and towards other people.

The overall quality and strength of the relationships within the family, particularly between the parents, are also associated to a highly significant extent with the occurrence of accidents (27). In this connection, in 1980, a WHO Technical Group (1) considered as risk factors: marital discord, marriage disruption (through divorce, separation or death), substance abuse and especially alcohol abuse by a parent or by both parents, serious illness of a family member, child neglect and large family size (28, 29). Thus, "instability in family life seems to have a negative influence on the child's social development and increases the risk of the child having an accident" (1).

Early education in the assessment of risks is provided mainly by the family but also by others, and by the physical environment. A judicious balance between protection by adults — "passive" protection — and the gradual transfer of responsibility to the child will ensure that he or she will gradually become more independent and learn to cope with increasingly varied and complex situations.

As the child grows it becomes increasingly evident that social factors are not concerned solely with the family, but with all the settings in which the person lives and develops. Both the school and the street contribute to the social "schooling" of the child and affect relationships, both with children of the same age and with those of different ages. The school environment has been extensively discussed in the scientific, sociological and psychological literature, and is outside the scope of this chapter. It is well known that the behavioural model provided by the teaching staff can influence the children.

Mention must also be made of a study recently carried out in the United States on a sample of nearly 800 children aged from 9 to 13 years (30). The authors investigated the challenges and social pressures imposed on the children by their classmates. The "dares" became more frequent as the age of the children increased, and were a cause of stress or even distress. About half the dares led to problem behaviour, placing the child or other children in risk situations. In older children, the risks for girls and boys are different, relating mainly to sexual activity for the former and to violence for the latter.

The earlier work of Bloch & Niederhoffer, among others, reported the same challenges and risk-taking behaviour among adolescents (31). The types of behaviour encouraged are often associated with the acquisition of a higher social status by the young adolescent, and may sometimes involve initiation rites, after which the adolescent becomes a full member of the group concerned or acquires the social status of an adult.

Life events and stress

The combined study of personal and social factors and of their interactions clearly shows that life events, changes in lifestyle and the stress suffered or felt influence the occurrence of accidents in childhood and adolescence. Notwithstanding the variety of tools used in the evaluations, and the fact that the children studied come from different continents and different social classes, the conclusions reached in the various studies are strikingly similar.

What emerges from them is the disturbance caused by life events and the associated stress, which interfere with certain mechanisms of adaptation to the conditions of everyday life and, in particular, reduce the ability to respond correctly to situations involving a high risk of accident. The conditions covered ranged from poisoning to serious physical injury, and the ages of those affected from birth to late adolescence (32–35).

The life events frequently mentioned, whether occurring in isolation or more commonly in association with one another, are as follows:

- number of moves and of changes in environment;
- number of jobs held by the father;
- death or illness of a close relative or friend;
- quarrels between parents;
- separation of parents.

The combined effect of these events is to create stress, which finds expression in various hormonal, neurological, vascular, muscular, behavioural and psychological changes. The effects of stress take the form of disturbances of the mechanisms of perception, and of the selection and classification of stimuli, as well as of the ability to take an appropriate decision quickly.

It is true that, for certain life events and changes in life-style, the health educator has comparatively few opportunities to take preventive action. However, other health promotion opportunities, in the broad sense, can be envisaged, such as social and political interventions aimed at reducing social inequalities. WHO attaches great importance to this kind of intervention. Members of an economically disadvantaged social class who are also poorly educated will be more affected by the life events mentioned above. One approach to primary prevention would be to educate children so as to increase their ability to cope with problem situations.

Finally, with regard to tertiary care after an accident has happened, it is often necessary to provide psychological assistance and support to children who have suffered or witnessed a serious accident. The majority of them, as Biermann has shown, suffer from serious psychological sequelae (*35*) (see also Chapter 4).

Theoretical framework

The WHO Technical Group developed an analytical framework covering the psychosocial factors involved in accidents to drivers of two-wheeled vehicles. The factors included were those considered suitable for use in preventive activities rather than those purely indicative of the risks involved (*1*). In the light of more recent analyses of this process, the model can be extended to include factors concerned

Fig. 6.1. Psychosocial factors involved in the chain of events leading to an accident (modified from *1*).

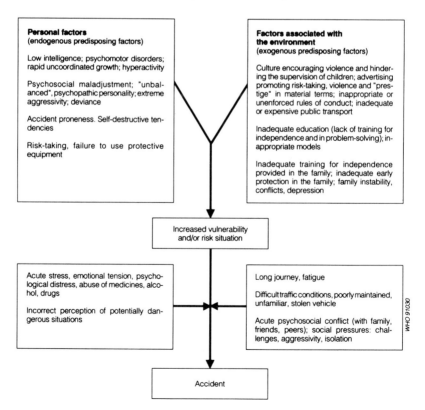

Personal factors
(endogenous predisposing factors)

Low intelligence; psychomotor disorders; rapid uncoordinated growth; hyperactivity

Psychosocial maladjustment; "unbalanced", psychopathic personality; extreme aggressivity; deviance

Accident proneness. Self-destructive tendencies

Risk-taking, failure to use protective equipment

Factors associated with the environment
(exogenous predisposing factors)

Culture encouraging violence and hindering the supervision of children; advertising promoting risk-taking, violence and "prestige" in material terms; inappropriate or unenforced rules of conduct; inadequate or expensive public transport

Inadequate education (lack of training for independence and in problem-solving); inappropriate models

Inadequate training for independence provided in the family; inadequate early protection in the family; family instability, conflicts, depression

Increased vulnerability and/or risk situation

Acute stress, emotional tension, psychological distress, abuse of medicines, alcohol, drugs

Incorrect perception of potentially dangerous situations

Long journey, fatigue

Difficult traffic conditions, poorly maintained, unfamiliar, stolen vehicle

Acute psychosocial conflict (with family, friends, peers); social pressures: challenges, aggressivity; isolation

Accident

WHO 91030

with, *inter alia*, the social and family setting, since health education efforts can usefully be made in this setting (see Fig. 6.1). In addition, feedback mechanisms must be added — both positive ones, through learning to be successful, and negative ones, particularly through conditioning by failure.

It is possible, at least in the medium term, to identify useful strategies for a prevention policy based on the factors mentioned above. Such efforts obviously go beyond the skills and roles of health personnel and health education teams alone. The impact of psychosocial factors on the occurrence of accidents in adolescence and childhood can be reduced only through a policy whereby personnel from other relevant disciplines also play their part.

References

1. *Psychosocial factors related to accidents in childhood and adolescence.* openhagen, WHO Regional Office for Europe, 1981 (EURO Reports and Studies, No. 46).
2. BERFENSTAM, R. ET AL., ed. *Prevention of accidents in childhood.* A symposium in the series of congresses and conferences celebrating the 500th anniversary of Uppsala University, held at the Department of Social Medicine, University Hospital, 5–7 October 1977. Uppsala, 1978.
3. WHO Technical Report Series, No. 118, 1957 (*Accidents in childhood: facts as a basis for prevention*: report of an Advisory Group).
4. JEANNERET, O. ET AL. *Les adolescents et leur santé*. Paris, Flammarion, 1983.
5. *Psychosocial factors and health*: Report by the Director-General to the Twenty-ninth World Health Assembly (WHO document A29/8).
6. NORMAN, L. G. *Road traffic accidents: epidemiology, control, and prevention*. Geneva, World Health Organization, 1962 (Public Health Papers, No. 12).
7. FABIAN, A. A. & BENDER, L. Head injury in children: predisposing factors. *American journal of orthopsychiatry*, **17**: 68–79 (1977).
8. SMITH, E. M. Relationship between intelligence and driving record. *Accident analysis and prevention*, **14**: 439–442 (1982).
9. MANHEIMER, D. I. & MELLINGER, G. D. Personality characteristics of the child accident repeater. *Child development*, **38**: 491–513 (1967).
10. FULLER, E. M. Injury-prone children. *American journal of orthopsychiatry*, **18**: 708–723 (1948).
11. DUNBAR, F. *Emotions and bodily changes*. New York, Columbia University Press, 1947.
12. PADILLA, E. R. ET AL. Predicting accident frequency in children. *Pediatrics*, **58**: 223–226 (1976).
13. PLATT, F. Operations analysis of traffic safety. *Traffic safety research review*, **2**: 17 (1958).

14. TRUDEWIND, C. *Trial of a taxonomy of out-of-school environmental conditions relevant to the genesis of performance-motivation.* Doctoral thesis, Ruhr University, Bochum, Germany.
15. *The influence of alcohol and drugs on driving.* Copenhagen, WHO Regional Office for Europe, 1981 (EURO Reports and Studies, No. 38).
16. JEANNERET, O., ed. *Alcohol and youth*, Basel, Karger, 1983, 211 pp.
17. LEVY, C. La mortalité par accident des enfants et des adolescents dans huit pays développés. *Population*, **35**: 291–320 (1980).
18. BROWN, G. W. & DAVIDSON, S. Social class, psychiatric disorders of mother, and accidents to children. *Lancet*, **1** (8060): 378–381 (1978).
19. WADSWORTH, J. Family type and accidents in childhood. *Child health and education studies*, **17**: 588 (1970).
20. BANDURA, A. *Aggression–a social learning analysis.* Englewood Cliffs, Prentice Hall, 1973.
21. ERON, L. D. ET AL. *Learning of aggression in children.* Boston, Little, Brown and Co., 1971.
22. LEFKOWITZ, M. M. ET AL. *Growing up to be violent.* New York, Paris, Pergamon Press, 1977.
23. SAND, E. A. ET AL. *L'échec scolaire à l'école primaire. Aspects psychosociaux. Prévention.* Brussels, Ministry of Education, 1982.
24. KNUDSON-COOPER, M. S. & LEUCHTAG, A. K. The stress of a family move as a precipitating factor in children's burn accidents. *Journal of human stress*, **8**(2): 32–38 (1982).
25. SOBEL, R. The psychiatric implications of accidental poisoning in childhood. *Pediatric clinics of North America*, **17**: 653–685 (1970).
26. HOLMES, T. H. & RAHE, R. H. The social readjustment rating scale. *Journal of psychosomatic research*, **11**: 213–218 (1967).
27. PLIONIS, E. M. Family functioning and childhood accident occurrence. *American journal of orthopsychiatry*, **47**: 250–263 (1977).
28. *Human factors in road accidents: report on a symposium.* Unpublished document of the WHO Regional Office for Europe, 1968 (EURO 0147).
29. *Prevention of road traffic accidents*: report by the Director-General to the Twenty-ninth World Health Assembly (WHO document A29/9).
30. LEWIS, C. E. & LEWIS A. L. Peer pressure and risk-taking behaviour in children. *American journal of public health*, **74**: 580–584 (1984).
31. BLOCH, H. & NIEDERHOFFER, A. *Les bandes d'adolescents.* Paris, Petite Bibliothèque Payot, 1963.
32. SIBERT, R. Stress in families of children who have ingested poisons. *British medical journal*, **3**: 87–89 (1975).
33. SHAW, M. T. M. Accidental poisoning in children: a psychosocial study. *New Zealand medical journal*, **85**: 269–272 (1977).
34. STUART, J. C. & BROWN, B. M. The relationship of stress and coping ability to incidence of diseases and accidents. *Journal of psychosomatic research*, **25**: 255–260 (1981).
35. BIERMANN, G. Unfallkinder [Accidents to children]. *Der Kinderarzt*, **13**: 1319–1322, 1690–1696 (1982).

Chapter 7

Psychosocial factors in the causation of accidents in adolescence

B. ZEILLER

Introduction

Adolescents are sometimes said to be reckless. This statement can be interpreted in two diametrically opposed ways, depending on whether recklessness is seen as something positive or something negative. Thus it can express admiration if the aim is to emphasize the character-building aspect of risk-taking, and as confirmation that the child is becoming an adult by gradually adopting—but more fully or more quickly than others—the modes of conduct and behaviour of his or her elders. In contrast, it may have a pejorative connotation, when behaviour leads to accidental injury or death, because risks and dangers have not been properly assessed.

The report of the WHO Technical Group on Psychosocial Factors Related to Accidents in Childhood and Adolescence, which met in Brussels in 1980 (*1*), placed great emphasis on the problems raised by such factors. In the previous chapter, Sand emphasized the fact that these psychosocial factors rarely act in isolation. Their inter-relationships make it difficult to determine the importance to be assigned to each of them (*2*).

The statistical data on adolescents are quite clear. They show that, in the majority of European countries, accidents are the leading cause of death in those aged under 20 years, and that the rates are particularly high for those aged 15–19. In France, in 1985, the mortality rates from accidents for those aged 15–19 were 62.9 per 100 000 for males and 22.4 per 100 000 for females, as compared with 16.4 and 7.0, respectively, for those aged 10–14. In fact, mortality from traffic accidents among boys increases with age up to the age of 21 years (*3*). Such data cannot simply be ignored. For professionals in the field of mental health, they raise the whole question of their role in the strategy of care and prevention.

Adolescence is not only a period of striking somatic and endocrine changes associated with puberty. It is also a stage in the development of the personality, with all the difficulties that involves for adolescents and those around them: establishing an identity, developing rivalries and antagonisms as a way of building a personality; trying things out and taking risks as a method of self-discovery. This construction and discovery of the self are a source of both pleasure and frustration. They come up against what is permitted and what is forbidden. At the end of the latency period, this process of maturation also leads to conflictive reactions towards the parent of the opposite sex (pre-oedipal and oedipal conflicts). Finally, the development of sexuality and of the emotions is one of the most important aspects of this stage. As far as intellectual development is concerned, Piaget (*4*) has described the emergence in adolescents of hypothetico-deductive or formal reasoning, with its cognitive and affective consequences.

Thus even the smallest manifestations of each of these changes could account for the individual and psychological causation of accidents. Adolescents who are involved in accidents rarely consult a psychologist or a psychiatrist because of them, since they are not, *a priori*, psychopathological in character. In addition, it is extremely difficult to appreciate the significance of a symptom and to connect it with the subject's mental state during one or two examinations or consultations. The difficulty is even greater in adolescents, since they are passing through a period of psychological maturation. Many diagnoses of a psychopathological condition in an adolescent, whether serious or not, can often only be made after several months of consultations, interviews, observation or psychotherapy. This shows the care with which the psychological factors that may be associated with an accident must be interpreted.

Adolescents at risk

Certain populations of adolescents combine a number of psychosocial and endogenous factors that tend to make them accident-prone. This is the case among those in whom, at one and the same time, psychological maladjustment and/or an unbalanced personality, sociopathological behaviour and family problems are combined (*1*). A longitudinal study of the medical histories of delinquent adolescents (*5*) showed that they had a higher accident rate (61%) than non-delinquent adolescents (41.7%). In a study on the health of adolescents said to be delinquent and admitted to an institution, a survey of traumatic lesions and intoxications was carried out (*6*). This showed once again a high incidence of road traffic accidents (60% of all accidents). This study was also important because the population studied consisted of adolescents admitted to an institution that was open to the outside world, who were assessed both from the educational and the medicopsychological point of view every day throughout their stay (2–3 years). Cross-checking of the data obtained with those of a study on the aggressivity of adolescents (*7*) admitted to the same institution makes it possible to come to some cautious conclusions as to the causation of the accidents observed.

Acting out

The propensity to acting out is a constituent of adolescent aggressive behaviour directed against others. It can account not only for the crimes that they commit but also for the outbursts of destructive behaviour in which emotional control is decreased or momentarily lost and during which adolescents are often injured. To a lesser degree, any group of young people who live or meet together is subject to such phenomena. Every day, the dispensaries of rehabilitation centres or educational establishments have to treat minor injuries that have occurred as a result of brawls or fights. This propensity to acting out, which is common in adolescence, appears to be linked most frequently to the following two factors:

– the extent to which young people can tolerate frustration. Certain adolescents, and particularly those who have suffered from a lack of affection, may not be able to tolerate apparently minor frustrations;
– the ability to verbalize. Where adults would use verbalization as a means of trying to resolve a conflict, adolescents quickly go over to acting out or physical force. They are thus sometimes simultaneously the aggressor and the victim.

The case of C., a boy of 16 who was not particularly athletic, may serve to illustrate this latter situation. As a result of a disagreement with a boy of his own age, C. struck him with his fist and kicked him. During this short brawl, C. fractured a leg in giving a particularly violent kick. Taken to a surgical department so that his fracture could be treated, he partially destroyed the furniture in the room because he could not stand being kept waiting. After leaving the hospital, he twice broke the plaster on his leg in the course of quarrels with his friends, during which he again started fighting.

This brief observation emphasizes the fact that the aggressivity of the adolescent towards others, because it is the most immediately obvious type of behaviour and the most difficult to tolerate, calls into question our own tolerance and our responses in preventing accidents and in providing care to the victims. In this context, there is a danger that an accident may be seen almost as a legitimate form of punishment. It is only too easy to think, wrongly, "after all, he got what he deserved". Here, there is a danger that the neurotic disorders of young people, their guilt and their self-punishment mechanisms (7) may be masked by the severity of the behavioural disorder.

Aggression directed against the self may also account for a large number of accidents among adolescents, whether or not associated with precipitating factors, such as the consumption of alcohol (8) or drugs (9).

The interrelationship between aggression directed against others and aggression directed against oneself raises the problem of the link between accidents and suicide.

The case of H., a 17-year-old, may serve to illustrate the complexity of this interrelationship. Although not in possession of a driving licence and not even knowing how to drive, H. stole a car after having consumed a large amount of alcohol. After driving a few metres, he hit another vehicle and destroyed a road sign. These five offences, which occurred within a period of a few minutes, resulted in his immediate imprisonment. However, he had been suffering for several weeks from depression and there was a danger that imprisonment would increase still further the risk of suicide. It proved possible to obtain his very rapid release so that he could continue to receive the necessary medicopsychological care.

Family problems

Family problems are common among adolescent accident victims and are found in 90% of those said to be difficult or delinquent (7). The family pattern is often characterized by an inadequate or absent father and a mother who may be possessive or suffer from serious personality disorders.

The interaction of psychosocial factors in adolescents means that accidents can represent a number of different things:

- the expression of inner conflicts through acting out rather than through fantasy;
- the coming together of these conflicts, with the contradictions that implies. This may lead the adolescent, consciously or subconsciously, to seek to patch together some way of reconciling them, which is liable to break down eventually. Young people are therefore confronted by their aggressive impulses, directed both at others and at themselves, their love of life and their wish for death, prohibitions and the wish to defy them, the pleasure principle and the reality principle.
- the unconscious and conscious guilt feelings with regard to these conflicts. These are more acute in people who have failed to resolve the oedipal problem.

The expression of these conflicts may give an accident not only the character of a parapraxis, but also that of an appeal and a cry for help.

The injury, whether trivial or serious, ultimately affects the only "object" of which the adolescent is the sole "proprietor": his or her own body.

References

1. *Psychosocial factors related to accidents in childhood and adolescence.* Copenhagen, WHO Regional Office for Europe, 1983 (EURO Reports and Studies, No. 46).
2. RENWICK, M. Y. ET. AL. Road fatalities in rural New South Wales: weighing the causes. *Medical journal of Australia*, 1(7): 291–294 (1982).
3. TAKET, A. Accident mortality in children, adolescents and young adults. *World health statistics quarterly*, 39(3): 232–256 (1986).
4. PIAGET, J. *La naissance de l'intelligence chez l'enfant.* Neuchâtel, Delachaux & Niestlé, 1966.
5. LEWIS, D. O. & SHANOK, S. S. Medical histories of delinquent children: an epidemiological study. *American journal of psychiatry*, 134: 1020–1025 (1977).
6. WAKS, K. *Manifestations somatiques chez 40 adolescents placés en foyer de semi-liberté.* Doctoral thesis, Faculty of Medicine, University of Paris, 1985.
7. ZEILLER, B. Les accidents chez les jeunes délinquants. *Revue de pédiatrie*, 17: 103–105 (1981).
8. STARY, M. Teenage use and abuse of alcohol. *Education annals*, 21: 10–13, 48 (1981).
9. JEANNERET, O., ed. *Alcohol and youth.* Basel, Karger, 1983.

Chapter 8
Child development and behaviour in traffic

B.-Å. LJUNGBLOM & L. KÖHLER

Introduction

One reason why children's accidents are a matter of such great public concern is that a child disabled or killed by an accident represents such a great loss, in WHO's phrase, of socially and economically productive life. It is unhappily the case that the accident risk per hour for a child is much greater than for an adult and depends on the developmental phase of the child as much as on the nature of the physical environment.

Development and maturation are two key concepts in all knowledge about children. The developmental aspect is so important that it influences the kinds of diseases that afflict children and the course and prognosis of these diseases. In addition, a child's strength, energy, capacities, abilities and behaviour must always be considered in the light of his or her development and maturation, which means that not only must physicians be aware of developmental aspects in their daily work with children and their problems, but also other professionals, such as psychologists, educationalists, social workers, architects, designers and town planners.

Analyses of child development have been connected with several theories, of which that of Gesell has been the most important for paediatrics (1). On the basis of his observations, Gesell formulated the following principles which are still seen as valid all over the world:

– development follows a definite sequence;
– development shows a cephalocaudal progression;
– development proceeds from gross undifferentiated skills to precise and refined ones.

These three principles are considered to be more or less fixed and immutable (2). The one aspect of development that Gesell accepted might vary was its rate, which is reduced under certain conditions and circumstances.

Piaget, the Swiss psychologist, has revolutionized thinking about cognitive development in childhood (3). The essence of development is seen as the individual's adaptation to his or her environment, and as a continuous process that proceeds stage by stage in a developmental hierarchy, where each reasoning process leads to the next, more complex one. In Piaget's theory, actions are important, both because they are the expression of cerebral processes and because thoughts are essentially internalized actions.

The stepwise development of the child's cognitive reasoning provides a good insight into the strategies of problem-solving and is a sound basis for developmental intervention and teaching programmes.

The psychoanalytical theories of child development (Anna Freud, Erik H. Erikson) have strongly influenced our understanding of children's emotional growth and stability, their attitudes, reactions and interpersonal relationships. They have demonstrated, in particular, the profound consequences that early childhood experiences may have later in life (4).

According to these theories, development follows certain laws, according to which there is an increase in ability and skill as the child grows older. All experience shows, however, that abilities and skills can vary, not only between different children of the same age, but also from day to day and from task to task in the same child. Thus, a child who for several days has been able to follow the rules for crossing the road may well forget them the following day.

Obviously, these and other developmental theories are useful when trying to understand children's behaviour in traffic. Often, accidents happen because children are not mature enough to manage their complicated environment, and it is not possible to eliminate risks solely by training, since children's learning ability is limited by their developmental phase.

Adopting a developmental approach, Stina Sandels and her co-workers in Sweden have investigated children's ability to manage traffic situations. They worked with normal children from 4 to 10 years of age and investigated how these children behaved in traffic before and after they had received special training (5, 6).

The spontaneous behaviour in traffic of children up to nine years of age is immature and marked by an inability to foresee dangerous situations. For instance, many children cross the street without looking at the traffic at all or if they do, it is at a late stage, after they have already started to cross. Furthermore, these children may behave completely unpredictably, treating roads and streets as playgrounds.

Children's capacities and instincts in traffic

Some systematic findings emerge from the studies by Sandels and her co-workers, which are crucial to an understanding of the basic problems of children's behaviour in traffic.

Impulsiveness

Children are guided by their impulses in quite a different way from adults. If they see something exciting on the other side of the road, they can forget all caution and everything that they have been taught about traffic and rush out into it, with total disregard.

Need for motion

Children have an inborn need to run, jump, and climb. For a child it is as unnatural always to walk calmly and quietly as it would be for an adult always to run. Automatically, this will increase the accident risk in traffic, where the basic assumption is that every pedestrian has the ability to walk in a disciplined fashion and is motivated to do so.

Fright and panic

Even when children are paying attention to traffic they are often not able to behave appropriately because traffic is so complicated and frightening that they can be scared by it and panic. A Norwegian schoolchild in the first grade described the situation in the following way: "Mostly I am afraid of the big lorries that drive so fast and sometimes come on to the pavement. Therefore, I run out on to the road but there are cars there too." Another child said: "Sometimes, on the pedestrian crossing, they nearly run into me. They run into children here, I have seen it in the paper" (7).

Vision

Children's field of vision has been found to be more limited than that of adults; as a result, they do not have the same ability to assess a traffic situation. Children are unable to concentrate on more than one object at the same time and and cannot change from near to distant sight as easily as adults. Thus, a child must first look at one object, then at a second, and finally at a third, in contrast to the adult who can see all three immediately. The ability to interpret fully in the brain what the eyes see is also a question of maturity, and this may not be reached until the age of 16, according to Piaget.

Height

If only because they are of short stature, children will find it difficult to assess traffic situations. A European seven-year-old child has an eye-height of about 100–125 cm while that of an adult is about 50 cm greater. In practical terms this means it is impossible for a child to see over the tops of parked cars and often not even over the bonnets. An oncoming car that would be seen immediately by an adult, will therefore be invisible to a child. Furthermore, the child will at the same time be invisible to the driver.

Hearing

Between 3% and 30% of six-year-old children incorrectly identified where a sound was coming from, depending on the direction from which it originated. An adult can also sometimes judge wrongly, but can more easily compensate for this. For a child, however, a mistake may have dangerous consequences; a wrong judgement can mean being run over by a car coming from an unexpected direction.

Ability to understand the meaning of words and concepts in traffic training

Children aged 6–10 years old were asked the meaning of important words and phrases such as "pedestrian", "pay attention to traffic" and "main road". It was found that young children did not understand the symbolic meaning of these words. At $7\frac{1}{2}$ years of age the children understood about half the words which at that time were routinely used in traffic training for five-year-old children. Subsequently, attempts were made to apply this finding and words are now used in traffic training that are understood by children at a given age, in accordance with their language skills. For this purpose, however, it is necessary to describe the complicated traffic system in such simple terms that the children still cannot understand how it functions in spite of the fact that they now understand the words. So the real issue is that of giving children information in such a way that it will help them to function adequately in traffic.

Ability to understand the meaning of important road signs

In the same way as for words, children's ability to understand the meaning of road signs was found not to be very good. A picture on a sign is a symbol that children often cannot understand. Thus, half of the six-year-old children studied understood at most 3 of 11 traffic signs that were particularly important for children. About 50% of eight-year-old children understood seven of them and about 50% of ten-year-old children ten of them. According to Piaget, it is not until they are teenagers that children begin to think in abstract terms like adults. Such results are therefore not surprising.

Ability to differentiate between left and right

The ability to think in abstract terms is necessary in order to be able to differentiate between left and right. Young children may be completely mystified by the fact that one side of the road is sometimes "the left" but on another occasion may be "the right" and vice versa. One investigation found that 58% of six-year-old children could differentiate between left and right; at seven years the proportion was 72%, and at nine years, 92%.

Ability to abstract and analyse impressions

The adult can hear, see, cross the road at a pedestrian crossing, and at the same time process all the available information and assess the overall situation, and then adjust his or her behaviour accordingly. Young children can only do one thing at a time, for example look or listen or decide to cross the road. This means that they can only absorb some of the information flow originating from cars driving fast and in opposite directions, various sounds, road signs and signposts. It is not surprising, therefore, that a gifted and traffic-trained girl, the daughter of intelligent parents, crosses the road in the following way: "First I look to the right, then to the left and then to the right again. Then I stand there trembling—and then I run" (7).

The information and observations presented above can be summarized as follows: children are not mature enough to cope with modern traffic, and education and training cannot change this. That is why a child, who behaves one day as a perfect pedestrian, may be totally unreliable the next. None of us expects a six-month-old child to walk. We all appreciate that the child's nervous system, musculature and skeleton are not sufficiently mature for this. But we seem to expect a seven-year-old child to be able to cross busy roads unaccompanied.

Children's behaviour in traffic before and after training

In their studies of children's behaviour in traffic, Sandels and co-workers simulated certain traffic situations. Behaviour in these simulated situations was found to be very similar to that in real-life traffic situations.

Behaviour before traffic training

The findings on behaviour in traffic before training can be summarized as follows:

(1) Crossing the road at a pedestrian crossing:
    6 years: less than 50% correct
    9 years: less than 75% correct
(2) Crossing a road, vehicles approaching from both directions:
    6 years: only occasionally correct
    7 years: less than 50% correct
    8–9 years: 50% correct
(3) Crossing a road, one parked car, no oncoming traffic:
    6 years: less than 50% correct
    7 years: 50% correct
    8–9 years: 75% correct
(4) Crossing a road, one parked car and oncoming traffic:
    9 years: less than 50% correct.

Behaviour after traffic training

An assessment of these training experiments suggested that it was possible to improve the children's skills, for example, in their understanding of road signs. It was also possible to improve their traffic behaviour through systematic training in real traffic situations, but only to a limited extent. Thus Sandels reports that it is possible to teach six-year-old children elementary traffic rules in some situations when they know that they are being observed.

In another set of extensive experiments with schoolchildren, the following results were reported (8) in a comparison of their traffic behaviour on bicycles before and after training:

(1) Looking behind before starting to cycle:

	Before training	*After training*
9–12 years	4%	60%

(2) Looking behind before turning to the left (across oncoming traffic):

	Before training	*After training*
9 years	10%	59%
10–12 years	20%	80%

(3) Stopping at the kerb before going on to the road:

	Before training	*After training*
9–12 years	50%	80%

Such findings seem to show that it is possible to improve many children's traffic behaviour by means of intense and systematic training. Unfortunately the investigation also showed—as one might expect—that a large number of children were unable to learn even very elementary precautions. Thus, for example, among 10–12-year-old cyclists, 1 in 5 could not learn to look behind before turning to the left. The investigations confirmed many of the most important findings from Sandels' surveys: appropriate training may give good results but a large number of children do not learn. The only way to protect such children in traffic is either to take direct control of them in some way, or to separate pedestrians and cyclists from the rest of the traffic. A Swedish study (9) showed that the risk of traffic accidents affecting children can be reduced by 80% by means of well designed traffic separation, and specifically by separating pedestrians and cyclists from motor traffic.

Adolescent behaviour in traffic

By the time they reach adolescence, children are in many respects as well equipped as adults, both intellectually and in terms of motor skills. They are, however, seriously handicapped by their lack of emotional and social maturity, the need to conform to the standards of the group to which they belong, and their desire to make an impression on friends, the opposite sex and adults. For many the results are tragic. Statistical evidence from both Norway and Sweden indicates that the risk per kilometre is extremely high for motorcyclists and riders of mopeds. Thus, for example, the risk of being injured in a collision with another vehicle is 3% for a 15-year-old riding a moped during the first year of use. The risk per kilometre is about ten times higher for a rider of a moped than for a car driver, and for the rider of a heavy motorcycle the risk is increased by a factor of about 25 as compared with the driver of a car (10).

Conclusions

The evidence produced by the studies reviewed here clearly confirms the view that, in accident prevention, it is necessary to consider the individual's maturity in all its aspects, i.e., in terms of motor skills, emotionally, socially and cognitively, in assessing capacity to behave appropriately in traffic. Maturation proceeds at varying speeds in these different fields and also varies from one individual to another. Age can therefore be no more than a broad indicator of children's ability to cope with traffic and of the kind of hazards that they will have difficulty in managing. The unpredictability of children's behaviour means that it is unrealistic to expect the total elimination of accidents.

However, certain steps can and should be taken at the local level to reduce the incidence of children's traffic accidents, as follows:

- Local accident prevention committees should be set up, on which all those directly concerned are represented, i.e., among others, paediatricians, accident surgeons, public health and school nurses, teachers and social workers, as well as politicians, parents and even children themselves. Their task will be to monitor the frequency, location, time of occurrence, cause and type of accidents, as well as the age and level of development of the victims and the nature of the injuries resulting from the accidents. These committees would be responsible for communicating the results and making recommendations to decision-makers in road planning, traffic control, public education on road safety, etc.
- In all planning of new roads, the design should be such as to separate motor traffic from pedestrians and cyclists. Wherever feasible, existing road systems should be modified in the same way.
- Public education and information for parents should emphasize both the link between age, development and traffic risks for children, and parental responsibility for the surveillance of children, particularly those under 12 years.
- To complement these local activities, further research on traffic behaviour training programmes for children of different age groups is necessary. The main aim should be to improve the learning and traffic behaviour of the less developed child and, for the youngest age group, to close the gap between understanding the vocabulary of traffic and behaving correctly in it.
- Further research on adolescent behaviour and the consequences of immaturity should enable public information and education programmes to be developed. These would be targeted on adolescents and young adults in order to encourage more mature and responsible traffic behaviour.

A child accident prevention programme including these components will be the natural consequence of any careful policy analysis based on the research findings. Properly implemented, the programme should result in a significantly reduced incidence of accidental injuries.

References

1. BALDWIN, A. L. *Theories of child development.* New York, John Wiley and Sons, 1968.
2. GESELL, A. *Studies in child development.* New York, Harper and Row, 1948.

3. FLAVELL, J. H. *The developmental psychology of Jean Piaget.* Princeton, NJ, Van Nostrand, 1963.
4. ERIKSON, E. H. *Childhood and society.* London, Penguin Books, 1967.
5. SANDELS, S. *Children in traffic.* London, Elek, 1976.
6. *Betänkende av barnolycksfallsutredningen.* [Report of the Committee on Accidents to Children.] Stockholm, Liber Förlag/Allmänna Förlaget, 1979 (SOU 1979:28).
7. RAUNDALEN, T. S. *Barnens vardag.* [The everyday life of children.] Stockholm, Awe/Gebers, 1979.
8. RYHAMMAR, L. *Barn och trafikundervisning.* [Children and traffic training.] Uppsala, Almqvist & Wiksell, 1979.
9. FORSKARGRUPPEN SKAFT. *Trafikolyckornas samband med trafikmiljö. Barnolyckor i Göteborg 1964–1966. Stadsdelsvis.* [Relationship between road traffic accidents and the traffic environment. Accidents to children in Gothenburg, 1964–1966, by district.] Göteborg, Chalmers tekniska högskola, 1969 (medeleande 23).
10. THULIN, H. *Traffic risk for different age groups and modes of transport.* Linköping, Swedish Road and Traffic Research Institute, 1981 (VTI-report 209).

Chapter 9

Education on safety and risk

J. R. JORDÁN & F. VALDES-LAZO

An analysis of the accidents that occur in infancy and childhood shows that the incidence of the different types varies as the child grows and develops.

Growth and development are inextricably linked, taking place simultaneously. Growth refers to the multiplication of cells and to changes in size, while development is concerned with the maturation of structures and their function, the whole process being extremely complex, with many interactions between the two. Growth is primarily quantitative in character; development more qualitative. The former is mainly a matter of anatomy, the latter more one of physiology. Growth relates to what one *is* (tall or short, lean or fat); development to what one can *do* (sit, stand, walk, run, speak, read, etc.) (*1*).

Paediatricians, as specialists in growth and development, have an important role as educators on safety and risk. They are well aware, in their daily practice, of the relationship between accidents and the child's age and level of development, of the predominance of boys and of children belonging to lower social groups, the increasing problems associated with urbanization and technology, and the vulnerability of children, particularly to accidents in the home and to road accidents (*2*).

Paediatricians, as children's advocates, are responsible for ensuring that their need for protection and education is recognized. Thanks to their knowledge of growth and development, they can act as counsellors to the parents and later to the children themselves; they can train health professionals and teachers in prevention and can use their influence to modify training courses for health professionals. Many have access to the mass media and even to policy-makers, advising on the need to take adequate measures, while always keeping in mind the possibilities and limitations of prevention. The awareness of their role in accident prevention is demonstrated by the numerous publications on the subject (*3–8*).

In 1966, at the World Health Assembly, the Member States of WHO adopted a resolution committing them to play an active role in accident prevention (WHA19.36). At the end of that same year, the first epidemiological investigation of morbidity due to accidents in children was carried out in Cuba. This study, involving nearly 8000 children, confirmed the predominance of boys over girls and the changing pattern of accidents as the child grows and develops (*9*).

It has been shown that injuries—the leading cause of death in children after the first few months of life—are related to the child's developmental stage. The link between children's developmental skills and the level of skill required by an activity may be particularly important. On the other hand, parents should be aware of children's increasing abilities and of the new hazards that these developmental milestones bring as they expand their area of action. The risk of injury in children can be related to the parental ability to judge and recognize correctly both the developmental skills of the child and the level of skill necessary for the safe completion of a task. Prevention involves either removing the hazards or changing the human factors by increasing parental knowledge of the children's level of development and their ability to interact safely with the environment.

A developmental approach that recognizes that children have different cognitive, perceptual, motor and language skills can provide many explanations of the occurrence of accidents. Although infants acquire the capacity to process information in the first two years of life, cognitive processes do not fully mature until adolescence. Children's mobility and progressive gross motor development place them at high potential risk of injury (see Chapter 8).

How accidents are linked to child development

It is easy to see that, as children develop and increase their potential abilities, the risk of accidents also increases. Health education is an important tool in accident prevention in children, both for the children themselves and for those who look after them. It is important, therefore, to warn those responsible for children, and especially mothers, about these developing potentialities. On the other hand, as children develop, their experience increases and they learn by trial and error what is unpleasant and dangerous. But this process is comparatively slow and children may frequently be tempted by curiosity or attracted by an unknown object or situation.

Fig. 9.1 shows the psychomotor development of the child during the first year of life (10, 11). The areas in which there is the greatest increase in skills during this period, which may contribute to accidents, are: gross motor, fine motor and adaptive. In our experience, accidents during this period are particularly common in developing countries. Environmental hazards and the insecure living conditions sometimes associated with overcrowded dwellings are major factors here.

In the newborn, the horizontal line representing the level of development crosses the base of the brain, indicating that no cortical control of voluntary movements is present. All movements, therefore, are involuntary, subcortical. Primitive reflexes are present (sucking, swallowing, Moro, grasping, rooting, etc.).

Fig. 9.1 Psychomotor development of the child during the first year of life. Horizontal lines have been drawn in sequence from the top downwards, one for each month of life, starting with birth.

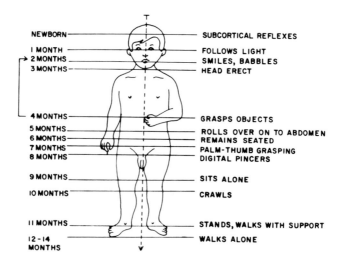

At the age of one month the line crosses the eyes: the child can now follow a bright object with the eyes. At two months, the line crosses the mouth indicating that at this age the child can smile and make babbling noises. At three months, the head can be held erect: the line crosses the base of the neck.

During the first three months, the main cause of accidental injury or death is obstruction of the airway, either by suffocation (compression by adults in the same bed or by the cords to which pacifiers are attached, soft pillows, ropes in the crib) or aspiration of food (e.g., as a result of being left in the supine position after feeding).

At four months, the line crosses the closed hand. Now both hands can meet and an object can be deliberately grasped. Objects are carried to the mouth. At five months, the child can roll over on to the abdomen: the line now crosses at this level. The child can first roll from the prone to the supine position and then the reverse. Another risk is now present: the child may fall from the cradle and in particular from a bed or table when lying unattended. Most cases of children falling from the cradle, bed or table are seen around this age. At six months, the line crosses the lower part of the trunk. Now the child can remain seated briefly, can lean forward on the hands to reach for nearby objects and carry them to the mouth, particularly by the age of seven months, when the line crosses the palm of the hand, indicating the thumb-palmar grasp.

Conditions become markedly more dangerous during the next stage of development. At eight months, the line touches the tips of the fingers indicating that now the child becomes able to grasp small objects like nuts, beads, etc. (index-thumb grasp or digital pincers). This adds other hazards, namely that such objects could be ingested or—much more seriously—breathed in with very dangerous consequences. The possible ingestion of dangerous objects, such as safety pins, increases the risk.

At nine months the child can sit steadily indefinitely and at ten months, the line passes through the knees, indicating that the child can now crawl, thus expanding the area of action. In moving around, the child may pick up dangerous objects, which may be ingested or drunk, and may fall down unprotected stairs. At twelve months, the line crosses the base of the feet, indicating that the child can stand alone and walk with support, and between twelve and fourteen months, the line passes below the feet: the child can now walk alone. The risk of dangerous falls now increases sharply when the child is not supervised by an adult. Again, it must be stressed that harmless falls are to be expected and overprotection should be avoided. However, supervision by an adult is imperative to ensure that the toddler does not fall into a bathtub, pail of water, or pool.

The ages shown in Fig. 9.1 indicate the average. Individual children may reach a particular stage several weeks earlier or later than indicated and parents should be aware of this.

Preschool children (1–4 years of age) are very curious and tend to explore their environment. To begin with, children regard the environment as part of themselves. They manage, by trial and error, to open doors and windows or to climb on to chairs and tables. All these activities are potentially dangerous. As their fine motor skills develop, they become able to open bottles which may contain toxic substances. Dangers also exist in the kitchen, where children may upset the contents of saucepans being heated on a stove.

As Gustafsson (*12*) has pointed out, the risk factors increase both with the complexity of the environment and the development of the child. At the same time, the child's development itself counterbalances these, as does adult supervision. The progressive development of the child's abilities thus makes itself felt everywhere in connection with the incidence and frequency of accidents, both increasing and diminishing the hazard, the latter as a result of experience. Motor and coordination skills lead the child to crawl, walk and run. The expansion of the range of action brings the child into the world outside the house. At the age of three years, children are able to talk and walk at the same time, but cannot then pay attention to what is going on in the immediate environment. From the age of five they are able to recognize colours and have good visual acuity (13). The majority can learn to ride a bicycle, but all their attention is devoted to stopping themselves from falling over and avoiding fixed obstacles. They have difficulty in judging the distance of moving vehicles. The concepts of space and of right and left begin at around six years, but even some adults find difficulty in identifying them quickly. At the age of seven, the behaviour of children in traffic is unpredictable and they should never be left alone in these circumstances (see Chapter 8).

In summary, those responsible for children should always be aware of the progressive development of skills with age so that they can take the appropriate precautions. It is clear that health education is an important tool in the prevention of accidents to children, but changes in the environment to make it safer are equally important.

Planning for prevention

Step 1: Reliable national mortality statistics

Statistics on births and deaths in Cuba are very reliable (14). Mortality due to accidents in children under 15 years of age in the country was analysed for the period 1979–1982. A total of 2371 death certificates were examined in which the cause of death was reported as an accident. Nearly 600 deaths occurred each year. The mortality by age group is given in detail in Table 9.1 (15).

The analysis of mortality due to accidents in Cuba showed that the main causes of death vary with age. In the light of the different risks that prevail at different ages, it should be possible to target education programmes to certain risk groups. Table 9.2 (15) shows mortality by

Table 9.1. Mortality in children under 15 years, Cuba, 1979–1982

Age (years)	No. of deaths	%	Rate per 100 000
< 1	279	11.8	55
1–4	529	22.3	22
5–9	704	29.7	17.5
10–14	859	36.2	18.3

Table 9.2. Number of deaths by age group and by type of accident, Cuba, 1979–1982

Type of accident	Age group (years)				Total
	< 1	1–4	5–9	10–14	
Traffic	9	153	317	344	823
Drowning	4	88	135	256	483
Burn	21	119	117	76	333
Choking	163	28	8	5	204
Fall	6	23	28	57	114
Electric shock	3	16	31	42	92
Mechanical suffocation	46	4	—	7	57
Electrocution by lightning	—	5	18	34	57
Poisoning	4	39	7	—	50
Foreign body in the airway	10	20	6	—	36
Falling object	—	—	13	6	19
Industrial	—	—	—	6	6
Other	13	34	24	26	97
Total	279	529	704	859	2371

age group and type of accident. In all the age groups, two-thirds of the victims were boys.

It is usually assumed that accidents are not an important cause of death during the first year of life; they are frequently disregarded in many publications, statistics being given for children over one year of age. This is because, in most developing countries, the infant mortality rate is fairly high and accidents are overshadowed by other causes of death, such as perinatal problems, infectious diseases and malnutrition. However, when the infant mortality rate decreases (in Cuba, the provisional rate for 1988 was 11.9 per 1000 live births) (16), accidents become a relatively important cause of death. It is clear that health education and accident prevention must start very early, even during pregnancy.

In the Cuban study, 58% of accidental deaths among those under one year were caused by aspiration of food during or after feeding. Another important cause of death was mechanical suffocation by the cords to which pacifiers were attached, small chains, necklaces and, more rarely, by being crushed by adults sleeping in the same bed

(16.5%). All these accidents took place in the cradle or in the adult's bed, particularly in the first few months of life. Burns and scalding, which mainly occur in the kitchen, accounted for 7%. In 3.6% the cause was a foreign body in the airway, followed by poisoning, particularly in the bedroom, kitchen or garden.

Fig. 9.2 shows the distribution of causes of accidental death for the age group 1–4 years. At this age, traffic accidents begin to increase as a cause of death. Nearly 30% are victims of these accidents, mainly as pedestrians. A further 22.5% die from burns and scalding, particularly in the kitchen. Another 16.7% are drowned in bathtubs or bodies of water around the house. Curiosity also often leads to other fatal accidents, e.g. poisoning (7.4%) or foreign bodies in the air passages (3.8%). Around 4% were killed by falls from a height and some 5%, particularly the younger ones, died as a result of food aspiration.

For the 5–9 year age group (Fig. 9.3) the expanding world of the child in conjunction with inexperience is reflected in the fact that 45% of deaths were due to traffic accidents; in most cases, the child was a pedestrian but some were passengers in vehicles. Drowning is important, accounting for 19.2% of accidental deaths. Burns, too, are important (16.6%) and electric shock accounted for 4.4%. Falls were the cause in 4%. Finally, 2.5% of deaths were a result of being struck by lightning.

In the 10–14 year age group (Fig. 9.4), children spend most of the time out of doors, so traffic accidents account for the highest

Fig. 9.2 Distribution of causes of accidental death at 1–4 years of age.

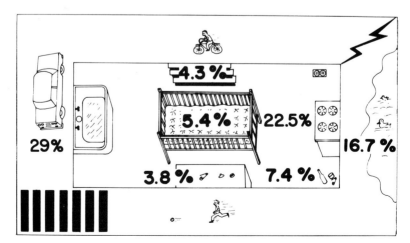

Fig. 9.3 Distribution of causes of accidental death at 5–9 years of age.

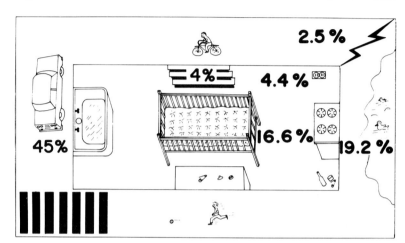

Fig. 9.4 Distribution of causes of accidental death at 10–14 years of age.

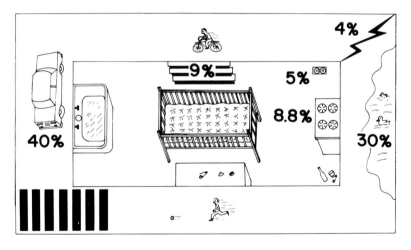

proportion (40%) of accidental deaths, followed by drowning (30%). Burns rank third (8.8%), followed by falls, now from greater heights (9%). Being struck by lightning caused 3.9% of deaths, mainly in the countryside.

In conclusion, the three main causes of accidental death in children aged less than 15 years in Cuba are: traffic accidents, drowning and burns. This information must be taken into account in establishing priorities and in health education programmes, while always bearing in mind the fact that risks vary with age and with the stage of development, and that the morbidity problem differs to some extent from that of mortality, so that studies specifically concerned with morbidity are necessary.

Step 2: Epidemiological studies of morbidity

As pointed out above, the second step in planning a national accident prevention programme is to carry out an epidemiological study of the morbidity due to accidents, since mortality is only the tip of the iceberg. Even morbidity is likely to be underestimated because the data cover only those cases that have been seen at health care facilities. In a pilot study carried out in Cuba in 1984, the questionnaire approved at a WHO symposium in Manila (2) was used. The survey was carried out over a period of one month in 22 health care centres randomly selected in eight of the 14 provinces of the country. A total of 2635 forms were completed, covering children from 0 to 14 years of age; 89.6% were from hospitals and 10.4% from policlinics. Two-thirds of the accident victims were boys and 79.6% of the accidents occurred in urban areas. Overall, more than half the accidents (52.9%) occurred at home, 24.7% outdoors, mainly on roads, and 21% in institutions such as schools, either in the school building or on the sports field.

During the first year of life, falls were the main cause of morbidity (70.9%), followed by blows from objects (9.3%) and burns (8.1%). In the age group 1–4, falls were again the most frequent cause of morbidity, followed by blows from objects, burns, poisoning, traffic accidents and animal bites. This age group accounted for 71.3% of all cases of poisoning; more than half of the cases were due to ingestion of kerosene in the kitchen, bedroom or garden. In the age group 5–14, the incidence of traffic accidents increased, children being injured mainly as pedestrians and cyclists. Apart from traffic accidents, falls were again the most frequent cause of morbidity.

Risks at different ages and at different places

Any health education programme must establish priorities on the basis of a pilot study or national survey to show which accidents occur most frequently and which are the most serious and likely to lead to death or permanent disability. In Cuba, the most important accidents during the first 15 years of life are traffic accidents, drowning and burns. Data from other countries also show the same picture. The priorities for the different age groups must also be considered. Certain types of accident predominate at certain ages and, as the child grows and becomes increasingly independent, the situation changes, some risks decreasing while others begin to appear.

As shown by the analysis of mortality over a four-year period (1979–1982) already mentioned, serious accidents during the first year of life occur mainly in the cradle or bed, and nearly all of them in the bedroom. In Spanish this is easy to bring out in a health education programme because, by chance, all the words for the various environments that the child encounters in its development begin with "C". Thus *cuna*, which means crib, cradle or cot in English, is followed by *cama*, which is bed in English and so on. The full list is as follows:

cuna	= crib, cradle or cot
cama	= bed
cuarto	= room
cocina	= kitchen
casa	= house
calle	= street or road
círculo	= day-care centre
colegio	= school
campo	= countryside.

Accidents change and the risk varies as the child acquires new skills. This fact must be made clear in all educational programmes for health workers, parents and teachers, and must be gradually introduced to the different target groups concerned with prevention.

In Spanish-speaking countries, we can use the slogan: *Cuidado con las "C"!* which means "Be careful with the Cs!". To illustrate this, some drawings have been prepared. In the first (Fig. 9.5) we see only the cradle or *cuna*. The second illustration is larger and shows the whole

Fig. 9.5 The cradle (*cuna*).

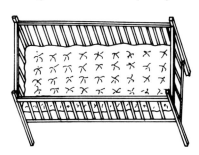

Fig. 9.6 The house (*casa*), showing kitchen, bedroom, bathtub, stairs.

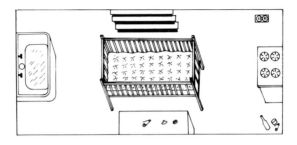

Fig. 9.7 The house and its surroundings.

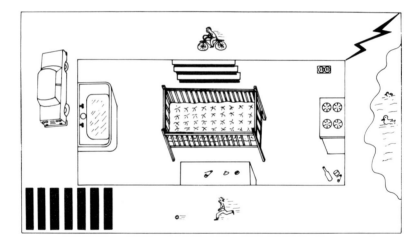

house with its various dangerous places (Fig. 9.6). Finally, Fig. 9.7 shows the road around the house and the surroundings, with the dangers of the agricultural environment and of nature itself, for example, cliffs, ponds and frequent storms.

Thus, on the one hand, we have the stages in development of the child and his or her new skills and, on the other, we have the successive spatial contexts, together with the new risks to which the child is exposed while still lacking knowledge and experience. Gustafsson's equation is relevant here: $HP \rightleftarrows SE$ (*12*), where H indicates the environmental hazard, P accident proneness or child's personality, S is supervision and E education (of both the child and the parents).

The same idea can be represented in the form of a balance of the kind shown in Fig. 9.8. The needle should be at the centre of the dial. If the

Fig. 9.8 The risk properly balanced.

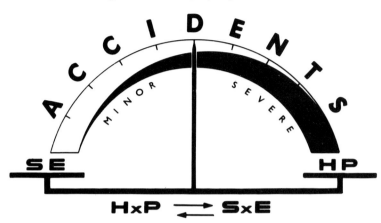

hazards and the child's personality shift the needle towards the right, more weight must be placed on the left, i.e., by increasing supervision and education, to restore the equilibrium. On the other hand, if the two last factors are present in excess, mild accidents (beneficial inasmuch as they "immunize" the child against more serious accidents) are avoided and this may be bad for the future, suddenly throwing the needle to the right when a risk appears.

Psychosocial factors in accidents in adolescence

The Cuban Child Growth Study (*17*), carried out in 1972–1973 on a randomized cross-sectional sample of the entire population aged up to 19 years, included a subsample of about 26 000 adolescents aged 10–19 years. A total of 15 anthropometric measurements were recorded, together with the stage of puberty and the degree of maturity of the bones of the hand and wrist.

It was found that, in general, puberty in girls started around 1.5–2 years earlier than in boys. However, there was considerable variation in both sexes in the age of maturation. In girls, at the age of 12 years, 10% had not yet started their breast development and 50% had no pubic hair. The situation was more variable in boys, where there were striking differences that may be the source of psychosocial difficulties (*18*).

At the age of 14, boys can be divided into three subpopulations: (1) those who are quite advanced in their maturation and have an almost adult morphology; (2) those at the half-way stage of pubertal development; and (3) the late developers, in whom practically no sexual maturation has taken place. These somatic changes, which are of great importance to adolescents, who are concerned with body image, are also associated with profound changes in function that increase muscular strength and capacity for exercise (*19, 20*). Those who mature early are not only taller and stronger, but are also better able to endure prolonged physical exercise.

These characteristics must therefore be taken into account among the endogenous factors that determine accident-proneness. Late maturers may be a high-risk group if they try to compensate for their temporary disadvantage; some may even adopt a systematic risk-taking behaviour. The normal variability of pubertal development must be carefully explained to the adolescent by parents, doctors and teachers, who should stress that variations in time and rate of development are perfectly normal and are not a cause for concern. People living in contact with adolescents should adopt an attitude of confidence and understanding in order to help them through this stage of life.

In the study of the different causes of accidental deaths in 1979–1982 in Cuba, mentioned earlier, the total number of deaths in the 10–19-year age group was 2207 (1651 boys and 556 girls). Among them, motor vehicle and other transport accidents were an important cause of death, accounting for nearly 45% of all accidental deaths. One out of four accidental deaths was due to drowning; 12.4% were industrial. A further 8.3% were caused by burns and there were three times as many girls in this group as boys. Most of these deaths occurred in the kitchen. Finally, in 5.3% of cases the cause was a fall and in this group there were 20 times as many boys as girls. Firearms caused 1.8% of deaths. In all prevention and education activities, this specific vulnerability of adolescents should be kept in mind.

Some general ideas on health education programmes

On the basis of the experiences in Cuba, some general ideas are put forward here on accident prevention programmes and how they can be presented to governments as a specific contribution towards achieving the goal of health for all by the year 2000.

National governments, through their ministries of public health and in cooperation with WHO and other international and nongovernmental organizations, should analyse statistics on mortality and, perhaps, morbidity, in order to determine the importance of the accident problem. On the basis of this information, programmes of varying degrees of complexity could be initiated, which should include a component dealing with health and safety education.

Health education should be based on the dual foundation of training and communication, with the emphasis on prevention. Health professionals (doctors, nurses, etc.) should receive training and they, in turn, should act as teachers at the undergraduate and postgraduate levels. In such training, the curricula should be adapted as appropriate to the local circumstances. Voluntary bodies can also supply educational and informational materials. The impact on individuals can be increased through the use of the mass media, with the aim of increasing awareness and thus changing both behaviour and the environment, and ultimately reducing the risk of accidents to children.

References

1. JORDÁN, J. R. The infant from 0 to 2 years of age: anthropometry and growth. In: M. Cusminsky et al., ed., *Growth and development. Facts and trends.* Washington, DC, Pan American Health Organization, 1988 (Scientific Publication, No. 510).

2. *Symposium on accident prevention in childhood: Report of a Symposium, Manila, 14–15 November 1983.* Unpublished WHO document WHO/IRP/ADR 218-22 2840E.

3. TAKET, A. Accident mortality in children, adolescents and young adults. *World health statistics quarterly*, **39**: 232–256 (1986).

4. BERGER, L. R. Childhood injuries: recognition and prevention. In: Gluck, L., ed., *Current problems in pediatrics*, Chicago, Year Book Medical Publishers, 1981.

5. BAKER, S. P. Childhood injuries: community approach to prevention. *Journal of public health policy*, **2** (3): 235–246 (1981).

6. MANCIAUX, M. ET AL. Epidemiology of children's traffic accidents in Europe. In: Kohler, L. & Jackson, H., ed., *Traffic and children's health*, Stockholm, Nordic School of Public Health, 1987 (NHV Report 1982: 2), pp. 37–55.

7. MANCIAUX, M. L'enfant et les accidents. In: *L'enfant en milieu tropical*, No. 123. Paris, Centre International de l'Enfance, 1980.

8. MANCIAUX, M. Accidents in childhood: from epidemiology to prevention. *Acta paediatrica scandinavica*, **74**: 163–171 (1985).

9. JORDÁN, J. R. Estudio sobre accidentes en el niño en áreas urbanas y rurales en Cuba. [Study on accidents to children in urban and rural areas in Cuba.] In: *Memorias del XII Congreso Internacional de pediatria.* Vol. III, pp. 240–243. Mexico City, Impresiones Modernas, 1968.

10. JORDÁN, J. R. Desarrollo psicomotor del niño. [Psychomotor development of the child.]. In: *Temas de pediatria* [Aspects of paediatrics], Havana, Editora Universitaria, 1976.

11. JORDÁN, J. R. Desarrollo psicomotor del niño (primer año de vida). [Psychomotor development of the child (first year of life).] Washington, DC, Pan American Health Organization, 1987 (Audiovisual slide tape programme, No. 95).

12. GUSTAFSSON, L. H. Children in traffic. Some methodological aspects. *Paediatrician*, **8**: 181-187 (1979).

13. LAGERKVIST, B. *Accident prevention in childhood: the foundation of pedagogical objectives and curricula based on various steps of the child's growth and development.* Unpublished paper presented at the Symposium on Accident Prevention in Childhood, Manila, 14–15 November 1983.

14. PUFFER, R. *Report of the quality and coverage of vital statistics on perinatal and infant mortality in Cuba.* Unpublished document of the Pan American Health Organization, 1974 (PAHO/AMRO Project 3513).

15. JORDÁN, J. R. ET AL. *Accident prevention and its relation to psychosocial development of children: experience with the Cuban pilot study on accidents.* Unpublished document presented at Havana, 16 November, 1984. Summary report IRP/APR/216 m3 1K(S) 4997E, 1985.

16. *Informe anual 1988. Annual Report.* Havana, Ministry of Public Health of Cuba, 1988.

17. JORDÁN, J. R. *El crecimiento del niño.* [Growth of children.] Barcelona, Editorial JIMS, 1988.

18. JORDÁN, J. R. Growth and development of the adolescent: a Cuban national study. In: *The health of adolescents and youths in the Americas,* Washington, DC, Pan American Health Organization, 1985 (Scientific Publication, No. 489).

19. TANNER, J. M. Growing up. *Scientific American,* **229**: 35–44 (1973).

20. PARISKOVA, J. & POUPA, O. Some metabolic consequences of adaptation to muscular work. *British journal of nutrition,* **17**: 341–348 (1963).

21. SCHELP, L. & SVANSTROM, L. *Community intervention and accidents. Epidemiology as a basis for evaluation of a community intervention programme on accidents.* Sundbyberg, Sweden, Karolinska Institute, 1987.

22. JANSSON, B. & SVANSTROM, L. *Agriculture and injuries. A system for injury surveillance in Swedish emergency care as a basis for injury control.* Sundbyberg, Sweden, Karolinska Institute, 1988.

PART III

THE TECHNOLOGICAL AND LEGISLATIVE APPROACH

Chapter 10

Environmental risks in the industrialized countries

J. GREENSHER

The environmental aspects of the most common injuries to children and adolescents will be reviewed in this chapter, with particular emphasis on the concept of active versus passive protection (see Table 10.1). Active protection requires the participation and cooperation of the individual involved; as a result, effectiveness depends on correct usage. Passive protection, which has proved to be the most effective means of injury control, does not require active individual participation; rather it is designed to act automatically. In the evaluation of the various factors, it is useful to distinguish between the pre-event, event, and post-event phases, using the framework developed by Haddon & Baker (*1*).

Traffic accidents

Motor vehicles

These are the greatest cause of mortality due to unintentional injury, producing about half of the fatal injuries in children and adolescents. Public health workers have made little distinction between trauma caused by motor vehicles and that caused by disease, and therefore have approached automobile-associated injuries by advocating preventive strategies, such as restraining systems.

In several studies and analyses, *safety belts* were found to reduce fatalities and injuries by about 50% overall. It was recognized early, however, that standard safety belts are not suitable for small children since they could cause abdominal injuries in a collision. Children under 4–5 years of age therefore need special restraining devices. Infants are especially vulnerable to fatal injuries in motor vehicle accidents, particularly when held on a passenger's lap. In 1980, the American Academy of Pediatrics initiated a campaign entitled "First Ride A Safe Ride", aimed at actively involving paediatricians in educating the public in the use of *safety seats*. Encouraged by the passage of a child passenger protection law in 1978 in the state of Tennessee and the positive effects of an educational and police enforcement campaign in reducing fatalities and injuries, all the 50 states of the USA and the District of Columbia now have laws making it mandatory for children in motor vehicles to be restrained. Federal regulations were also developed requiring dynamic testing standards for systems used to restrain children in motor vehicles.

Table 10.1 Accidents in industrialized countries: environmental risks and prevention strategies

Cause	Prevention strategy	
	Passive	Active
Motor vehicles	Fitting of seat-belts	Use
		Enforcement
	Fitting of children's car	Correct use
	restraints	Education
		Enforcement
	Airbags	Maintenance
	Reduction of speed	
	Lower speed limits	Enforcement
	Reducing alcohol consumption	Enforcement
	Raising the legal age	
	Increasing the price	
	Raising the minimum age for	Education
	obtaining a driving licence	
	Making roads and vehicles safer	Appropriate
	Separating vehicles from pedestrians	clothing for
	Legislation regarding reflectors on	pedestrians
	bicycles	
Drowning	Physical barriers	Maintenance
	Installation of warning signs	Observation and
		enforcement
	Safe pool design	
	Reducing alcohol consumption	
	Legislation	Enforcement
	On-site rescue and resuscitation	
	Equipment availability	Use and knowledge
		Learning to swim
Burns	Use of flame-retardant materials	
	Construction	
	Clothing	
	Furniture	
	Cigarettes	Reduced
		consumption
	Self-extinguishing	
	Increasing the price	
	Installation of automatic sprinklers	
	Installation of smoke detectors	Maintenance
	Provision of fire exits	Maintenance
	Establishment of burns centres	

Table 10.1 (*contd.*)

Cause	Prevention strategy	
	Passive	Active
Falls	Installation of window barriers Protective surfaces Rounded corners and edges	Enforcement

Bicycles,
motorized
bicycles
motorcycles,
all-terrain
vehicles
	Safe construction
	Protective clothing
	Legislation
	   Age of use
	   Minimum age for alcohol
	     consumption
		Enforcement
		Training and
		   enforcement

	Crash helmets Legislation	Enforcement

Poisoning	Packaging
	   Legislation
	Establishment of poison control
	   centres
		Enforcement

The state laws have not been totally effective in ensuring use of restraints for children, the major problem being that of enforcement. An additional problem has been improper use. In recent studies, 70% of the child safety seats in use were being used incorrectly: without tethers, without seat belts, with an unsafe harness assembly, or incorrectly positioned. To achieve more uniform and correct use, the National Transportation Safety Board recommended public education, legislation, research, enforcement and training. A number of states organized child passenger safety, restraint education and loan-a-seat programmes as a way of solving the problem of misuse.

Seat-belt use by adolescents, young adults and drunk drivers is particularly poor. Automatic seat-belts would be most effective in this high-risk group, even though their theoretical effectiveness is somewhat less than that of three-point belts.

Airbags offer passive protection automatically for occupants of the front seats, particularly in frontal crashes. They offer only minimal protection in side-on collisions, roll-overs or ejections. It is felt that a combination of airbags and seat-belts offers maximum protection.

Alcohol is a major contributing factor in many types of injuries and plays a significant role in automobile injuries in teenagers. Efforts to reduce alcohol consumption have met with mixed success and have produced only limited results. Price appears to be a factor governing consumption of alcohol by teenagers, and increasing its cost could result in reduced consumption and a lower accident rate in this high-risk group. Raising the statutory drinking age to 21 years has also been found to result in a reduction in accident fatalities among teenagers, which has led to the upward revision of the permitted drinking age in many states.

Another environmental factor that must be considered is *road characteristics*. Mortality rates per vehicle–mile on the main interstate roads in the United States are only a third of those on other roads.

The *age of the driver* must also be considered. Teenage drivers have a significantly higher involvement in fatal crashes. Driver education for teenagers in schools resulted in a higher rather than a lower fatality rate by enabling a larger number of teenagers to become drivers. Increasing the driving age could reduce the fatalities in this age group.

Pedestrian injuries and fatalities, which account for half of all automobile-associated deaths, represent a significant challenge. Appropriate vehicle design and better separation of vehicles and pedestrians are essential if any significant reduction is to be achieved. Speed is an important factor in determining the severity of injury. Use of reflectors on clothing and bicycles would make pedestrians and cyclists more easily visible. An increase in the duration of the amber phase of traffic lights can ensure safer traffic flow at intersections. Lower bumpers can reduce the incidence of hip fractures in pedestrian victims. Increased use of traffic lights, stop signs, and overpasses or underpasses at danger zones are effective means of protecting pedestrians.

Bicycles and other two-wheeled vehicles

The *bicycle* comes first in the list of hazardous products maintained by the Consumer Product Safety Commission in the United States. In 1980 there were 100 million bicycles in the country. Of 1200 deaths associated with their use, 35% were of children under 14 years of age. The average annual accident rate for riders aged 5–12 years is 2%, an estimated 20% of the accidents resulting in fractures and an estimated 5% in concussion. In one series of 107 injured children, of whom 20% had been involved in a collision with an automobile, trauma to the head was the most common injury.

Minibikes are particularly dangerous because of their poor handling characteristics due to the short wheelbase, small tyres, insufficient acceleration, inadequate brakes and small size. Lack of safety devices or defective or poorly constructed components were implicated in one-third of accidents involving these vehicles. Short of banning them altogether, action to make wearing of helmets and protective clothing mandatory for riders and limitation of their use to designated hazard-free areas appear to be the only possible responses to these unsafe vehicles.

Mopeds are low-speed, lightweight motorcycles with some of the operating characteristics of both bicycles and motorcycles. Acceleration is often inadequate for city traffic and their low speed is inappropriate on the highways. Injuries to the head and lower extremities are the most common serious injuries. Helmets will protect the head, but not the neck, from injury.

The death rate for riders of *motorcycles* in the United States is estimated at approximately 43 deaths per 100 million miles, as compared with the overall death rate for drivers of motor vehicles of 2.55. Approximately 90% of motorcyclists involved in accidents are male and 60% are under 25 years of age. Over 30% of the fatal accidents involve persons under 20 years of age. The protective effect of helmets has been shown for all types of head injury. A rider without a helmet is twice as likely to suffer a minor head injury and five times as likely to sustain a severe or critical injury as a rider wearing a helmet.

All-terrain vehicles

The three-wheeled versions of these off-the-road vehicles, which have begun to appear over the past few years, are producing an escalating number of injuries and deaths associated with their use. According to the United States Consumer Product Safety Commission (CPSC), over 1000 deaths related to the use of all-terrain vehicles (ATV) have occurred since 1982; they estimate that over 85 000 ATV-related injuries are treated in hospital emergency rooms yearly. A review of the fatalities indicates that 50% of victims are under 16 years of age and 23% under 12 years of age. The causes appear to be related to the inherent instability of the vehicles, difficulty in controlling the vehicles, inexperienced drivers, carrying of passengers, speeding, and alcohol abuse. Serious spinal cord injuries are occurring as a result of rollovers. Children under 16 seem to be at greatest risk. A major effort was made by the CPSC to obtain a detailed analysis of ATV use and to determine whether regulation was needed. In 1988, an agreement was reached between the US Justice Department and manufacturers, banning the sale of all three-wheeled ATVs and restricting the four-wheeled vehicles to riders over 16 years of age.

Drowning

Drowning ranks second as the cause of death in the 0–14-year age group in the USA. The rates are especially high at ages 1–2 years and in males 17–20 years of age. Drownings occur most frequently in natural bodies of water, swimming pools and bathtubs. Swimming-pool deaths occur predominantly in the 0–4-year age group, accounting for 57% of pool deaths in one report. Swimming pools were cited as being involved in 13% of the drowning deaths for all ages and in 23% of those of children 0–14 years of age.

Efforts to prevent drowning have been aimed both at young people and at the sites of drowning. Modification of the physical environment, e.g., by installing physical barriers at sites of high risk, on river banks, around swimming pools, etc., and by marking hazardous bodies of water to indicate the depth, undertow, etc. has had some success in reducing the risk of drowning. Studies in Australia have suggested that fencing around pools can markedly reduce the number of deaths from drowning in the 0–14-year age group. Swimming pool design, including adequate fencing and self-latching gates, has received a great deal of attention. Since the introduction, acceptance and use of automobile safety restraints for children, drowning is beginning to replace motor vehicle accidents as the leading cause of death in the young age groups in states of the USA that have large numbers of swimming pools (California, Arizona). Standards must therefore be developed for the safe design of pools, including safety features such as adequate fencing, non-slip surfaces, appropriate lighting, covers, on-site rescue and resuscitation equipment, etc.

In teenagers and adults, the association of alcohol consumption with boating accidents and drowning poses a special problem. Significant blood alcohol levels have been found in drowned persons over 15 years of age.

Diving accidents causing death and morbidity in the form of paraplegia or quadriplegia should be mentioned here. A campaign to call attention to the dangers of diving into unfamiliar natural bodies of water is necessary in order to prevent the debilitatig and costly consequences of the head and neck injuries that may result.

Burns

Fire is the third most common cause of death in children in the United States, the majority taking place in the home. House construction is an important factor in fires. Older houses are more flammable and faulty electrical and heating systems are leading causes of fires. The mortality rate from fires is higher among low-income families. Cigarettes are also a main cause of fires; self-extinguishing cigarettes would reduce fire hazards.

Smoke detectors have been found to give early warning of fire, and morbidity and mortality can be markedly reduced by their use. The use of smoke detectors would be the single most effective means of preventing death and injury due to fire in children. Automatic sprinkler systems can effectively reduce the spread of fire but are very expensive. Mandatory fire codes should be aimed both at primary prevention and at the secondary containment of fires.

Ignition of clothing was a common cause of burns in children in the USA prior to the 1960s, especially in young girls. A change to more tight-fitting clothes and use of less flammable fabrics led to a significant reduction in the fatality rate from this cause. The introduction of flammability standards for children's nightclothes further markedly reduced the morbidity and mortality. The finding that Tris, a commonly used flame-retardant chemical, was potentially carcinogenic hampered efforts to extend the concept to other materials.

The development of modern burn centres has had a significant effect on survival rates after burn injuries.

Falls

The great majority of deaths from falls occur in the elderly and are predominantly the result of the subsequent complications. Falls from a height are a category peculiar to children. These deaths most frequently involve young children falling from high, unguarded windows.

Modification of the environment by installing childproof barriers and walkways would reduce the injury rate. In the programme "Children can't fly" in New York City, the emphasis was on direct passive prevention. The city made available lightweight inexpensive window bars that could be easily installed in high-rise apartment buildings, and this resulted in a 47% reduction in the number of deaths due to falls among children under 16 years of age. Recent reports indicate that such programmes must be followed up if the gains are to be maintained.

Additional environmental factors contributing to high morbidity from falls among children are sharp edges and corners. Furniture, especially low tables, is particularly important in this respect. Hard surfaces, particularly in playground settings, increase the severity of any injuries.

The design of playgrounds, houses, and furniture to take into account the potential for causing injury would help to reduce morbidity and mortality from this source.

Poisoning

The past 15 years have seen a marked decrease in the number of deaths due to poisoning among children in the United States from over 400 to approximately 50 per year in children under four years of age. Changes in the environment of the child, particularly from the point of view of passive prevention, have played a significant role in bringing about this reduction.

A reduction in the lead content of paint, and the change from coal gas to natural gas (containing a lower concentration of carbon monoxide) have created safer products. Reducing the number of junior aspirin tablets available in a bottle to less than the toxic dose, and the requirement that childproof containers should be used for many drugs and poisons, have led to a dramatic decrease in poisonings from these products as compared with those that are not required to be packaged in this way. Unit quantities of dangerous household products such as lye were introduced as a method of prevention but were poorly accepted by the public; further research is required in this area.

The development of poison control centres across the United States to respond to the large number of ingestions occurring led to improved access to accurate information on toxicity and more appropriate treatment. Regionalization and the development of appropriate standards for these centres represented an important step forward.

Unsafe products—unsafe people

Articles commonly available around the home—bicycles, toys, chemicals, tools—are frequently involved in significant numbers of deaths and injuries. In the United States, the Consumer Product Safety Commission (CPSC) was created in 1972 to "protect the public against the unreasonable risks of injuries and deaths associated with consumer products". A major objective of the CPSC was to promote research and investigate the causes and methods of prevention of product-related deaths and injuries. The CPSC was further required to maintain a National Injury Information Clearinghouse to collect, investigate, analyse and disseminate injury data and information.

To allow the CPSC to set priorities for further investigations or action, data collection was essential. The National Electronic Injury

Surveillance System (NEISS) was therefore created in 1972 and redesigned in 1978. It is a two-level system for collection of data on injuries, consisting of hospitals selected as statistically representative of the USA and its territories. NEISS performs two functions. First, national estimates of the number and severity of product-associated injuries treated in hospital emergency rooms are made. Second, injury victims can be located, if necessary, to obtain further information. Additional information is gathered from death certificates, consumer complaints, etc.

NEISS data originate from patients attending the selected hospital emergency departments, who are routinely questioned by clerks as to how the injury occurred. Every day, a NEISS coder reviews the records for product-related injuries. The product is coded as precisely as possible by means of a coding manual. The information is transcribed on to a coding sheet and entered into a dedicated computer terminal installed for this purpose. The computer system edits the data and prepares a daily summary and detailed case print-out for review by the staff of the Directorate for Epidemiology, which then become part of the permanent data base.

The redesigned (1978) NEISS updated and improved the sample, thereby increasing the validity of the estimates. The 1972 sample included only hospitals within the contiguous United States; the revised sample included Alaska, Hawaii and overseas territories. The redesign also provided a means of making changes in the sample while maintaining the basic sampling plan. The operational procedures were also improved so as to decrease coding errors and minimize under-reporting. The collection of more detailed data was also instituted. Reports now provide for two product codes and an indication of the involvement of a third product where necessary. Motor vehicle accident data were also added. At the first level, i.e., surveillance, NEISS provides a measure of the size of the problem of product-related injury as reflected by the number and severity of injuries treated in hospital emergency rooms throughout the USA. The data generated provide valuable management information for use in selecting priorities. Since only product involvement, not accident causation, is measured, a second-level or in-depth investigation is needed to determine how the accidents happened.

Hospital emergency rooms were selected as the source of injury statistics because they provide a large reservoir of cases and offer a cost-effective means of evaluating product-related injuries. Only about 40% of such injuries are treated in emergency rooms, however, so that the data thus obtained do not provide a measure of the entire injury problem. They do, however, give a good approximation to it.

Attempts are made to ensure uniform reporting by the use of study manuals and forms, periodic site visits and regular contacts between those collecting the data and those with overall responsibility for the process. It is thought that the quality-control procedure keeps reporting errors to a minimum. Some misclassification does occur however, because of the difficulty of obtaining precise product descriptions from emergency-room records. Proper treatment of the injured, in fact, does not necessarily require the identification of the product concerned. For this reason, it is suggested that, in general, the estimates provided by NEISS do not fully reflect the actual incidence of product-related injuries in the population.

References

1. HADDON, W. & BAKER, S. P. Injury control. In: Clark, D. & MacMahon, B., ed., *Preventive and community medicine*, Boston, Little, Brown & Co., 1981, pp. 109–140.

The Injury Prevention Program (TIPP) and the manual *Injury control for children and youth* of the American Academy of Pediatrics (PO Box 927, Elk Grove Village, IL 60009–0927) cover a vast amount of material on the various matters dealt with in this chapter.

Chapter 11

Injury control for young people: technology, biomechanics and product safety

D. MOHAN

Introduction

Childhood injuries have given rise to a great deal of concern in the industrialized countries over the past 20 years. This has resulted in many expensive campaigns of education, publicity and propaganda aimed at reducing the incidence of such injuries. These have very often been accompanied by research programmes and the introduction of regulations, standards and design guidelines concerning products commonly used by children. Regulations that would not normally be accepted by society in general are sometimes adopted when children are involved. Similarly, safety standards can be promulgated for products used by children but not as easily for those used by adults: children's nightwear must satisfy standards of flammability in many countries, but similar standards do not exist for adult clothing. No attempt has been made to reduce the temperature at which cigarettes burn or the time for which they can continue to burn on their own, although it is accepted that such standards might reduce the incidence of fires caused by unattended cigarettes. This shows that it is easier to initiate safety measures when children are involved.

The situation in the less industrialized countries is somewhat different. While societal concern for the well-being of children in these countries is similar to that in the developed countries, such concern is very often not translated into effective control over the safety of products and the environment, mainly for the following reasons.

- Morbidity and mortality due to diseases are perceived to be a more serious problem than injuries as far as children are concerned.
- In general, play areas, dwellings and equipment used by children are not controlled by centralized agencies. Toys and recreational equipment are very often made by small manufacturing units. This makes it very difficult to enact and enforce laws, regulations and standards.
- Housing, living and working conditions in developing countries make it difficult for parents to pay much attention to the safety of their children as they themselves risk their lives and health in the everyday living and work environment. Their working conditions do not allow them to look after their children as they would like to. Similarly, parents who are constantly worrying whether their

children are suffering from the malnutrition and endemic diseases prevalent in tropical regions may have different concepts of risk as far as morbidity due to injuries is concerned.

- Many countries do not have effective controls on, or knowledge of, the safety of imported products.
- Though it is possible that childhood injury rates are fairly similar in both developing and developed countries, the causal factors may be so different that perceptions of the problem will vary greatly from country to country.

In the light of the foregoing, this chapter has been divided into the following three parts:

- A summary of basic information on biomechanical, thermal, electrical and chemical aspects helpful in product and environmental design.
- A listing of countermeasures applicable to both products and the environment that are likely to be effective in reducing the incidence and severity of injury among children and young people around the world.
- Areas where more research and evaluation are required

Technical considerations in product safety

Biomechanical considerations

Biomechanics is an interdisciplinary field which links physics, mechanical engineering, anatomy and physiology in an attempt to understand the properties and functioning of the human body. In the past few decades, a great deal of data have been generated which are useful in designing safer products, thereby reducing the probability and severity of injury in accidents.

Impact injury
Not enough is known about the biomechanical properties of human tissues and body segments of children under 15 years of age. However, for purposes of product design, enough knowledge is available to enable some basic safety criteria to be established.

The probability of head injuries increases dramatically when the height of a fall (on to a rigid surface) is greater than one metre. Studies show that even thin rugs over hard floors, wooden floors and hard mud-packed surfaces reduce the probability of severe injury in a fall. The risk of injury from falls from 2–4 metres can be reduced to some extent if the impacting surface is loose sand or a thick soft mattress.

Feet-first falls on to rigid surfaces start becoming hazardous for teenagers and older persons from heights of 2–3 metres. Similar data for toddlers are not available. However, falls of infants and toddlers from heights of less than one metre do not generally cause serious injuries; in contrast, falls from 1.5 metres have been known to cause fractures of the cranium (star fractures) and of the collar bone.

The mechanisms of brain injury are not entirely understood; this applies particularly to impacts that do not cause easily identifiable cerebral lesions but do result in amnesia, recurring headaches, changes in behaviour patterns and epilepsy. It is generally accepted, however, that acceleration and deceleration of the head should be kept to a minimum, and in general to less than $200\,g$ in short-duration (10.0 ms) impacts. Such criteria can be used in designing helmets for use by riders of two-wheeled vehicles and in sports. Studies show that it is possible to reduce head acceleration levels to acceptable limits by appropriate use of cushioning material in helmets.

Child strength

Children can at times exert much greater force than might be expected and can either break or deform toys and other recreational equipment, making them more dangerous than anticipated by the manufacturer. They may also force some part of their body into an opening or gap that would normally be too small for them. Toys and equipment should therefore be designed to withstand such forces and available data on the subject should be made available to manufacturers, designers and regulatory bodies.

Anthropometry

Age- and sex-specific anthropometric data for North American children are now available. These data are essential in designing toys and furniture for children so as to ensure that it is not easy for their fingers or limbs to become trapped in small gaps and openings. Such gaps should either be designed so that children's limbs are unable to enter them at all, or they should be large enough to allow free movement. These principles have been used to set standards for slats in crib design and for establishing guidelines for holes which do not trap children's fingers.

Corners and edges in furniture, steps, toys and other equipment routinely cause cuts, lacerations and severe bruises in very minor impacts. While it is impossible to eliminate such injuries completely, their incidence and severity can be greatly reduced, e.g., by using rounded corners and edges.

Whether or not a pointed object punctures the skin involves a complex relationship between the diameter of the point, the properties of the skin and the force applied. The probability of puncture is significantly reduced as the diameter of the point increases. However, children's skin is much softer than that of adults and they are also likely to poke their own eyes or those of others in play or anger. It is therefore advisable not to leave pointed objects within their reach.

Sports equipment and activities

Injury mechanisms in sporting events have been analysed in a number of studies and this has made it possible to suggest specific design criteria to make sporting activities safer. The notable examples include the analysis of jogging and running shoes, ski-bindings, protective equipment in hockey and football, etc. Such studies are concrete proof that it is possible to redesign equipment to make it much safer, using biomechanical criteria.

Thermal considerations

There is a well known relationship between contact time and temperature for various levels of thermal injury. Skin contact with an object at a temperature of 70 °C for between 0.5 and 1 second will result in a burn that can be completely cured. If contact is for more than one second, irreversible injury is likely. The extent of the injury will obviously depend on the size of the heat source: a hot needle will burn a small superficial layer of skin, whereas a hot cooking pot could cause an extensive deeper burn. Apparently the body can tolerate contact with hot air for somewhat longer periods than solid objects at similar temperatures.

It is also important to remember that children's skin and tissues are more sensitive than those of adults. In general, therefore, children should not be exposed to surfaces hotter than 55 °C; grilles of space heaters should be designed so that they do not reach temperatures higher than 55–60 °C.

Electrical considerations

Electric shock may result in localized burns, cardiac fibrillation, respiratory failure, neurosystem damage or instantaneous death. The extent of the damage will depend on the voltage, frequency of the current, the quality (wet or dry) and extent of the contact area, and the quality of grounding of the human body. There are large variations in all four parameters so that it is not easy to set clear exposure limits for all situations. Children, however, generally encounter voltages of 220 volts or less, and frequencies of 50–60 Hertz or DC. In general, any voltage greater than 40 volts is dangerous and there is not much to choose between 110 and 220 volts. Alternating current frequencies of 50–60 Hz are about the most hazardous as they result in tetanic muscular spasm. Since all countries have adopted household voltage standards of around 120 volts or 220 volts, young children should be kept away from all electrical appliances. All electrical toys should operate at voltages of less than 40 volts.

Chemical considerations

It is not possible to set a single standard for the maximum permissible dose of chemical poisons as the mode of action, lethal dose and after-effects vary so greatly. In addition, little is known about the long-term effects of low-level exposure to many toxic chemicals. Toxicity is defined in terms of the lethal dose for 50% of a test population of animals (LD_{50}) and toxic substances are rated accordingly. One of the classifications used is the following:

	Lethal dose per kg of body weight
Super toxic	Less than 5 mg
Extremely toxic	5–50 mg
Very toxic	50–500 mg
Moderately toxic	500 mg–5 g
Slightly toxic	5–15 g
Practically non-toxic	more than 15 g

Since young children (say, of less than 20 kg in body weight) can easily gulp down 20 ml of liquid or eat 20 g of powder, they can quickly ingest almost a lethal dose of chemicals classified as moderately toxic. Young children should therefore be protected from all chemicals, and completely isolated from all but the slightly toxic and practically non-toxic substances.

The foregoing does not take into account the long-term effects of chronic exposure to, and ingestion of, chemicals.

Product and environmental safety

Product and environmental safety involves the development of design criteria that reduce both the probability of an accident occurring in the first place and the severity of the injury sustained if one does occur, and design features such that the severity of the injury is not increased after the actual event. Once these criteria are established, some will be adopted voluntarily by manufacturers and builders, while others will have to be made mandatory by regulation. Both actions are generally the result of public awareness of safer designs and pressure to adopt them. Standards are then enforced through effective controls and sanctions.

This system has worked reasonably well in developed countries, though there has been some resistance, depending on the political and economic mood of the country in question. In developing countries it is more difficult, for the reasons already outlined, to enforce standards. Design criteria and standards for developing countries should therefore be established with the following in mind:

- Standards are more likely to be implemented when products are manufactured in centralized locations or large factories.
- When products are made in the informal sector or in small manufacturing units, safety criteria should be such that they are both easily identifiable and demonstrably safer, so that public pressure will ensure that safer products are manufactured (this, of course, must be supplemented by publicity about safer designs). Design features that require little maintenance or effort by the user are more likely to be successful.

A serious problem in the developing countries is that many imported products are either banned or severely restricted in the countries of manufacture. The most glaring example of this is the export to developing countries of certain pesticides that are banned in most of the countries of Europe and North America. Similarly, safety standards are often not followed in the case of cars and motorcycles, Tris-treated nightwear, toys and medicine containers exported to developing countries. While it is true that safety standards for many products would not be the same in developed and developing countries, this would apply largely to those products whose use is country-specific. For most other products traded and manufactured internationally, design standards will be very similar in both types of country.

Table 11.1 shows a few examples of injuries caused by products, and the possible countermeasures.

Conclusions

Many of the problems previously mentioned can be solved by prohibiting the product or activity concerned, for example, firearms, fireworks, etc.

Table 11.1 Injuries caused by products and possible countermeasures

Injury or cause of death	Product	Countermeasures
Burns	Fabrics, furnishings	Flame resistance and flammability standards.
	Cooking stoves	Energy-efficient wick stoves instead of stoves using kerosene under pressure. Stable base and low centre of gravity.
	Space heaters	Protective grilles that remain at a temperature of less than 60 °C.
	Matches, match boxes	Strike bars on back of book matches, slow burning rate, rapid extinction.
	Fireworks	Low explosive content, design such as to discourage handling during ignition or while burning, low-temperature combustion.
Cuts/lacerations	Toys, furniture, playgrounds	No sharp edges, corners or points. No needle-like parts of rigid material such as steel. Axles, etc., should be of pliable plastic. Objects should not cause serious injury, even if children fall on them or throw them.
	Machinery, implements	Used mainly by teenagers. Considerations similar to those for adults; ergonomic design, low force requirement in operation.
	Razor blades	Phase out old-fashioned razor blades.
Drowning	Pools	Fencing around pools at least 1 metre high with self-locking door which cannot be opened by young children. Prominent "no diving" notices on sides of pools in shallow areas.
	Wells	Fencing around wells, covered tops.
	Boats	Prominent maximum load indicators.
Impact injury	Houses	Compulsory grilles on windows. Minimum height of 1 metre for walls around terraces and roofs. Landings after every 1.5 metre drop in staircases or break in direction.
	Transport	Bicycles that allow feet to touch the ground, two-wheelers painted in conspicuous colours, e.g., yellow and orange, provision of reflectors, conspicuous jackets, helmets for children. Children to be transported in appropriately designed child seats. Road design to keep vehicle velocities low in urban areas. Motor vehicles with front ends and radiator grilles that absorb shocks.

Table 11.1 (*contd.*)

Injury or cause of death	Product	Countermeasures
	Playgrounds	No equipment to have surfaces more than 1 metre above the ground unless soft landing surfaces provided. Safe equipment can be designed at low cost with less demanding maintenance requirements.
	Sports equipment	Same countermeasures as for playgrounds.
	Occupational hazards	Provision of guard rails at least 1 metre in height at heights above 2 metres. Provision of soft landing areas where falls likely.
	Furniture	Furniture for infants and toddlers should not have surfaces more than 1 metre above the ground without adequate restraining systems and protection. Provision of rugs and carpets in areas where children play.
Amputations/ mutilations	Motor vehicles, agricultural implements and other occupational tools	Same guidelines as above. (Children should not use equipment of size and weight designed for adults.)
Electric shock	Household gadgets	Wiring should be bite-resistant. Use of flat pin connectors and self-closing sockets. No male connectors on far end of cable connected to mains. Foolproof earthing systems in equipment and mains.
	Toys	Should operate at less than 40 volts.
Poisoning	Medicines, drugs	Pills in blister packs or childproof containers. Liquids in small volumes in childproof containers.
	Pesticides	Clear and effective labelling describing effect on humans in local languages. Safer application procedures (prohibition of the most hazardous pesticides).
	Cooking fuels	Special, low-volume containers with narrow necks. Colouring (blue) and bitter agents added.
	Paints/dyes	Lead content to be limited to 0.5% and toxic dyes eliminated.

Table 11.1 (*contd.*)

Injury or cause of death	Product	Countermeasures
	Chemicals	To be sold in childproof containers, small packages and dispensers which allow use only of small amounts at a time.
	Storage cabinets	Fitted with latches which cannot be opened by young children.
Suffocation/ strangulation	Toys/furniture	Avoid use of ropes/strings. Gaps and holes should be small enough so that no child can put its head through or large enough for head to pass through freely.
	Plastic bags	Should have holes, warning labels or be very small in size.
	Beads, toys	No parts of sizes such that they can lodge in the throat or nose.
Penetrating	Firearms	Locking mechanisms that cannot be operated by children.

Labelling of products is very important, but has not been considered here. Many countries have specific labelling requirements, but these may not suit all cultures and countries. Both symbols and wording must be designed for the target audience. Labelling is often inadequate and ineffective; pesticides sold in developing countries are generally marked with the words "dangerous", "poison", or "caution", and colour-coded, but these are not necessarily effective as workers using them may not know the language used, or appreciate the subtle difference between danger and caution. Labels must be in local languages and must spell out clearly what the consequences are likely to be if the product is not used as instructed.

Research priorities

Research is necessary on the following:

- Development for cotton and synthetic materials of flame retardants that do not wash out or degrade cloth quality.
- Simple guidelines on grille design for heaters.

- Cigarettes that do not burn for more than two minutes.
- Fireworks that burn at low temperatures.
- Playground equipment that gives children the impression that they are taking risks but that is relatively safe, inexpensive and needs little maintenance.
- Standardized guidelines for edges, corners, and points for toys and furniture, and simple testing gadgets.
- Safer front ends of cars, buses and trucks.
- Cheaper and safer helmets for use in sports.
- Suitable childproof containers for use in families that include people with little education and the elderly.
- Introduction of bitter agents into toxic substances.
- Safer and less toxic pesticides; long-term effect of pesticides on children.
- Epidemiological studies of morbidity and mortality in agriculture and other occupations in developing countries.

Chapter 12
The role of legislation

J. HAVARD

Public health legislation usually involves interference with various freedoms; it must therefore be based on sound epidemiological evidence, and the measures that it seeks to enforce must have been scientifically evaluated. Failure to observe these principles will only lead to the discounting of such legislation by the community. In the case of child safety, the community is generally willing to accept measures that it is not yet willing to accept for the community as a whole. Whereas only 22 states in the USA compel the wearing of seat belts in cars, every state requires children to be restrained in them. Many member states of the Organisation for Economic Co-operation and Development (OECD) require children's nightwear to satisfy flammability standards, but similar standards do not exist for adult nightwear. On the other hand, levels of safety that are acceptable for adults are frequently inadequate for children or, for that matter, for the elderly. Examples include safety standards for gas and electrical equipment in many countries.

The political and social implications of legislation on child safety require the most careful consideration of the evidence upon which it is based. The maxim that "anything that sounds reasonable will be effective" should be avoided at all costs.

Recognition and detection of factors increasing the risk to children

Mortality

The early recognition and detection of risks is a characteristic feature of countries with well developed medico-legal systems of investigation. Such systems include legislation requiring the early notification of violent or unexplained deaths of children to the appropriate authority, e.g., the coroner or medical examiner, and providing for a competent medico-legal autopsy to be carried out irrespective of any objections that might be raised by parents or guardians.

It should be more generally realized that certification of the cause of death in young children is an inexact science and requires the most careful attention to detail by doctors experienced in paediatric pathology if important evidence is not to be missed.

Morbidity

Legislation requiring the notification of non-fatal injuries resulting from accidents to children is very much less satisfactory than that covering fatal accidents. The attention given to the notification of relatively unimportant infective conditions in childhood, such as scarlet fever, contrasts strangely with the lack of legislation requiring the notification of accidents involving children, such as motor vehicle accidents, which are the most important single cause of death or permanent disability in children in developed countries.

In this respect, legislation is usually regarded as the responsibility of authorities other than the health authorities, and the information that it yields is generally unreliable and defective insofar as it fails to provide a scientific basis for the introduction of countermeasures. The gross under-reporting by the police and the transport authorities of injuries received by child cyclists is a good example. A recent survey in the United Kingdom showed that fewer than half of the children known to have received medical treatment for injuries received on cycles could be accounted for in the official statistics of road accidents. The provision of reliable statistics on morbidity from accidents in childhood is also important insofar as it provides a baseline for the evaluation of countermeasures. In this respect, reporting systems such as the Home Accident Surveillance System in the United Kingdom and the National Electronic Injury Surveillance System in the USA should be strongly encouraged.

Product safety

Legislation can require manufacturers, importers, distributors and retailers to notify the appropriate authority whenever it is discovered that a product might present a substantial risk of injury to the consumer; thus the Consumer Products Safety Act in the United States is known to have drawn attention to a considerable number of products dangerous to children.

Preventive measures

Legal obligations of the parent or guardian

In most countries a general legal obligation is placed on parents or guardians not to expose children to unacceptable risks of injury from accidents. This obligation is generally reinforced by powers given to the appropriate authorities to take the child into care where the danger is judged to be unacceptable. Clearly, the risk is highest with small children because of their greater liability to falls, suffocation, poisoning and burning.

Legal obligations of children

For the older child, a number of age-related legislative provisions exist aimed at reducing the risk of injury. They include restrictions on the sale to children of firearms and certain other dangerous products, on the use of swimming pools, and on access to alcohol. Raising or lowering the age at which alcohol can be sold to young people has been shown to have a significant effect on the incidence of accidents. The provisions governing the issuing of driving licences invariably specify that such licences can be issued for the different categories of motor vehicle only to those above a certain age.

Environmental legislation

In many countries, the risks of injury to children have been substantially reduced as a result of legislation requiring manufacturers to meet certain safety standards, e.g., for flammable clothing, electrical fittings, toys, etc. In some instances, the environmental factors have not been fully taken into account, e.g., it is often not appreciated by town planners that the siting of a new school will determine the pattern of child pedestrian casualties for some years to come. The need for building regulations to take account of risks to children is also not sufficiently well understood. In some cases, even superficial examination of prize-winning architectural designs has revealed obvious hazards to children. In developing countries, the risks to children of hazards associated with rapid mechanization and with exposure to situations with which they are unfamiliar can be particularly dangerous, and legislation to avoid such hazards is important.

Product safety

A comprehensive review of legislation governing product safety in relation to accidents in childhood cannot be attempted in the space available. It is certainly a well documented topic and has been the subject of numerous recommendations by international organizations. The most recent reivew of the subject can be found in the report on product safety measures to protect children, drawn up by the OECD Committee on Consumer Policy, which was published in 1984 (1).

Legislation is generally aimed at enforcing the national or international standards adopted by the country concerned. A common method is to require all products coming within the scope of the legislation to comply with the published standards. Another is to provide that products made in accordance with specified published standards will be "deemed to satisfy" them, although this method is less effective.

The main problem faced by governments seeking to introduce adequate safeguards is the need to avoid creating technical barriers to international trade. Directives of the European Economic Community under Article 100 of the Treaty of Rome (the purpose of which is to eliminate technical barriers to trade) have given rise to anxiety in some countries that they may interfere with national, or even international, safety standards. Where approved international standards exist, the problem is minimal. The Council of the International Organization for Standardization (ISO) has requested all its technical committees and member bodies to take account of the specific needs of young children when drafting international standards, and the ISO secretariat has set up an international working group to develop documentation on child hazards, which will support all standards work in the future. Difficulties may arise where no international standards exist for the product. These can be avoided by accepting certificates issued by recognized or accredited organizations in the country of origin. Conversely, countries should not allow products that fail to meet their own safety standards to be exported to other countries; the OECD report has recommended that legislation should be passed to that effect. Specific legislation can apply to a very wide range of products, such as poisons, foods, vehicles, pesticides, etc.

Road traffic accidents

As about half the fatal accidents to children and young people in the industrialized countries occur on the roads, it might be expected that the prevention of road traffic accidents would be the subject of a considerable body of specific legislation. In practice, this is not the case. Apart from injury prevention legislation, such as that making it compulsory for the occupants of vehicles to wear restraining devices (safety belts) and for motor cyclists to wear crash helmets, there is very little specific legislation other than age-related provisions governing the issuing of driving licences for motor vehicles.

As far as child pedestrians are concerned, there is very little legislation apart from the general provisions governing road safety. The kinds of injury sustained by children struck by motor vehicles have been extensively studied and related to design features, particularly with regard to the front of vehicles. However, it is unusual for regulations governing vehicle design to take account of the special risks to small children. One of the commonest causes of serious injuries to child pedestrians occurs when children emerge from behind a parked car while crossing the road. The parked vehicle obstructs both the child's view of the approaching car and the driver's view of the child. However, there is very little evidence that legal restrictions on the parking of cars in residential streets take this important factor into account. The main consideration is usually the need to ensure an unimpeded, and therefore a faster and more dangerous, flow of traffic in urban areas.

Legislation on speed limits in residential areas is particularly important in preventing child pedestrian casualties, and the relatively low level of enforcement in many countries is a matter of concern. The time taken between the point at which the child is seen crossing the road and the point at which the vehicle stops or takes other appropriate avoiding action depends to a large extent on its speed.

The carrying of children on bicycles should also be prohibited by legislation because of the inherent instability of the latter and the increased risk when a child is carried as a passenger.

The age at which a young person is allowed to drive a motor vehicle is the subject of legislation in almost every developed country; it will obviously depend on the category of motor vehicle concerned. The conditions attached to the issue of a driving licence for the various categories of vehicle are also important, bearing in mind that the peak incidence of involvement of drivers in accidents is in the 15–19-year age group in many countries, where such accidents may account for more than half the male mortality in that age group.

As with all public health legislation, it is particularly important that regulations governing the driving of motor vehicles should be properly enforced. In many countries they are not, particularly where speed limits and alcohol consumption are concerned. It is important to realize that young drivers are heavily over-represented in accidents involving excessive speed and the use of alcohol. Special age-related legislation has already been introduced to deal with the problem in certain countries, and is under consideration in others. Examples include speed restrictions for a fixed period following the granting of a driving licence and the imposition of a lower blood alcohol limit for young drivers. Unfortunately it has not yet been possible to obtain conclusive evidence that such measures are effective.

General considerations

While voluntary agencies supported by charitable contributions have played a major part in reducing child accidents, their effectiveness is inevitably limited in the absence of the ability to secure the necessary evidence in support of countermeasures and to enforce them.

Legislation is necessary to provide adequate financial support and to ensure the cooperation of the various government departments involved. Research must be directed along the right channels, and the activities of the various bodies concerned with different kinds of accidents coordinated. Provision of adequate baseline epidemiological data to enable the effects of different countermeasures to be evaluated is essential and will require the cooperation of government departments and agencies. Examples include the Home Accident Surveillance System (HASS) in the United Kingdom and the National Electronic Injury Surveillance System (NEISS) in the USA. Such systems are costly, but they do provide reliable information from which risks can be assessed so that appropriate countermeasures can be introduced. The recommendations of international organizations and their specialized agencies are particularly important in this respect.

Reference

1. *Product safety: measures to protect children.* Paris, Organisation for Economic Co-operation and Development, 1984.

Chapter 13

Isolated measures and integrated programmes

A. HITCHCOCK

The meaning of integration

Mortality and morbidity among young people due to accidents may be reduced by reducing the incidence of accidents, by modifying the environment in which they occur so that the severity of their effects is reduced, or by improving techniques of medical treatment and reducing the delay before treatment is made available. In most cases, improvements related to treatment of injuries can be implemented by the medical professions and health authorities acting alone, but the others usually require changes to be made in areas that are the responsibility of other public or private authorities. Obvious examples include changes in the design of machinery, the use of glass in house construction, practices in hang-gliding clubs, and the phasing of traffic signals. In all these cases, furthermore, selection of an appropriate form of intervention will involve expertise of a non-clinical nature. Indeed, in many of them a health professional representing a large public organization can find himself regarded as just another lobbyist for a private sectional interest.

It is noticeable, moreover, that designers of machinery do include guards and other safety features without being urged to do so by public health professionals, and that road and traffic engineers have developed elaborate disciplines of accident investigation, analysis and prevention without much input of a clinical nature. Similarly, many clinical advances have been made in the treatment of traumas without excessive concern for the mechanisms by which they occurred. Nevertheless, cooperation between authorities with different areas of responsibility has been found useful in almost every field where it has been tried. It can:

- improve the identification of problems;
- facilitate the establishment of priorities;
- make possible modes of intervention that were not previously possible or even conceivable;
- provide an improved basis for research into the mechanisms (physical, psychological, environmental and physiological) of causation, and so into countermeasures.

Such improvements are achievable only with intricate institutional and professional cooperation, which requires a great deal of skill and patience. Cooperation can sometimes, under strong external pressure, be achieved on the basis of "you co- and I'll operate", but such arrangements do not last long. Every party to such cooperation has policy concerns other than accident problems—the transport engineer is concerned with the economic benefits to individuals of the movement of people and goods, the clinician with improved health in non-accident contexts, the police with crime prevention, and so on. Each, too, has a different perspective on the problem being tackled, and a professional approach to it that may not easily be appreciated by the others. In practice, too, considerations of power, prestige and public recognition at both the personal and institutional levels intervene. For these various reasons, cooperation between disciplines in safety matters is often not achieved and, if it is, remains fragile for many years.

The need for interdisciplinary cooperation is one of the forms of programme integration with which this chapter is concerned. Another form relates to the idea that various forms of action by the community are necessary simultaneously to deal with different aspects of the same problem. If, for example, there is a disproportionate number of children aged 5–9 years among road traffic accident victims in a particular location or jurisdiction, simultaneous actions may be needed to train the children, educate their parents, warn motorists, modify the road environment, redesign vehicles and improve techniques for dealing with, e.g., bone damage in children of this age; all these should be seen as part of a single programme. This type of approach has been persuasively promoted in a recent report from the Organisation for Economic Co-operation and Development (OECD), though the present author has not found it particularly useful. (1). Of course, all easily available and competing options should be examined, but in practice actions in different fields require different time scales.

The purpose of this chapter is to present the concepts of other disciplines than health and to describe their approaches to the problems of accidents to children and adolescents. The discussion will be restricted to road accidents, and refer mainly to the United Kingdom; the conclusions, however, are generally applicable.

Accident analysis and epidemiology

The idea that road accidents can usefully be treated as a public health problem to which epidemiological techniques can be applied is relatively new. Road designers and traffic engineers in some countries have considered accident prevention to be an aspect of their work since at least the late 1940s. The idea that vehicles should be designed in such a way as to reduce accidents (lights, properly maintained steering, brakes and tyres) goes back even further, but the concept of designing vehicles to reduce injury in an accident seems to have arisen more recently, and to have been fairly quickly associated with the interest of epidemiologists in the area.

Econometric approaches

From the point of view of the traffic engineer or transport planner, however. the reduction of mortality and morbidity is only one of a series of conflicting objectives. While it is not always easy to say so publicly, it is not of such overriding importance in the minds of the professionals, the political decision-makers or the general public that it automatically outweighs all features of any scheme. A number of more or less formal analytical techniques have been described in the literature for resolving conflicting interests. In the United Kingdom, it is usual to try to quantify the various factors, by assigning a monetary value both to savings in travellers' time, and to mortality and morbidity. The type of decision involved might be a choice between different road schemes intended to reduce accidents, the route of a new road, or the formulation of a standard or code of practice for use by professional engineers. By quantifying each aspect, the choice of design for, e.g., a road junction becomes a simple question of maximizing a function. As would be expected in a country that prides itself on its pragmatic approach to political problems, this optimum is then regarded as one input into a multicriterion decision analysis, in which predicted levels of accidents also figure. The logic of this is open to question, but the decision process does not seem likely to be changed.

This technique of economic analysis permeates the thinking of all those engaged in transport. One consequence is that sensitivity to safety considerations is incorporated in the earliest stages of any design. The Institution of Civil Engineers, for example, defines traffic engineering as concerned with the "safe, economic and efficient" movement of people and goods. This outlook, in practice, is an integral part of the training of engineers at undergraduate level.

The same is true of other transport decisions. For example, in the debate about subsidization of fares on public transport in London, the belief that high subsidies would reduce accidents was a significant element in the proposition. When the subsidy level changed abruptly, a careful quantitative analysis of the effect of high subsidies on road accidents was made (2). The effect was indeed significant, and all parties to the dispute acknowledged the fact, while differing as to the relative emphasis that should be placed on it.

Data collection

Such an econometric approach can be adopted only if quantitative estimations of very detailed effects can be made. This means that, for example:

- in choosing locations for actions to improve safety, the most serious accident sites are given appropriate priority;
- in publicity schemes, messages are not only clear and understandable, but directed towards serious problems.

To this end, data on accidents need to be collected in standardized form in considerable detail and with high reliability. It is also necessary to have measures of exposure.

In the United Kingdom, the national accident data system is based on: (1) the police record of every reported accident (there is a legal obligation to report any road accident in which any injury was sustained by those concerned; in practice not every accident is reported); and (2) counts of traffic on the road system. Both of these are collated nationally, but local authorities also keep accident records, often in greater detail than those held nationally, and make traffic counts.

The police record is known as STATS 19. This form (3) consists of a 26-item list of circumstances surrounding the accident—time of day, nature of road and road lighting, weather, road surface, manoeuvres being undertaken, and so on. A second set of forms (24 items) describes each vehicle involved and a third (19 items) each casualty. The forms relate to accident prevention only. The police officer may in addition be required to collect evidence for possible prosecutions, to call for medical assistance or to control traffic. STATS 19 is not part of this procedure and the officer is not required to form any judgement, or to act as an amateur counsel, clinician, ophthalmologist or moral arbiter. The concept of blame has been found by experience to be irrelevant to accident prevention, and police officers' opinions on the other matters so variable as to be of no use statistically. Some importance is attached to providing feedback to individual police officers of examples and accounts of the results of their efforts.

Exposure data are based on continuous axle counts at 50 points randomly selected on the urban and rural road system, supplemented by a further 200 quarterly classified counts, and a four-year rolling programme of 8000 classified counts covering the main and secondary road system. A periodic 1000-point count enables figures for minor roads to be obtained. This system is currently being replaced by one using automatic machines.

The system is not considered to be adequate. Its most important defect is the lack of data on the exposure of pedestrians, but others include the lack of clinical information and of the previous accident (or conviction) record of the participants. Attempts are being made to remedy these defects.

Similar systems exist in other developed countries. In France, continuous classified counts which distinguish between different kinds of vehicle are made automatically at a number of points in the main road system. In the USA, two systems for recording accident data exist. The National Accident Sampling System (NASS), unlike STATS 19, considers only a small ($\sim 5\%$) sample of all road injury accidents, but employs 87 full-time specialist teams. This permits elaborate observations to be made on the nature of vehicle damage and on the reconstructed circumstances of the accident, so that is becomes possible to relate injuries to particular impact directions, velocity changes, and deformation characteristics of the vehicle during the crash. Each record describes the vehicle and the damage to it in terms of 100 data items, the accident in a further 38, and the output of the CRASH computer program in 58. A further 50 items describe each driver, 30 each occupant (including some clinical data), and about 25 each person who was not in a motor vehicle. As is appropriate in view of the distribution of responsibility between state and federal government in the USA, these data are intended mainly for use in improving vehicle design, since this is a federal function. However, the data are also used for other purposes: the National Highway Traffic Safety Administration (NHTSA) report for 1983 (4), for example, contains articles on elderly people and on drinking and driving.

The United States Government also collects a separate series of reports through the Fatal Accident Reporting System (FARS). As with the NASS series, full-time specialist staff are employed for this purpose, but the series covers all fatal road accidents. FARS data describe each accident in terms of 96 data items, each person involved in 48, and each vehicle and its driver in 45 (5).

The NASS/FARS system is significantly more elaborate than the STATS 19 one, in particular because it includes clinical data. However, STATS 19 has been running for significantly longer and its coverage is also greater (100% of all injuries reported to the police, while for NASS/FARS it is around 5% of injuries, with 100% of fatalities). Both clearly are very much more extensive than records of other conditions leading to morbidity or mortality, including even such well researched topics as atheroma.

Similar systems exist in a number of other developed countries, notably Australia, Japan, New Zealand and Scandinavia. In developing countries, some police-based systems do exist—Sri Lanka and Papua New Guinea both maintain records—and more recently, other developing countries are establishing not only accident data banks, but also accident investigation teams. Egypt is a leading example.

It will be seen that the volume of data available is vastly greater than that available to epidemiologists in disease-related fields. Some road accident researchers have recently begun to familiarize themselves with the methods and techniques of medical epidemiologists, in the hope of finding ways of improving their own methods. They find it remarkable that medical experts have achieved as much as they have with such imperfect data bases.

Road engineering

In-depth studies of road accidents divide contributory factors into vehicle faults (5%), road environment faults (25%) and human faults (95%). (There is usually more than one contributory factor.) While most progress to date has been made by changing the road environment, this does not mean that only road engineering factors are considered. For example, not infrequently particular road layout contributes to a failure of perception (a human fault) or to a tendency to make errors of judgement in a situation where many factors have to be taken into account at once. Changing the environment can therefore reduce human error.

Very few accidents are associated with vehicle design faults, although vehicle design can, of course, affect the probability of injury after impact. Of the vehicle-related factors identified in two in-depth studies (6, 7), some 90% were related to defective tyres or poorly maintained brakes.

Publicity

Human behaviour can be affected, as every salesman knows, by advertising and publicity. In the case of road safety, the main difficulty is that the gains from unsafe behaviour are obtained at once, while the losses, though large, are extremely infrequent. Most people do not die in road accidents; indeed, most go through their lives without incurring any significant trauma. Safety is difficult to sell. In the United Kingdom, it is accepted that all publicity campaigns should be evaluated, if not in terms of accident reduction, at least in terms of change in behaviour. Experience enables the following generalizations to be made:

- Messages should be precise (*"Look out for child cyclists"*) rather than general (*"Take care"*). Research of the kind already described can draw attention to relevant messages.
- Messages should be targeted to a particular population.
- The campaign should be of limited duration.
- When a campaign has been evaluated, the results should be reported to those responsible for it.

It is in this area that voluntary bodies are most active. A county is often too small a unit to design and evaluate its own campaign, and several private bodies—notably the Royal Society for the Prevention of Accidents—produce publicity material which they sell to local authorities or sometimes to other private bodies, such as parent–teacher associations. The UK Government is also active in this field.

Education and training

Education is an area in which monitoring has not yet demonstrated, and probably cannot be expected to demonstrate, significant results in terms of reducing accident rates. Some specific training programmes can, however, be shown to have an effect on accident rates, but in general one is obliged to be content with observing effects on behaviour, or retention of information. The author is not aware of any work in which general education about safety has been shown to reduce accidents; the presumed effects are too remote in time and so confounded by other factors that confidence limits are invariably very wide.

Nevertheless, it does seem self-evident that the communication of examples and information, whether in schools or more informally, will have value, provided that the information is comprehensible to the child, is suitably reinforced, and is precise. In the United Kingdom, following a review in the 1970s of material available in schools, much attention has been devoted to devising suitable educational packs, either single-subject or combining traffic education with other disciplines. Preliminary evaluation indicates that at least some of the information is retained. County road safety officers and local schools (which, in the United Kingdom, are largely autonomous in the choice of the subjects to be taught) do in fact cooperate, often with the encouragement of parents' associations and professional teaching bodies.

It is not easy to devise techniques for advising parents about the traffic abilities of their children, and research indicates that many people grossly underestimate the complexity of tasks, such as crossing a road or judging the speed of vehicles. Here too, trials are in hand in London, based on Scandinavian models, but their impact has yet to be evaluated.

"Causation" of accidents

The concept of accident causation gives rise at a deep level to a number of intellectual or philosophical difficulties which can become practically significant and a source of confusion in the application of countermeasures. It is often better to avoid the problem by speaking of associated or contributory factors. Other difficulties can arise, especially where responsibilities are divided among several institutions or professions. For example, most countries have standards for the design of roads and the layout of junctions. In the major developed countries, such national standards are dependent on traffic levels, but are carefully balanced, often on the basis of economic calculations, so that an appropriate compromise is achieved between initial cost, traffic delay, ease of maintenance, reliability and user safety. When such standards are applied, it sometimes happens that, because of some special site characteristic accident rate is unexpectedly high. It is customary in the United Kingdom to wait until there is confidence that this is not an abnormal random variation, and then to make a careful analysis, on the basis of which changes to the design are proposed. In some countries, however, those responsible for road construction consider that their responsibility is at an end if they are able to demonstrate compliance with the standard—and indeed they are not legally empowered to take an alternative view. An impasse thus arises, which can only be resolved, if at all, by political negotiation. Essentially, this is the consequence of extending the belief that non-standard layouts are a common cause of road accidents (which has some validity), considering that they are the single cause under the control of, in this case, the public works authority.

At a different level, political groups in many countries rightly observe that a cause of many road accidents is culpable human error, which can be deterred by severe legal sanctions. Such political groups campaign for legal penalties to be imposed for example, on those causing injury by driving while drunk. The problem here, in part, is that the process of political campaigning, if it is to be effective, involves advocacy, which must be partial; in many cases, however, it is fired by the belief that drink is the single cause of all accidents in which it is a factor, and this could lead to inappropriate emphasis in accident prevention policy.

Integration

There are those who urge that an integrated approach covering attempts to prevent accidents occurring, ameliorate the trauma caused by them, and improve treatment thereafter, is appropriate in every case (8, 9). Such an approach has been found institutionally acceptable and useful in the USA, but not in the United Kingdom and in some other countries. This is because there are inevitable cultural differences between the modes of achieving the necessary interprofessional and interdisciplinary cooperation in different countries. What is common to the successful approaches is a willingness, once data have been collected, to rely on them. In the United Kingdom, which has been used as an example here, it is the integrating principle to rely on the data, and to be prepared to resist attempts, however common-sensical they may seem, to impose coutermeasures that are not supported by them, as well as to discard ideas that monitoring shows to be unsupported.

In practice, every culture must find its own integrating principles, in both intellectual and institutional terms. This is not easy, and requires unaccustomed humility on the part of all concerned. But the rewards in terms of saving lives and reducing injuries are large, real and well worth while.

References

1. ORGANISATION for ECONOMIC CO-OPERATION and DEVELOPMENT. *Integrated road safety programmes.* Paris, OECD, 1984.
2. ALLSOP, R. E. *Fares and road casualties in London.* London, Greater London Council, 1983.
3. DEPARTMENT OF TRANSPORT. *Instructions for reporting accident statistics.* London, HMSO, 1980 (STATS 20).
4. NATIONAL HIGHWAY TRAFFIC SAFETY ADMINISTRATION. *National Accident Sampling System, 1985.* Washington, DC, US Department of Transport, 1985.
5. NATIONAL HIGHWAY TRAFFIC SAFETY ADMINISTRATION. *Fatal Accident Reporting System, 1983.* Washington, DC, US Department of Transport, 1984.
6. SABEY, B. E. *Road safety and value for money.* Crowthorne, Transport and Road Research Laboratory, 1980 (SR 581).
7. TAYLOR, H. & SABEY, B. E. *The known risk we run: the highway.* Crowthorne, Transport and Road Research Laboratory, 1980 (SR567).
8. HADDON, W., Jr. The changing approach to the epidemiology, prevention and amelioration of trauma: the transition to approaches etiologically rather than descriptionally based. *American journal of public health,* **58**: 1431–1437 (1968).
9. HADDON, W., Jr. On the escape of tigers: an ecologic note. *American journal of public health,* **60**: 229–234 (1970).

PART IV
PREVENTION AND EDUCATION

Chapter 14
Evaluation of educational projects in Australia

S. WHITELAW

Defining the problem

Establishment of the facts should be the starting point in developing any accident prevention programme. An epidemiological study should be carried out in order to identify the areas where there is the greatest need for preventive strategies, and should:

- describe the distribution and the demographic, social and economic characteristics of the problems affecting the community;
- identify the determining factors in the problem and provide the data necessary for the planning, implementation and evaluation of services for prevention and control;
- provide the data necessary to determine priorities in the light of the limited resources available for health care, or identify the biological characteristics that have an impact on the problem.

Strategies for evaluation

The main objective of epidemiology is to determine high-priority or need areas, distribution and causation. The procedure used for this purpose consists of the following three phases:

- descriptive epidemiology: determination of the frequency, the type of person at risk, and where and when accidents occur;
- formulation of a hypothesis: once a picture emerges from the analysis and interpretation of the descriptive epidemiological data, a statement or hypothesis can be formulated which can be tested in phase 3. For example, it may be hypothesized that the greater prevalence of trauma caused by road accidents in males as compared with females is due to the fact that there are more male than female drivers;
- analytical epidemiology: two types of analytical epidemiology are used in observing groups in order to discover whether a particular characteristic is a determinant:

  - a comparative study of people who have had an accident; a determinant will be more apparent or occur more frequently among those in a given situation than among those who have not been so exposed. For example, in a group of people who have had a road traffic accident, there may be a high proportion of individuals who drink and drive.

– a comparative study of people possessing the characteristic in question and those who do not possess it; a larger proportion of people who possess the characteristic should have had an accident as compared with those who do not.

Evaluation measures

It is universally accepted that the most reliable evaluation measure is a reduction in mortality or morbidity; however, the lack of a comprehensive accident data base limits the use of morbidity as an indicator in many countries.

Structured evaluation of satisfaction, knowledge gained, change of attitude and self-reported behavioural change are of limited value for evaluation. The most reliable method of evaluation consists of the independent observation of change of behaviour incorporating time series analysis so as to avoid confusion. The need for an appropriate comparison group cannot be too strongly emphasized (*1,2*).

Objectives

The establishment of objectives serves as the initial step in the strategic planning process, providing guidance for the coordinated efforts of involved individuals and groups, and ensuring that everyone is working towards the same desired results. Objectives also make it possible to establish expected performance standards and provide the means for evaluation and control.

Methods

The three methods mainly used in the evaluation of educational programmes are discussed below.

Survey method

The sensitive nature of many accident problems often reduces the effectiveness of a self-administered questionnaire. As a way of solving this problem, survey information can be obtained through personal interviews using a structured questionnaire. The interview, which should be carried out by trained interviewers, will reduce the possibility of non-response that exists with a self-administered questionnaire. The method is also governed by the rules for sample size, response rates and standard error.

Cohort studies

Cohort studies begin with the identification of a group of people who have shared a common experience, e.g., involvement in a traffic accident. Such people can be identified by means of an epidemiological data base.

Observational studies

Attitude change and self-reported behavioural change are not as reliable as behavioural change observed by an independent researcher. It should be noted that a return to earlier behaviour patterns is often seen during stressful situations. Numerous surveys have pointed to stress as a contributing factor in the occurrence of accidents.

Human, social and environmental systems

All accidents are the result of the complex interaction between variables associated with human, social and environmental systems; accident prevention programmes must therefore be based on a systems approach, requiring an intervention in one or more of the systems concerned.

In any consideration of the environment, it must be realized that it does not consist solely of physical, tangible features, such as buildings, products and equipment (the environment in the strict sense of the term), but also of intangible characteristics, such as standard of living and stress created by external forces (the psychosocial aspects).

Human behaviour depends both on the information possessed by the individual, namely his or her awareness of the accident risks and of the preventive measures available, and on attitudes and motivation. Any definition of education must include both formal and informal educational programmes.

Accident awareness study

To ensure the correct targeting of messages about accident prevention, a baseline investigation is necessary in order to assess the following:

- the awareness of accident risks among specific groups;
- awareness of preventive measures;
- attitudes towards accident prevention;
- the corresponding behaviour;
- awareness of first-aid measures;
- awareness of past programmes and promotions.

The results of such a study can provide a basis for setting priorities, initiating activities and developing new accident prevention and educational programmes based on known rather than assumed needs (3).

The study should be repeated periodically for purposes of comparison and to enable existing programmes to be appropriately adapted in the light of the awareness, attitudes and behaviour of specific community segments, to demonstrate how effective programmes have been, and to change programmes in line with changes in community needs.

The study can also be used to obtain a clear indication of the type of communication medium that is relevant to a particular target group.

Community-based programmes—networking

Networking constitutes a new approach in the prevention of childhood accidents, based on the concept of community development. The objective is to maximize the availability and accessibility of safety education in the community, thereby contributing to a safer environment for children.

In South Australia in 1981, a community-based network of "child environment advisers" was established on an experimental basis, to promote the involvement of parents in accident prevention. The function of the network was not to replace but to supplement existing preventive programmes, utilizing untapped community resources and seeking out those sections of the community that would otherwise remain unaware of accident prevention messages. According to information obtained in an accident awareness study, people in the lower socioeconomic and in certain ethnic groups were unaware of the educational services available to them, and were not influenced by brochures, media promotions or posters.

The concept of community development is based on the belief that the people who really know the environment are those who live in it, and that it is they who are in the best position to influence their immediate surroundings. Community development is by no means a new concept; there are many examples from other countries of attempts to foster this idea. However, until 1983, only in Sweden had the concept been applied to accident prevention.

During 1983, the Child and Home Safety Centre in South Australia developed a programme calling for the recruitment of volunteers from a local community, who would be responsible for assisting parents in identifying and solving problems in matters of safety in the home. The pilot programme was conducted in an area occupied by people of low socioeconomic status which also had a relatively high percentage of ethnic minorities. The project was publicized through the media, lectures, committee meetings, local notice boards and personal approaches; use was also made of the ethnic churches and community leaders in order to gain acceptance. Volunteers participated in a series of workshop sessions to prepare themselves for their role as child environment advisers. They came from a variety of cultural backgrounds, giving them the obvious advantage not only of speaking the relevant languages but of sharing a common culture and thus of evoking a greater response from the parents.

These child environment advisers were viewed primarily as catalysts of change; they visited families in their homes, gave advice and motivated parents to make improvements that would increase the safety of their children. Consequently, their role was not to impose safety measures on parents, but rather to assist them in developing an awareness of safety factors. The volunteers reported environmental hazards, such as unsafe playground equipment, to the local council, surveyed supermarkets, and took positive action to remedy problems. A collection of household poisons was organized in order to reduce the incidence of child poisoning.

During a 12-week period, the child environment advisers increased safety awareness in the community, and were able to overcome the cultural barriers of language and customs. They were successful in reaching ethnic communities and groups of low socioeconomic status who were often not reached by conventional methods.

Accident prevention—an integral part of health promotion

Positive results from the evaluation of the child environment advisers project encouraged the Child and Home Safety Centre to consider an extension of the community network to other local authority areas, and to broaden the basis of the original concept from accident prevention and emergency casualty care to comprehensive preventive health.

The *Self-help health care manual* was produced with the aims of increasing knowledge and management skills, of developing a critical attitude towards the preventive approach to health, and of increasing the community's confidence in its ability to manage minor health problems in the family. As part of an ongoing programme, this manual was translated into Bulgarian, Cambodian, Greek, Italian, Polish, Serbo-Croat, Spanish and Vietnamese to enable programmes to be conducted and a network established for each ethnic community (*4*).

Evaluation showed that participants demonstrated a positive attitude and behaviour in relation to health and accident prevention, and achieved a better understanding both of their own health and of that of their family.

Health education—in state government schools

In 1973, the South Australian Education Department established a project team to develop and implement a health education programme for primary and secondary schools. A survey in 1977 indicated that the course was having little impact on accident prevention; despite the fact that teachers of health education considered the section relating to accident prevention to be one of the most important, it was the least frequently taught. A more extensive evaluation was carried out, targeted on prevention of burns and first aid. The aims of the study were:

- to determine the impact of health education courses and the knowledge and attitudes of students towards burn prevention and first aid;
- to explore the effectiveness of a range of methods of teaching the topic;
- to monitor teacher behaviour and opinions regarding the teaching of accident prevention.

To assess the influence of the health education course, the following strategies were explored, based on practical rather than theoretical considerations: the method of presentation of information; the type of incentive offered to students to learn the information; and the age group to which the information was presented.

Statistical analysis of tests on 12-year-olds and 14-year-olds revealed that the knowledge of, and attitudes towards, accident prevention among students receiving health education were no better than those of students not receiving such education. Warning students that they were to be tested did motivate them to learn factual information; however, it had little influence on attitudes. None of the teachers regarded their lessons as being successful in achieving their objectives. Lack of appropriate resources, such as films, slides and literature on accident prevention topics, hampered teacher cooperation.

Road trauma and road safety activities

Trauma from motor vehicle accidents is known to be the most common cause of death among people between the ages of 15 and 45. Epidemiological surveys have shown that alcohol is a major contributing factor, especially in young male drivers. Legislation on licensing, seat-belts and crash helmets, together with improvements in road and vehicle design, has had an impact on mortality rates.

Drink driving education kit

In line with the philosophy that schoolteachers require suitable resource materials if they are to cover accident prevention as part of the health curriculum, the "drink driving education kit" has been produced. It was originally developed in New South Wales and adopted in 1984 in South Australia; every state secondary school has now been provided with a copy. Initial results indicate that teachers are using this kit, which contains teachers' notes, transparencies, slides and video presentations.

Road Safety Instruction Centre

In 1970, the South Australian Government amended the Highways Act to provide for a specific allocation of one-sixth of the cost of every driver's licence to the Road Safety Fund. As of June 1985, 825 849 licences had been issued in South Australia, while approximately 30 000 new licences are issued annually. The Road Safety Instruction Centre was established from the income received. The Centre covers almost 72 000 m² and includes a large-scale road system, a skid pan, lecture facilities and an open area on which all aspects of driver education can be practised. The role of the Centre is to provide:

- further education for licensed vehicle drivers and motorcycle riders;
- in-service training for teachers involved in road safety education in schools, and facilities for a student driver education programme;
- courses for licensed drivers wishing to become professional drivers or driving instructors;
- road safety education for children, pedestrians, cyclists, motorcyclists and drivers.

In addition, there are six children's road safety centres located in the metropolitan and country areas throughout the State. An extensive evaluation of the facilities provided by the road safety centres has been undertaken to improve the service provided to the community (5).

Promotional media campaigns

Use of television and radio has been shown to be an effective means of creating community awareness of a given accident problem. Many promotional campaigns have been aimed at influencing the attitudes and behaviour of drivers, and particularly of males in the 16–25-year age group.

"Mr Hyde" campaign

In 1984, the South Australian Department of Transport launched a media campaign (6) targeted at 16–25-year-old males, aimed at:

- creating an increased awareness on the part of both motor vehicle drivers and passengers of the problems created by alcohol and careless driving;
- promoting a change in the attitudes of the offending drivers and passengers;
- promoting a change in the attitude of other drivers and passengers who are placed at risk by the offenders.

An extensive radio and television campaign was conducted together with a supporting programme in which posters and information sheets were sent to elderly citizens' clubs, since children and the elderly account for a disproportionately large number of pedestrian accidents.

The "Mr Hyde" campaign proved to be highly successful both in creating awareness and in changing attitudes towards drinking and driving. Significantly, a reduction in the numbers of women passengers of drivers under the influence of liquor has been recorded.

The campaign has received three "Cleo" (advertising industry) awards, two for the television commercials and one for radio content. It was entered as a road safety initiative in a competition held in Hong Kong in November 1985.

"Tunnel vision" campaign

In 1983, the Departments of Transport and Education launched a road safety campaign (7) designed, not only to provide education, but also to establish a data base on male drivers, covering their driving and drinking habits, their accident and offence records, when they learnt to drive and who taught them, as well as their attitudes towards road safety.

An evaluation of the campaign also covered the extent of freedom parents allowed their children on the roads and the amount of road safety instruction that they received during school road safety programmes. The success of road safety campaigns was evaluated in terms of the effect on attitudes and driving habits, and an attempt was made to determine which groups of young drivers and parents were most affected. The campaign was based on creating an awareness of the limited peripheral vision of young children, and emphasized driver responsibility in the prevention of injury to child pedestrians.

Questionnaires were circulated to parents and drivers both before and after the campaign. The results of the evaluation showed that awareness of the campaign was extremely high and that 89% of the sample population, as compared with 5% before the campaign, had some appreciation of driver responsibility. Radio and television commercials were supported by public debate, thereby increasing awareness of the campaign. Of young male drivers aged 16–24 years, 87% understood the meaning of the term "tunnel vision", as compared with 41% before the campaign. In the case of parents, 97% were aware of, and understood what was meant by that term.

"Road show": a new approach to road safety

M. Fahey, the Chairman of the New Zealand Road Show Trust, promoted throughout Australia a road accident prevention pro-gramme targeted specifically at teenage drivers. Statistics from both Australia and New Zealand show that young men working in unskilled or semi-skilled jobs are either most at risk on the roads or most likely to cause problems to other road users.

In 1982, a pilot study was carried out in Christchurch, New Zealand, in which a stage show, making use of modern electronic media, and a live stage performance with modern dancing and music were shown to 22 000 secondary school students. A group of 1800 students were subsequently interviewed, and demonstrated a marked attitudinal change towards road safety. An increased number of students wore seat-belts, more girls drove rather than allowing their inebriated male companions to do so, and the girls drew up a list of boys that they were not prepared to drive with; that list was still in use two years after the initial showing of the programme. A subliminal message presented during the performance resulted in a 600% increase in the demand for professional driving instruction.

In 1983, a statistically significant reduction in serious accidents and fatalities was recorded. In many cases students were able to influence the driving pattern of their parents, more of whom took taxis rather than driving under the influence of alcohol.

The "Road Show" concept was supported in the schools by the provision of a kit containing prepared studies based on the long-term effects of serious road accidents, films and discussion papers on tragedies and disasters in New Zealand.

Prevention of drowning

According to Pearn, a noted authority in Australia on childhood drowning, Australia has the second highest rate of child mortality from drowning in the world (8). During the period 1973–1983, the figure for accidental drowning of both children and adults in Australia showed a reduction of 21%, while the reduction for South Australia during the same period was 69%. Credit for this remarkable achievement should go to the Department of Education's Water Safety and Swimming Programme, which is based on the philosophy that swimming should become part of an overall safety programme rather than safety being part of a swimming programme (9).

The aims of a water safety programme should be:

- to provide sufficient opportunities for children to gain positive experience, skills and an understanding of water safety, mobility in and on the water, survival, self-rescue, and safe rescue of others;
- to provide opportunities for children to enjoy the water;
- to teach correct swimming strokes and the use of safety skills and resuscitation;
- to encourage a realistic relationship between swimming and water safety and other aspects of education;
- to encourage children with special difficulties to use water as a form of recreation and therapy;
- to provide children at upper primary school level with an opportunity to take part in a variety of aquatic activities;
- to enable secondary school students to progress beyond the basic level of aquatics and acquire advanced skills in an activity of their choice.

The South Australian Education Department provides free instruction for all children attending both state and independent schools. A total of 230 centres throughout the State employ 1200 part-time instructors during the January vacation, and 600 part-time instructors during the school year to teach the programme. A further ten major centres provide aquatic programmes offering fishing, snorkelling, sailing, canoeing, board sailing, water skiing, surfing and boating. Instructors are provided with educational material based on a cartoon character called Silly Billy. The Education Department's programme is supplemented by posters, overheads, videos, television commercials and a children's book.

The reduction of the drowning rate in South Australia from 4.2 to 1.1 per 100 000 over the past 12 years is also the consequence of two items of legislation:

(1) the *Home Pool Fencing Act 1972*, which requires all private swimming pools to be fenced; and
(2) the *Boating Act 1974*, which requires power boats to be registered, operators to be licensed and safety equipment to be carried.

Numbers of drownings in home swimming pools have fallen significantly since 1972; however, it is believed that the surrounding publicity and public debate, rather than the legislation itself, were the major contributing factors. In contrast, South Australia's comprehensive boating legislation has had little impact in reducing the number of boating deaths. Statistics show that adult males are at the greatest risk.

Park et al., in their paper on the epidemiology and prevention of drowning (9), clearly state that 47% of all persons aged 15 and over who are involved in drowning accidents have been drinking alcoholic beverages. South Australian statistics support this statement. Children who took part in water safety programmes in the early 1970s in South Australia are now teenagers and young adults. The long-term plan of educating primary and secondary school students in aquatic centres may be successful in ensuring that young adults and parents will be better informed about accident prevention than parents in the previous ten years.

Conclusions

In summary, a consistent pattern emerges in programmes that are shown to be successful, either by formal evaluation or by a reduction in mortality or morbidity (*10*). Such programmes have the following characteristics:

- They are based on sound epidemiological data.
- The underlying philosophy has been defined.
- They are aimed at achieving long-term success in the reduction of mortality and morbidity.
- They have been developed as an integral part of an overall health concept.
- They are community-based, and provide resource material and training for community volunteers.
- They avoid the use of scare tactics in the promotion of messages about accident prevention.
- They provide the information needed for a particular action in a specific situation rather than aiming at bringing about a change

in everyday behaviour, e.g., the use of cold water for the treatment for burns.
- They are supported by legislative and environmental systems.
- They are supported by the media in creating an awareness of a given problem.

This multifaceted approach seems to be the key to success.

References

1. WHITELAW, S. *Directives for research methodology for accident prevention and health promotion.* Unpublished paper presented at the Joint MCH/MNH/APR Workshop on Research Development in Childhood Accidents, Havana, November 1984.
2. O'CONNER, J. P. Strategies for accident prevention through evaluation. In: *Proceedings, ANZAAS Jubilee Congress,* Adelaide, 1980.
3. DEPOLD, R. ET AL. *What do mothers know about accident prevention?* Adelaide, South Australian Health Commission, 1983.
4. SCANDRETT-SMITH, M. *Road safety campaigns in South Australia.* Adelaide, South Australian Department of Transport, 1985.
6. STEIDL, P. S. *Mr Hyde campaign.* Adelaide, Profile Management Consultants, 1984.
7. FISCHER, A. J. & LEWIS, R. D. *Tunnel vision road safety campaign.* Adelaide, South Australian Department of Transport, 1984.
8. PEARN, J. *Drowning.* Unpublished paper presented at a seminar of the Institute of Ambulance Officers (Australia), Queensland, 1981.
9. PARK, E. ET AL. Drowning. Epidemiology and prevention. *American journal of public health,* **64** (4): 303–312 (1974).
10. KIRK, M. *Education for accident prevention. The South Australian programme.* National Safety Council of Australia, South Australian Division, 1985.

Chapter 15

Education and training in injury control

L. R. BERGER

Introduction

Despite the profound importance of injuries as a social, medical, and public health problem, training activities in injury control have been limited in scope and few in number. Fatalistic attitudes towards injuries as "accidents", minimal levels of funding, and a paucity of skilled teachers are major obstacles. The recognition that injury control must be based on epidemiological data and scientific countermeasures is not yet part of the public consciousness.

The future of training in injury control, however, appears bright. There are now a multitude of agencies and organizations with related interests. Innovative community programmes and educational efforts have developed a range of strategies, materials, and guidelines for action. This chapter provides a brief survey of ideas and resources to assist educators and injury-control specialists in generating new training opportunities.

Resources for education and training

Several recent publications can serve as textbooks for courses in injury control. *The injury control fact book* (*1*) contains mortality data for the major types of injuries in the United States of America. The book examines the circumstances under which deaths due to injury occur, the etiological agents, and the populations at risk. Robertson's book on injuries (*2*) complements *The injury control fact book* by reviewing injury research, strategies for injury control, economic costs, and public policy issues. Waller's *Injury control* (*3*) provides a broad survey of data, theory, and strategies for action. Each of these books contains numerous references.

Another possibility is to use *Injury prevention in developing countries* (*4*) as a textbook. This contains the proceedings of a conference held at the Johns Hopkins School of Public Health and co-sponsored by the World Health Organization. It includes concise reviews of epidemiology, the principles of injury control, and injury problems affecting developing countries. The appendices contain analyses of specific injury issues by course participants, an extensive bibliography, written exercises, and a list of audiovisual resources.

Journals devoted exclusively to injury control include *Accident analysis and prevention* and the *Journal of safety research*. Important articles on injuries are also to be found in *Pediatrics*, the *American journal of public health*, the *Journal of trauma*, and the *Journal of occupational medicine.*

Several organizations in the USA publish regular reports or newsletters containing information on recent publications, conferences, and action programmes. These include the National Safety Council (*NSC, Accident facts*), the Insurance Institute for Highway Safety (*IIHS, Status report*), the National Highway Traffic Safety Administration (*NHTSA, Highway safety literature*), the National Child Passenger Safety Association (*NCPSA, Safe ride news*), the Consumer Product Safety Commission (*CPSC, NEISS news*), and the American Academy of Pediatrics (*AAP, Accident prevention newsletter*). Each of these organizations also serves as a clearing-house for injury-control information in its specific area of interest. For example, the CPSC collects injury data via an electronic surveillance system based in hospital emergency rooms, publishes in-depth epidemiological studies, and distributes professional and public information materials on a wide variety of consumer safety topics. The IIHS and NHTSA perform similar functions for traffic-related injuries. The Injury Control Division of the Center for Environmental Health, Centers for Disease Control (CDC), is becoming a repository for information on programmes in all areas of injury control.

Training would be assisted by the following improvements in information sources:

- coverage of injury control journals in computerized reference publications such as the *Index medicus*;
- an international listing of educators and researchers in the field of injury control with their major areas of expertise and interest;
- an annotated listing of educational materials, including audiovisual materials and curricula, for major areas of injury control. This would list each programme's name, intended audience, time needed for presentation, educational content, and source agency;
- a manual of action programmes briefly describing each programme's objectives, activities, outcomes, and contact person from whom further information can be obtained.

Developing training programmes

Most courses for the education of professionals consist of a series of lectures designed to convey specific information. In fact, a variety of training methods should be considered in addition to lectures. The advantages and disadvantages of a number of different approaches are presented in Table 15.1.

To design an educational programme:

1. Determine the professional roles for which the learner is to be trained.

Table 15.1. Advantages and disadvantages of training methods

Method	Advantages	Disadvantages
Lectures	Can be quickly prepared, kept up to date, offered to large numbers of learners, and tailored to different audiences; students can ask questions	Place learners in a passive role, may take longer than simply reading information, lecturers vary in quality
Films, video-tapes, slide programmes	Can be replayed many times for different groups, realistic examples, entertainment value	Expensive, require special equipment, difficult to tailor to different audiences
Self-instructional lessons	Learners can do the work in any setting and at their own pace; answers can be checked quickly	Require much time and skill to prepare, cannot provide practice in skills such as observing and interviewing
Job aids, such as manuals and hand-books	Can be organized for easy reference and used on the job whenever needed	Learners may lack motivation to read through a manual; explain tasks without providing practice; questions cannot be answered if not in the manual
Apprentice-ships and on-the-job experience	Learner practises in real work situations, gains clearer idea of what information is important for practical application, assists training agency or establishment	May be difficult to find experienced personnel who are also good teachers and student supervisors; work may be slowed down because of teaching demands
Group discussions, role-playing, simulations	Learners become actively involved; entertaining, a good way to practise tasks involving communicating with people	Learners may be uncomfortable in groups, some may become confused by the variety of opinions expressed; information may not be efficiently conveyed

2. Specify the teaching objectives based on the knowledge, skills, and attitudes required to fulfil these roles.
3. Select the methods and materials appropriate to the educational and sociocultural background of the learners.
4. Evaluate the teaching programme by obtaining feedback from the learners and by assessing their competencies.

Physician training

Physician training encompasses the teaching of medical students, residency programmes, and continuing medical education for practising physicians.

The role of physicians in injury control includes:

- the identification of preventable hazards;
- the education of other health-care providers and families;
- participation in community action programmes;
- treatment of injury victims.

Until recently, only the last function has received attention in training programmes. It is unrealistic to expect that every physician will become an injury-control expert or an agent of social change. However, a minimum desirable set of educational objectives for every physician might contain the following:

- *A knowledge*:

  - of methods of registering preventable injuries;
  - of the most common and serious injuries occurring in different age groups;
  - of the populations at high risk for specific injuries;
  - that injury countermeasures include community action and technological changes, as well as education;
  - that injuries are a leading cause of morbidity and mortality in all age groups.

- *The skills to enable him or her to*:

  - recognize preventable injuries in a clinical setting;
  - counsel patients effectively regarding injury prevention for themselves and their families;
  - record in the medical charts of injury victims important epidemiological data, especially patient characteristics (e.g., occupation) and the circumstances of the injury.

● *The attitude that*:

 – injuries are preventable, not random "accidents";
 – the scientific method—not common sense or moral judgements—should guide injury-control efforts;
 – injury-control research and action are important aspects of health care.

Training directed towards these "core" objectives can form part of each stage of physician training.

Medical student education

A number of efforts have been made to develop injury-control courses for medical students. Waller, for example, has outlined a 20-hour curriculum combining emergency medical instruction (11 hours) with discussions of injury epidemiology and control (*3*).

The effort required to introduce any new course into a medical school curriculum is monumental. Injury control is such a multi-disciplinary field that the usual interdepartmental conflicts are magnified. Furthermore, injury control as a topic must compete with such "new" educational priorities as aging, alcoholism, patient education, occupational health, rehabilitative and emergency medicine, and human sexuality. Health education, for example, is not a required course in any of the 120 medical schools in the United States of America.

Advocates of injury control must develop ways to integrate the subject into existing preclinical and clinical settings, rather than waiting for medical schools to insert entire new courses into their curricula. For example, instructional guides and audiovisual materials can be designed as flexible modules for adaptation by the staff in the basic sciences, preclinical, and clinical departments. To maintain the enthusiastic attention of a medical student audience, the modules should consistently combine epidemiological and preventive issues with clinical information. A module on burn injuries, for example, might include the items shown in Table 15.2. The American Academy of Pediatrics is currently preparing such a modular curriculum.

Among the instructional settings where injury-control topics could be incorporated are:

 – biostatistics and epidemiology;
 – behavioural sciences: adolescents and risk-taking, seat-belt use, alcohol use and motor vehicle accidents, intentional injuries (suicide, child abuse, homicide, rape);

Table 15.2. Examples of items to be included in a burn injury teaching module

Epidemiology	Clinical	Preventive
House fires leading cause of fatalities	Identify burns caused by abuse	Install smoke detectors
Scalds leading cause of emergency visits	Burn depth is a function of time and temperature	Reduce water temperatures
Sex differences in causes of burns	Burn therapy: shock, sepsis	Legislation governing use of flammable fabrics

- orthopaedics: falls in the elderly, sports injuries;
- pathology: forensic pathology, mortality data;
- paediatrics: developmental aspects of injuries;
- surgery: dynamics of car accidents, firearms injuries, burns.

Staff with experience in injury control can teach the subject by inviting medical students to committee hearings, community meetings, and news conferences. In addition to diagnostic and management issues, discussions with students about injured patients can include aspects of prevention.

Training of interns and residents

Physicians in residency programmes ("house officers") often work 60–80 hours a week. Nevertheless education in injury control can be provided during this phase of professional training. Visiting professorships, sponsored by medical organizations or private funding, could enable injury-control experts both to lecture and to join residents in their discussions of patient care. House staff may opt to pursue particular injury problems in greater depth during elective months. Often their interest may be stimulated by a patient in their care, as in the following example:

A resident examined a 3-year-old boy in the emergency room who was unconscious. His parents said he had been in excellent health until 30 minutes previously when they found him on the floor of the bathroom next to an empty bottle of mouthwash. The child's blood alcohol level was markedly elevated. The child recovered uneventfully.

The resident spent an elective month researching the issue of alcohol in mouthwash. He learned that every brand was distributed in at least one bottle size that contained enough alcohol to kill a toddler of average weight. None of the manufacturers responded to the resident's question as to why mouthwash contained up to 27% alcohol and no federal agency chose to act on the information. The results of his research were published in the journal *Pediatrics* (5).

Post-residency training and continuing education

Education on injury control for practising physicians can be provided in the form of hospital lectures, workshops and seminars at professional meetings, action programmes sponsored by medical societies, and fellowship training. Examples of these approaches are given below.

Short course on injury control for community hospitals

Two paediatric surgeons, a trauma nurse, a paediatrician, and a public health professor have designed a 2–3-hour course on childhood injuries. Expert clinical talks attract large audiences of doctors and nurses eager to learn about the latest resuscitation techniques and approaches to the child with multiple injuries. Injury-prevention topics—such as the epidemiology of childhood injuries, control strategies, and community action—are also presented. Teaching elements include a resource manual, posters, and "interest centres". These last are exhibits both of clinical topics (fluid therapy, intubation) and prevention issues (car safety seats, burns prevention). A major objective is to sensitize health professionals to injury control so that they will participate in future research, educational, and legislative efforts.

Workshop on injury control

With small groups, use can be made of active learning techniques. One two-hour workshop begins with a short (15-minute) lecture on prevention strategies (human, vehicle, and environmental factors; three phases of injury). The participants then divide into groups of 4–6 people and choose a specific injury topic, such as motor vehicle accidents or scalds. Each group then spends an hour answering the following questions:

- What factors might contribute to a high rate of this type of injury?
- What kinds of information about these injuries (e.g., age of victims) would you like to have before designing an intervention for your target community?

- How might these data be obtained?
- What are the possible approaches to preventing this injury?
- Choose one approach that you think is feasible. Which groups would support it and which would not? Why?

The remainder of the workshop is devoted to reports from each group on their deliberations. Many aspects of injury epidemiology, data collection, and countermeasures are inevitably discussed.

An action programme involving paediatricians

In 1980, the American Academy of Pediatrics (AAP) launched a campaign to promote the safety of child passengers in motor vehicles. A national task force was established to identify goals and strategies. Local AAP chapters throughout the country formed child passenger safety committees and elected chapter coordinators to educate paediatricians and promote community action. The AAP assisted the chapter committees by: distributing professional and patient information on the importance of motor vehicle injuries and how to prevent them; preparing manuals on legislative action and enforcement; mailing a newsletter, *Safe ride news*, about chapter activities and resources; suggesting specific ways that paediatricians could promote child passenger safety in their offices; and making available grants for innovative action programmes. Within five years, all 50 states had child passenger safety laws and AAP activities were expanded to address seat-belt use, automatic passenger protection, and motor vehicle injuries in adolescents.

A fellowship programme in community health

A two-year fellowship in child protection consisted of clinical work, formal instruction in public health disciplines such as epidemiology and biostatistics, and an action research project. Supervised within a department of pediatrics, the fellow also chose a "community base" in which to work. This was a governmental or voluntary agency dealing with child health issues—a setting in which to learn about the administrative, financial, and programmatic aspects of social action. The majority of time in the second year was spent designing and implementing an action research project. Agencies involved with injury control would be ideal sites for fellowship training.

Schools of public health

In addition to teaching students, important roles for schools of public health in the field of injury control include the training of programme managers, research, the development of instructional materials, and advocacy. The most extensive injury-control programme is at Johns Hopkins University. The programme director holds joint appointments at the school of public health and the medical school and has established close ties with the medical examiner's office, trauma units, and emergency medical services. Three courses in injury control are regularly offered, namely: "Issues in injury control", a survey of preventive concepts and policy issues; "Epidemiology of injuries", including data sources, high-risk groups, and programme evaluation; and "Emergency medical services", which covers current programmes, problems, and policy issues.

Motor vehicle injuries are the subject of a 10-week course developed at the University of Illinois for graduate students in public health. Topics include the epidemiology of motor vehicle injuries, the impaired driver, occupant restraints, and the role of the health professional in prevention.

The Injury Control Division of CDC has promoted training through national workshops and the development of case studies in injury epidemiology and prevention. Each case study addresses the following four aspects of a specific injury:

- issues and problems related to data acquisition;
- methods of analysing data;
- devising appropriate strategies for injury control;
- designing evaluation techniques to determine the effectiveness of countermeasures.

Each case will consist of a data set based on existing morbidity or mortality data, an instructor's guide, and questions for students. Case studies can be used as a primary teaching approach for courses and workshops or as supplementary exercises.

Training programme managers

Perhaps the highest priority in injury-control training should be given to the managers of public health and related agencies. The integration of injury-control activities into existing action programmes can have an immediate impact. Lead agencies can sponsor community demonstration projects, establish injury data systems, and influence legislative and regulatory decisions. Once programmes are initiated, the agencies can become sites for training in injury control, both of community health workers and of students from many disciplines (public health, medicine, engineering, nursing, and law, for example).

Table 15.3. Knowledge and skills required by programme managers

---

1. Data collection and assessment of needs
   - Types of data
   - Sources of data
   - Collection of local data (from medical records, telephone inquiries and field studies)
   - Analysis of epidemiological data
2. Formulation of a strategy
   - Establishment of objectives
   - Choice of groups
   - Choice of appropriate measures: education, regulation, technological modifications, community action
3. Implementation
   - Organization and management of the programme
   - Community involvement
   - Preparation of material
   - Training of personnel
4. Evaluation

Table 15.3 outlines the knowledge and skills that programme managers require in order to initiate injury-control activities. CDC has provided management training and technical assistance to local health departments through its Injury Control Division. A number of excellent publications designed for public health agencies address the general programmatic aspects of injury control. There are also detailed guides for specific injury-control activities, such as conducting household hazard surveys, ensuring the safety of playgrounds, and reviewing laws and regulations.

An innovative approach to management training is the concept of a "community laboratory" workshop. Workshop facilitators accompany participants to sites in a community where injury-control problems have arisen. These might be bodies of water where children have drowned, neighbourhoods with a high incidence of residential fires, or roadways where the number of motor vehicle occupant deaths has been high. Experts in environmental design, alcohol control, community action, and other injury-related disciplines then interact with participants. The final step is the development of injury-control strategies to address the issues raised by the site visits.

Conducted over two or three days, such a workshop can convey both the conceptual and practical aspects of injury control through active learning experiences. The group interaction can also lead to networks for further collaboration among participants in both injury research and action programmes. A substantial benefit to the host community is that the participants may put forward ideas for effective action programmes to address serious injury problems.

Training community health workers

Community health workers (CHWs) include public health nurses, emergency medical personnel, outreach workers, and other primary health care staff. The knowledge and skills that they can apply to community-based injury-control activities are shown in Table 15.4, which also includes suggested methods for the training of CHWs.

Counselling families on preventive measures is a familiar role for CHWs. A curriculum for home care and the prevention of childhood injuries has been developed for personnel working in a clinic for migrant farmworkers. Group instruction by clinic staff is provided in four 2-hour sessions. The course manual also serves as a reference guide for home use by families.

The Injury Prevention Program (TIPP) is an innovative approach to providing childhood injury-control counselling in a time-efficient manner. TIPP materials are available from the American Academy of Pediatrics.

TIPP includes age-appropriate safety questionnaires that are completed by parents and reviewed by the provider to determine target areas for discussion; safety information sheets for parents to take home; a schedule for age-specific counselling (Table 15.5) and

Table 15.4. Knowledge and skills required by community health workers and suggested training methods

Required knowledge and skills	Suggested training methods
Knowledge of the commonest and most serious injuries in the community and in high-risk groups	Lectures Correspondence courses
Investigating the risk of accidents in the home and in the community	Supervised field trips Use of slides or videotapes
Reporting hazards to the competent authorities	Field manual
Providing advice on safety matters	Role-playing
Demonstrating safety equipment, e.g., car seats and smoke detectors	Demonstration kits

a counselling guide. Because only "at-risk" answers are discussed, average counselling time is only 3 minutes per family.

The TIPP package was developed for urban and suburban communities in the USA. However, the use of age-specific questionnaires to target a few common and serious injuries for discussion is a valuable approach in any primary care educational programme.

Table 15.5. TIPP early childhood safety counselling schedule[a]

Preventive health visit	Minimal safety counselling		
	Introduce	Reinforce	Materials
Prenatal/ newborn	Infant car seat Smoke detector Crib safety		
2–4 weeks	Falls	Infant car seat	
2 months	Burns—hot liquids	Infant car seat Falls	Questionnaire 1 Safety sheet, 0–6 months
4 months	Choking	Infant car seat Falls Burns—hot liquids	Safety sheet, 0–6 months
6 months	Poison Burns–hot surface	Falls Burns–hot liquids	Safety sheet, 7–12 months IPECAC Syrup Poison centre sticker
9 months	Water safety Toddler car seat	Poison Falls Burns	Safety sheet, 1–2 years
1 year		Poison Falls Burns	Safety sheet, 1–2 years
15 months	Specific to need— optional		Questionnaire 2
18 months		Poison Falls Burns	Safety sheet, 1–2 years

Table 15.5 (*contd.*)

Preventive health visit	Minimal safety counselling		
	Introduce	Reinforce	Materials
2 years	Falls—play equipment, tricycles Auto—pedestrian	Auto-restraints Poison Burns	Questionnaire 3 Safety sheet, 2–4 years
3 years		Auto-restraints, pedestrian Falls Burns	Safety sheet, 2–4 years
4 years		Auto-restraints, pedestrian Falls—play equipment Burns	Specific to need

[a] Source: American Academy of Pediatrics.

Training community health workers to incorporate injury control into home visits is another effective strategy. The home is where the vast majority of injuries to young children occur. In addition families for whom safety information would be most valuable are often the least likely to attend lectures or read educational brochures.

Home visits by CHWs were a major component of the Statewide Childhood Injury Prevention Project (SCIPP). Home visitors used a checklist to identify hazards (such as dangerous cribs and frayed electrical wires). A household educational manual was used to inform families about age-specific injury-prevention measures. Simple safety measures—such as reducing the temperature of water in heaters—were taken on the spot. Building and fire code violations were reported to city authorities so that the necessary repairs could be made. In New York City, CHWs made home visits to install free window guards in apartment buildings. In two years, the number of young children dying as a result of falling from windows was reduced by half.

Schoolteachers

Recruiting teachers to the injury-control cause requires excellent instructional materials for classroom use and model programmes of demonstrated effectiveness. The Center for Health Promotion and Education (CHPE) of the CDC has developed health education programmes that include grade-appropriate curricula, teacher training guides, and parental involvement. A module for teenagers is devoted exclusively to injury prevention. CHPE has also compiled a list of model school health curriculum projects in the USA. The CPSC distributes a child safety planning guide for kindergarten teachers. This contains information on common childhood hazards, questions and answers for class discussions, suggestions for student activities, and resource materials. Several teaching programmes dealing with motor vehicle injury prevention are available from the National Highway Traffic Safety Administration.

Injury prevention should not be restricted to health education classes. Lesson plans in many subjects can incorporate injury-related topics, as follows:

- physics: analysis of crash forces;
- mathematics and computing: formulae for analysing the economic costs of injuries;
- English and journalism: articles on public policy decisions; development of public service announcements;
- arts/graphics: design of safety information materials;
- social studies: carrying out surveys of knowledge of and attitudes towards injury issues; discussion of seat-belt or helmet laws.

Classroom instruction should be only one component of safety education. Innovative approaches are needed in order to generate student involvement and enthusiasm, as illustrated below:

A task force on motor vehicle injuries was formed at an Albuquerque high school. Students, teachers, administrators, and athletics trainers participated. Activities promoted by the group included: the production of two videotapes by the students on why teenagers do not use seat-belts and how a teenager's life was changed by a serious car crash; rides on a "convincer" sled that simulated a low-speed car crash; design of educational materials on seat-belt use incorporating school themes and logos; and formation of a Students Against Drunk Driving (SADD) chapter at the school. Observations of seat-belt use made outside the student car park will be used to evaluate the programme's impact.

It is necessary to obtain the support of school administrators before teachers can implement any new programmes, especially ones that include out-of-classroom activities. A school physician can help to mobilize administrative support. Providing incentives for teachers to invest time in injury-control activities—for example, by allowing them to attend workshops on professional leave or by giving cash rewards to teachers whose students are observed wearing seat-belts—is an important means of overcoming hesitation to take on one more teaching responsibility.

Funding for education and training

The list of potential audiences for injury-control education is a lengthy one (Table 15.6). However, development of educational materials, curricula design, and training workshops all require funding. The following are some suggested methods of generating financial support:

1. Approach corporations and small businesses: a manufacturer of child car seats supported the development and distribution of a comprehensive child passenger safety package that included films and slide programmes: a pharmaceutical company helped sponsor the TIPP package that includes poison-prevention information.
2. Establish a safety institute: an "institute" is a collaborative group representing many disciplines and areas of expertise. Institutes for highway safety at the Universities of Michigan and North Carolina have conducted research and training in the bio-engineering, environmental, and behavioural aspects of motor

Table 15.6. Potential audiences for training in injury control

Teachers	Physical and occupational therapy
Day-care providers	students
Police	School nurses
Architects	Engineers
Lawyers	Media persons
Medical students	Urban planners
Clinical nurses	Public health managers
Practising physicians	Physicians-in-training
Paramedical personnel	Nursing students
Social workers	Community health workers
Housing inspectors	Health educators
Business school students	Fire officers
Business managers	Public health students
Policy-makers	Consumer groups
Preschool, elementary and high	Employees
school students	Government legislators

vehicle injuries. The University of Washington is establishing an institute to address all types of injuries. The staff currently consists of a paediatrician with public health training, an epidemiologist, a data specialist, and a health educator. A multi-disciplinary team can generate a comprehensive research agenda and compete for grants and contracts much more effectively than an individual researcher.

3. Develop training ties with existing action programmes: graduate students can perform many programme tasks for agencies, especially in fieldwork and data analysis. Not only does the student gain practical experience, but the host agency may contribute towards the cost of the development of educational materials, the presentation of workshops, and other expenses.

References

1. BAKER, S. P. *The injury control fact book*. Lexington, MA, Lexington Books, 1984.
2. ROBERTSON, L. S. *Injuries: causes, control strategies, and public policy*. Lexington, MA, Lexington Books, 1983.
3. WALLER, J.A. *Injury control. A guide to the causes and prevention of trauma*. Lexington, MA, Lexington Books, 1984.
4. *Principles for injury prevention in developing countries.* Unpublished document of the WHO Regional Office for Europe, IPR/ADR 217–40, 1985 (available from the Injury Prevention Programme, World Health Organization, Geneva, Switzerland).
5. WELLER-FAHY, T. ET AL. Mouthwash: a source of acute ethanol intoxication. *Pediatrics*, **66**: 302–305 (1980).

Chapter 16
Accident prevention: the role of research

J. A. WALLER

Introduction

Current knowledge of injury as a health problem has drawn upon
a range of methods, especially those of epidemiology, and laboratory
and clinical sciences. Of these, the tools of the epidemiologist have been
the most important to date. Traditionally, epidemiological research has
focused on determining the distribution and causes of disease
phenomena within populations. In recent years, however, the role of
epidemiology has been recognized to be considerably broader and to
include the study and evaluation of health services as well as health
problems. None the less, throughout the world, and even in countries
in which a great deal of research is carried out, some of the most basic
facts about injury, its treatment and effects remain unknown. The
research needed to fill these gaps can be divided into four basic areas,
as described below.

Basic data on morbidity and mortality

For each geographical area of the world, the following questions need
to be answered. What is the overall frequency of injury and injury-
related death among children and adults? What is the frequency of
injuries attributable to different types of events and of different
severities? How do these differ from one area to another? Can new
problems be identified quickly as they arise? What are the immediate
and long-term costs and effects of injuries, to individuals and their
families and to entire communities and countries? Who pays these
costs?

Data on injury causation to guide planning

It is becoming increasingly clear that injury-causing events and their
outcomes are commonly the result, not of single causes, but rather of
a complex interaction between human, product (or energy carrier) and
environmental factors. Furthermore, these factors play their roles over
the three separate phases that make up the injury event, namely
a pre-injury or pre-event phase that determines whether or not an event
with the potential of causing injury or damage to property will occur,
an injury or event phase that determines the occurrence of the injury
itself and its initial severity, and a post-injury or post-event phase that
determines the ultimate outcome over time. The human factors that

affect all three phases vary with age, sex, and cultural background, while environmental and product factors vary, not only from one geographical area to another, but also with socioeconomic status and over time. Far more research on the interaction between factors in each phase is needed, since much of the research carried out so far focuses only on single factors, and sheds little light on how those factors interact with others to produce or avoid injury events, injuries, and their outcomes.

Data for programme evaluation

Research on the selection and evaluation of safety interventions is a relatively new but promising field. There is a great need for work aimed at identifying how interventions are chosen from the range of those possible. Research aimed at evaluating the effectiveness, efficiency, and costs of possible interventions, and at determining how the costs and effects are distributed among those individuals in greatest need of protection is also needed.

Research into new or improved methods of data collection and analysis

While the methodological problems involved in the study of injury are probably no more difficult to solve than those associated with the study of many other health issues, these problems have contributed to the serious gaps that exist in our knowledge, and many of them are correctable (see Chapter 3).

Obstacles to research

The number of trained persons currently conducting research programmes on injury is extremely low compared with those undertaking research on other health problems. This shortage is in large part a reflection of limited and episodic funding for research in this area, deterring those who would otherwise seek careers in injury research and cutting short or otherwise limiting promising activities that have already begun.

Furthermore, research on many aspects of injury is often seen by health professionals as not an appropriate area of medical interest, and the relevant personnel and literature are widely scattered and difficult to identify, especially for the newcomer to the field. As a result, injury definitions and research methods that could benefit from standardization and refinement often remain in disarray, and important opportunities for ensuring the comparability of data from individual studies or from different geographical areas are lost. The five subject areas described below could particularly benefit from standardization and refinement.

Problems in defining injuries or injury events

There is no standard accepted definition of the term "injury" itself. Depending on the circumstances and type of activity, an injury may be defined as damage that results in the persons concerned seeking health care, needing hospitalization for a specified period of time, or losing the ability to perform their usual activities for a stated period, usually a minimum of one day, but sometimes longer. Certain fatalities, such as sudden deaths in infants, or deaths from the medical complications of falls in the elderly, may or may not be recorded as injury-related, depending on local policy and practice. This lack of uniformity in definition severely limits comparisons between different countries and between age groups within certain countries. The fact that different definitions may be used means that no means of examining the relative degree of hazard exists, even for comparable activities. A WHO conference in 1978 specifically sought to achieve a definition of injury that would be acceptable to a wide range of Member States (1).

Need for more comprehensive definitions of severity

The definitions of injury severity in use in both research and official data collection systems have a wide range. At one extreme, there are simple schemes lacking validity and reliability (such as those in common use by police departments), which divide injuries into three or four broad categories, ranging from uninjured to fatal. At the other extreme are schemes of internationally documented validity and reliability, such as the Abbreviated Injury Scale (AIS) (2) and, derived from it, the Injury Severity Score (ISS) (3). These latter schemes have proved quite useful, especially for studies of blunt trauma in transport accidents, but are somewhat less applicable for penetrating injuries. To date, they have been most accurate when injuries are coded by medically trained personnel.

They were specifically designed, however, to provide a high degree of correlation with threat to life. Both AIS and ISS have been found to be far less useful for examining such questions as the need for health care services, long-term costs, and the duration and type of disability (4). New severity scoring systems, that can be applied accurately by non-medical personnel, therefore need to be designed for use in research on these important problems. These new systems may be particularly relevant to studies of very young and very old people, where injuries may have effects greater or smaller than the average based on the threat to life. It is essential that all such systems should be developed in such a way that they can be used not only for sophisticated research in highly industrialized countries, but also in the less industrialized ones, where trained personnel and financial resources for research may be much harder to find.

Injury rates based on exposure data

Except for road traffic accidents, injury and fatality rates are generally specified relative to the size of the population, or occasionally relative to a number of products, based on the underlying assumption that all people or products have similar types and amounts of exposure. Thus, if differences in injury rates are found, it is commonly concluded that they are the result of differences in hazard inherent in the person or the product, rather than that they may simply reflect different amounts or types of exposure or use.

In reality, persons or groups with very low injury rates per number of persons may have such low rates simply because of limited exposure; they may, in fact, have very high rates per unit of exposure. Thus, for example, it might be decided that children with epilepsy may swim without any additional precautions being taken, as previous experience has shown that they have few seizures while swimming. However, this could well be because they have been avoiding swimming, believing it to be dangerous, rather than because there really is no increase in risk. Agreement is needed among researchers as to which types of activities can most benefit from determination of injury rates based on exposure, and which exposure measures are the most appropriate and the easiest to obtain.

Better measurement of impact forces in relation to body characteristics

Accelerometers and similar instruments for measuring the relationship between body impact and resulting trauma are being used increasingly in laboratory research. To date, however, this research has tended to collect data primarily on the tissues of healthy young adult males, so that little information is available as yet on possible differences in effect on the tissues or organ systems of children or of the elderly. Such laboratory research needs to be carried out, and its practical applicability determined through the linkage of laboratory, clinical, and epidemiological studies.

Better anthropometric data on children

While much is known about the dimensions and development of children in some highly industrialized countries, such information may not exist in developing areas.

Even in countries with good data, certain information important to safety, e.g., on the development of grip strength, may not be available. Adult dimensions and behavioural patterns may vary from one country to another and among ethnic groups within countries. It cannot be assumed, therefore, that anthropometric data collected in one part of the world will be applicable to other geographical areas or ethnic groups.

Research on the amount, effects and costs of injury

The collection of comprehensive information on the amount and costs of injury is both time-consuming and expensive, and to date has proved to be beyond the capability of all countries. The compilation of accurate data on the numbers of deaths from injury per year and their distribution according to age, sex, and type of event should be a goal of all WHO Member States. However, valuable data about less serious events and their outcomes may be obtained at lower cost through special survery techniques and other special research methods.

At its most basic, countries and areas within countries need information on the frequency and severity of different types of non-fatal injuries and their distribution according to age, sex, place of occurrence and type of care received, and to be able to update this information periodically in order to identify trends.

Morbidity

Two different types of morbidity information should be collected. The first consists of very limited data received regularly from a small number of representative locations by means of a permanent collection system. In the United States of America, the National Electronic Injury Surveillance System (NEISS) of the Consumer Product Safety Commission obtains a simple count from 80 hospitals throughout the country of the numbers of injuries seen each day involving various products. This system permits annual estimates to be made of product-related injuries according to age, sex and area of the country and serves as an early warning system for new patterns of injury that may suddenly become important as new products are brought on to the market (see Chapters 3 and 10).

The second type of morbidity information involves more intensive studies carried out periodically. In some developing countries, where virtually no morbidity information is currently available, it may be necessary to begin by collecting only limited information for short time-spans, such studies being repeated annually or even less frequently. Studies of this type have been carried out successfully by means of brief one-week national or regional surveys in several developing countries (5). It is possible, for this purpose, to use volunteers or the unemployed.

Care must be taken to ensure that these surveys reach broad sectors of the population and are not limited only to those who receive medical or hospital care, or to schoolchildren. The availability of both education and medical care varies widely according to urban/rural area, socioeconomic status and national pattern. Studies limited only to schoolchildren or to those who obtain medical or hospital care, therefore, may in some cases provide an inaccurate picture of the true injury situation in the country as a whole. Where marked seasonal variation occurs, an attempt should also be made to collect data during two or more seasons in order to reflect the effects of weather and of seasonal changes in living patterns.

Injury severity

As far as injury severity, as assessed at the time of injury, is concerned, the AIS and ISS should be used where possible. Where this is not possible, other simpler systems that can be tested against AIS for validity and reliability and that are compatible with it need to be developed. Children develop so rapidly up to the age of five that data should be analysed for one-year age categories, rather than for all children under that age. In this way, it will be easier to identify the true importance of certain injuries, such as poisoning or injuries while crawling or toddling, whose peak occurrence may be limited to only a 6–24-month developmental span.

Long-term effects and costs of injury

It is more difficult, but nevertheless important, also to collect information on the long-term effects and costs of injury. One method is to carry out special studies whereby injured children are followed over a year or longer, information being collected periodically about continuing disabilities and costs. This method provides information on the proportion of injuries of specific types that result in long-term disability. In order to ensure comparability between areas and over time, it might be appropriate to examine disability existing at the time of discharge from hospital and one year after the injury occurred.

Another method is to survey a population of children at a particular time, determine which of them have certain specified disabilities, and inquire into their causes and duration. This provides useful information on the long-term impact of injury within a population, but does not indicate what proportion of all injuries or of specific types of injuries result in such disability. The methods used for disability assessment can be very simple, e.g., whether or not a person is able to see light or to count fingers held at one metre from the eye.

In determining the long-term costs of disability or death in children, the willingness-to-pay method of projecting lost earnings (6) is to be preferred to the human capital method (7). The former is based more specifically on probable future value to society whereas the latter, which is useful when applied to persons already in the workforce but not to children, bases its projections of the future entirely on previous earning capacity. A combination of both methods has also been developed and is applicable to children (8).

Data on who pays the costs of injury may be particularly useful. One study in the USA, for example, showed that the bulk of the medical and health care expenses for head injuries to young motorcycle riders who did not wear helmets was borne by the community rather than by the individual, the family or the insurance company (9).

Research on causation of injury

While epidemiological and survey methods are most useful for determining injury frequency, distribution, effects and costs, a wider range of research methods is appropriate for determining causation. Hypotheses concerning causation are often based on clinical observation (for example, a sudden rise noted by physicians in skateboard injuries among children), and may be tested by means of the research methods used in epidemiology, experimental psychology, biomechanics or other disciplines.

As noted earlier, it is common for two or more factors to contribute simultaneously to the occurrence of an injury event or to its outcome. In falls on stairs, for example, intrapersonal factors such as extreme youth, cerebral palsy or old age may affect locomotive patterns, while slip resistance characteristics and the presence or absence of visual defects and distractions may accentuate or mitigate the effects of such personal limitations (*10*). The presence of a railing may enable individuals to stop themselves from falling and thus reduce the injury potential even if a mis-step does occur. This body of information has resulted from a series of studies to compare persons who have fallen with those who have not, stairs on which falls have occurred and those where they have not, and to investigate average injury severity in falls of different types. Laboratory studies have been carried out on the slip resistance of different types of shoes and walking surfaces, while videotape recordings of behaviour on stairs have documented the characteristics both of stairs and of the personal actions most and least often associated with mis-steps, falls, and injury. The summary report of a recent WHO workshop on childhood injury contains an outline of important human and environmental factors in injury (*11*).

The results of the crash testing of school buses with instrumented dummies suggest that, for buses meeting current US Department of Transportation design standards, the use of seat-belts may actually increase the severity of injuries to children (*12*). Such testing, on the other hand, has clearly demonstrated the benefits of occupant restraints for both adults and children in automobiles, and of helmets for motorcyclists.

Two other problems besides the failure to take account of interactions between factors have limited the conclusions that can be drawn from much previous and current research. One of these is the limitation of the research to the injured population alone, without comparing it with an uninjured population, or the failure to examine the frequency of injury not only in the presence of a given factor but also in its absence.

A second related problem is that many studies that do include such comparisons of injury frequency in the presence and absence of the factor concerned fail to determine the extent to which it exists, i.e., to determine rates of injury per unit of exposure. As an example of both problems, initial conclusions based only on clinical observations and impressions suggested that a new "high-rise" bicycle style was associated with an increase in injuries to cyclists (*13*). Subsequent study using comparison techniques showed that high-rise bicycles were associated with more injuries than standard ones simply because they were more likely to be used by boys, who had higher injury rates no matter what type of bicycles they used (*14*). Still later research that took the amount of exposure into account found that boys covered greater distances on their bicycles than girls and in fact had injury rates per unit of exposure no higher than those of girls (*15*). What originally appeared to be a product-related problem therefore turned out to be primarily a reflection of the extent of exposure to hazards that were similar for both old- and new-style bicycles. Especially in children and young adults, where both the extent and type of exposure to environmental hazards may vary widely because of developmental age, sex, personality, regional or other child-rearing patterns, and other characteristics, it is important, in research, for an attempt to be made to control for such exposure characteristics in order to avoid reaching erroneous conclusions regarding cause.

Research on the selection, application and effectiveness of interventions

Two separate but related issues are important here. First, to what extent is a given intervention successful in achieving its stated objectives and at what costs in terms of money, resources or altered life-style? Second, given the choice that often exists between two or more possible interventions which may require either behavioural or environmental change in order to succeed, or which may separately affect only the pre-event, event or post-event phases, how are the intervention strategies commonly selected at both the individual and community level? While more is known regarding the first of these issues, neither has been explored to any substantial degree and both are therefore fertile and important fields for future research.

What is currently known is that, in some cases, intervention programmes shown to have little likelihood of success are nevertheless continued, while in others highly effective and cost-effective countermeasures are passed over in favour of less effective ones. In still other cases—such as the use of seat-belts—teenagers, those who consume alcohol, and others at highest risk of injury have been found to be the least likely to use protective devices either voluntarily or when required by law, although use by lower-risk groups can be improved substantially by introducing legislation making it compulsory (16).

Evaluation should be incorporated into all safety programmes, especially if they involve measures that: (a) are being tried for the first time; (b) are being tried in a new population or under circumstances different from those in which they were previously applied; or (c) have not been properly evaluated previously. Such evaluation can be aimed at assessing several different levels of outcome. First-level outcomes include changes in skills, knowledge, attitudes or resources. These may (or may not) lead to observed changes in behaviour (self-reporting of changes in behaviour has often been found to be unreliable). Finally, behavioural change may (or may not) lead to reductions in morbidity and mortality, improved cost-effectiveness or fewer side-effects as compared with previous interventions. While some safety interventions have been "evaluated", the evaluation method most often used has been simply a before-versus-after examination of injury experience without such comparisons being made, as is necessary, both in the population where the intervention is taking place and in a "control" population not exposed to the intervention.

Both evaluation and studies aimed at determining why individuals or communities make certain decisions regarding injury prevention can benefit from the expertise of specialists not generally used in injury research, such as economists, political scientists, and ethicists. In particular, research is needed to identify which types of interventions can best be applied by physicians, public health personnel and other health professionals. The assessment of economic costs and benefits is a useful tool in programme planning and evaluation, but also has important limitations and should not be used as the sole arbiter of programme value (*17*). Wakeland has developed an excellent scheme for examining the potential implications for different parts of new safety programmes (*18*).

Finding and coordinating research resources

As already pointed out, research funds and personnel for injury research are less readily available and more fragmented than is the case for the study of most other health problems. In particular, few specialists in biomechanics, economics or political science have given more than passing attention to this field. Under these circumstances, programmes aimed at ensuring that trained personnel are available in the future need to be undertaken (see Chapter 15), while new approaches are used in order to find and utilize the scarce research resources currently available. Such approaches could include the following:

(1) *The establishment in each country of an injury research networking committee, clearing-house or similar organizational structure,* which can identify persons with relevant interests or skills, sources of funding or other resources, current literature, etc., and can also, where these resources fall short of needs, promote corrective action. If possible, such a network should include or identify and use persons with skills in medicine, epidemiology, biostatistics, human factors, engineering, psychology, mechanical engineering, biomechanics, economics, education, political science, urban planning, law, sociology, and ethics.

(2) *The development of regional collaborative activities* involving funding from, and the personnel resources of, two or more

countries for research problems of common interest. An outstanding example of such a collaborative activity has been the provision of technical resources by the Transport and Road Research Laboratory in the United Kingdom to various developing countries in Africa and Asia. The WHO Injury Prevention Programme serves such a function itself, as well as helping to identify and promote potential collaborative activities among Member States.

(3) *The establishment of a clearing-house*, with the collaboration of WHO or otherwise, to give injury-control professionals access to important research and programme papers that may not be easily obtainable. Few of the important injury-control journals, for example, are listed in the *Index medicus* and the *Index* may itself not be readily available to personnel in some developing countries.

(4) *The establishment of an inventory of existing knowledge and needs*, utilizing one or more of the above approaches, with regard to injury research in each of the Member States; this should also identify goals and lay down a timetable in line with the priorities specified. The 1980 health objectives of the US Department of Health and Human Services, which include the reduction of death and disability from injury, are an example of this strategy (*19*), as is the complementary report of the National Research Council's Committee on Trauma Research (*20*).

References

1. *Road traffic accident statistics: report on a WHO ad hoc Technical Group (Prague, 1978)*. Copenhagen, WHO Regional Office for Europe, 1979 (EURO Reports and Studies, No.19).

2. COMMITTEE ON INJURY SCALING. The Abbreviated Injury Scale: 1980 revision. Morton Grove, IL, American Association for Automotive Medicine, 1980.

3. BAKER, S. P. ET AL. The injury severity score: a method for describing patients with multiple injuries and evaluating emergency care. *Journal of traumatology*, **14**: 187–196 (1974).

4. MACKENZIE, E. J. ET AL. Predicting post-trauma functional disability for individuals without significant brain injury. In: *28th Annual Proceedings of the American Association for Automotive Medicine, 8–10 October 1984, Denver*, Morton Grove, IL, American Association for Automotive Medicine, pp. 173–187.

5. *Study Group on Assessment of Country Surveys on Accidents in Childhood, Ankara, 1982.* Unpublished WHO document IRP/ADR, 216–221, 1742 M.[1]
6. JONES-LEE, M. W. *The value of life: an economic analysis.* Chicago, University of Chicago Press, 1976.
7. MUSHKIN, S. & COLLINGS, F. Economic costs of disease and injury. *Public health reports,* **74**: 795–809 (1959).
8. LANDEFELD, J. & SESKIN, E. The economic value of life: linking theory to practice. *American journal of health,* **72**: 555–566 (1982).
9. *A report to the Congress on the effect of motorcycle use law repeal: A case for helmet use.* Washington, DC, National Highway Traffic Safety Administration, US Department of Transportation, 1980.
10. ARCHEA, J. ET AL. *Guidelines for stair safety.* Washington, DC, National Bureau of Standards, US Department of Commerce, 1979 (NBS Building Science Series 120).
11. *Summary report of Workshop on Research Development in Childhood Accidents, Havana, 15–16 November 1984.* Unpublished WHO document IRP/APR, 216 m 31 k (5), 4979E.[1]
12. *Highway loss reduction status report,* **20** (5), 11 May 1985.
13. HAMELL, T. R. Accidents and those bizarre bicycles. *Pediatrics,* **42**: 214 (1968).
14. WALLER, J. A. Bicycle ownership, use and injury patterns among elementary school children. *Pediatrics,* **47**: 1042–1050 (1971).
15. PASCARELLA, E. A. *A study of youthful bicycle riders in an urban community.* Chapel Hill, NC, Highway Safety Research Center, University of North Carolina, 1971.
16. WILLIAMS, A. F. & O'NEILL, B. Seat belt laws: implications for occupant protection. *Transactions of the Society for Automotive Engineers,* **88**: 106, abstract 790683.
17. WALLER, J. A. *Injury control. A guide to the causes and prevention of trauma.* Lexington, MA, Lexington Books, 1984.
18. WAKELAND, H. H. An array of social values for use in analyzing the need for safety regulations. In: *Proceedings of the 4th International Congress on Automotive Safety, July 14-16, 1975.* Washington, DC, National Highway Traffic Safety Administration, Department of Transportation, 1975, pp. 875–906.
19. *Promoting health/preventing disease. Objectives for the nation.* Washington, DC, Department of Health and Human Services, 1980.
20. COMMITTEE ON TRAUMA RESEARCH. *Injury in America: a continuing public health problem.* Washington, DC, National Research Council, 1985.

---

[1] Available on request from Injury Prevention Programme, World Health Organization, 1211 Geneva 27, Switzerland.

Chapter 17

Research and prevention: still a largely unexplored area

C. J. ROMER & M. MANCIAUX

General considerations

Accidents and their consequences form part of a complex process characterized by the interaction of a large number of factors resulting in a transfer of energy between a vector (the injuring agent) and a host (the individual) in an environment (physical, cultural or socioeconomic), which may affect health status, particularly of vulnerable population groups such as children, adolescents, some groups of workers or old people. Because of this essentially multidisciplinary and multisectoral character, there are a number of inadequacies in the management of this major health risk, particularly in the areas of research, application of research, and prevention programmes.

The safety sector is the very poor relation of public health research in general, even though accidents are among the leading causes of death in young people and their cost to society is as great as, if not greater than, that of heart disease or cancer. Furthermore, the establishment of priorities and hence the allocation of resources concentrate on the clinical aspects and give little prominence to research on appropriate prevention techniques that seek either to act on the environment or to promote safety in the same way that health is promoted at the different levels of society.

Chapter 16 broadly marked out the field of research on accidents, stressing the lack of qualified research workers, the shortage of resources despite the magnitude and complexity of the problem, and the extremely varied avenues that ought to be explored. Here, we intend to develop further Waller's main suggestions, while making no claim that the list presented is exhaustive or that it implies any order of priorities, which will depend on the situation prevailing in a particular country or region.

Clinical research

Clinical research, which is usually hospital-based, is concerned with the patient and the injury. It deals essentially with improving techniques of care. Nevertheless it may play an important role in prevention; by providing more precise estimates of the overall severity of injuries treated and by following up injured people after their discharge from the hospital or the rehabilitation centre, it should provide an answer to a question that is of crucial importance for the formulation of prevention policies: is the reduction in accident mortality observed in many industrialized countries accompanied by an increase in long-term or even permanent sequelae and disabilities? Annex 1, which presents the protocol for a research study currently under way in one region of France, shows what can be done in this area.

Clinical research has its limits, however, as is clearly shown in Table 17.1 which compares the clinical, epidemiological and ergonomic approaches to the study of accidents (1).

Epidemiological research

The importance of epidemiological surveys (2) seems all the greater since they can provide not just a simple statement of facts but a basis for the rational prevention of accidents. The epidemiological study of accidents therefore needs to be given new life through new surveys. These could take the form of descriptive surveys intended to provide information, analytical surveys, or experimental epidemiological approaches.

Descriptive surveys

Descriptive surveys carried out at the national level would probably prove far too expensive, complex and difficult to interpret. Preference should be given to local studies, aimed at clarifying certain precise problems. Indeed, epidemiological surveys in this field cannot be purely descriptive: they should also provide an opportunity for careful research on the etiology of accidents.

Descriptive and analytical surveys

In these surveys two approaches are possible. One approach starts from observation of accidents at the institutions providing care, e.g. hospitals, general practitioners' surgeries, clinics. Through questioning of the parents of children involved in accidents, an attempt can be made to define the causes. Such surveys should be conducted in various environments, for example, in urban and rural areas, and may cover either all accidents or one particular type of accident.

However, it would be useful to supplement this conventional approach, which involves a retrospective analysis, by a prospective study, starting from certain well defined observation zones. It would be useful to monitor accidents within a defined community, to define the individual circumstances of the accident, and to analyse the characteristics of the local houses, playgrounds, etc., in order to identify what, in surveys of road accidents, have been called "black spots".

Table 17.1. Comparison of the three main approaches to research on accidents in childhood and adolescence.[a]

	Clinical approach	Epidemiological approach	Ergonomic approach
Object	The patient Injuries	The characteristics: – of high-risk situations – of high-risk groups – of the risk factors – of the three classical elements: victim–agent–environment	The interface and interaction between the elements involved
Relevant questions	To whom (host, victim)? What (what injuries)?	How many cases? When? Where? To whom (victim)? Why?	How?
Advantages	Availability of hospital records	Possibility of collecting quantified data on: – exposure – the above-mentioned characteristics – the events	Possibility of transposing the concepts and the experience acquired with occupational accidents
Drawbacks	Records omitting the features of interest to epidemiologists Customary bias towards hospital cases	Low predictive value of risk factors Difficulty of direct observation Exhaustiveness of data: – difficult in the case of accidents – virtually impossible in the case of other events Complexity of the causal network	Ergonomists lack experience in the area of child and adolescent development
Level of prevention	Secondary Tertiary	Mainly primary, active	Mainly primary, passive

[a] From: Jeanneret (1)

To conduct a valid epidemiological survey, it is also necessary to take into account all risks, since minor accidents have the same epidemiological significance as severe accidents. This was done in France, for example, in the early 1980s, at the instigation of the Ministry of Health (*3*). This means that the survey must be confined to a relatively small population that is geographically homogeneous and readily accessible. Particular attention must be given to the conditions that are conducive to the accident process, since it is on these conditions that action can subsequently be taken. The frequency of accidents should be related to the population actually exposed, which will require determination of the length of time of exposure to risk; by determining the time that the child spends on different activities, it will be possible to compare domestic hazards, hazards at school, hazards in playgrounds, etc.

Experimental epidemiology

Alongside analytical epidemiological studies, it would be useful to develop an experimental approach. This could cover the child's environment and changes to the layout of apartments, the location of schools, and the organization of traffic.

This will involve different areas of basic and experimental research, whose existence and lessons are not well known to physicians; this subject, called "accidentology", has been applied mainly to the study of traffic accidents and has been used essentially to develop passive safety measures.

Ergonomic research

If the hazards of the domestic, work, leisure and road environment are to be reduced to the minimum, and consumer products made safe, coordinated multidisciplinary research and action are needed in fields such as ergonomics and the biomechanics of impacts, particularly with regard to vulnerable groups, such as children and old people. This type of research, which studies the physical and physiological responses of bodies to injuries, is a sector where an alliance between biology and engineering can help create a safer environment and prevent a considerable number of deaths and disabilities (see Chapters 10 and 11).

The study of what actually happens in an accident is the first stage in the search for safety. To take traffic accidents as an example, the injuries seen in the victims, the environmental factors (e.g., passenger space and external features of a car), how the injuries were inflicted, the relationship between the lesions and the severity of the accident—all these components must be considered. The analyses are conducted by multidisciplinary teams of physicians, to study the injuries, and engineers and technicians, to look at the technical data on the accident (impacted areas, buckling, trajectories of the victims, assessment of the energy levels involved at the moment of impact). The data thus accumulated can be used to guide research towards the most frequent and dangerous accident configurations, and towards the mechanisms that provoked the most serious injuries.

Once the "standard" accidents have been defined the research worker can use dummies to reproduce the accident process. High-speed cameras and measuring instruments attached to the dummies and vehicles provide an accurate record of the forces to which the dummies are subjected and analyse their action. These results can be used to refine the analysis of accidents, e.g., in the evaluation of collision speeds, or the relation between the injuries observed and the zones of impact. On the basis of these observations, the research worker may suggest protective measures or countermeasures, aimed at eliminating the most dangerous features of the accident or reducing its severity. Next, these countermeasures can be developed and optimized in the light of the various possible configurations (height of subjects, level at which protection needs to be applied, optimization of technical resources, etc.).

There is currently less information on children than adults, and research is needed to overcome the specific problems presented by this group of users. However, protection of children inside cars is currently the subject of intensive research, covering harnesses and bucket seats for children under six years and abdominal seat-belts for older children.

Other examples of research in progress include studies to optimize the shape of the front of vehicles so as to reduce the severity of collisions and protect child pedestrians, and studies to improve the efficacy of helmets worn by motorcycle riders.

Other avenues to be explored

Health economics

Economic research can provide useful information for decision-makers by determining the medical and social costs of accidents, comparing these costs with those of other health problems and, with a view to rationalizing budgetary decisions, giving indications of the cost/benefit ratio of the possible forms of action (see Chapter 5).

Behavioural science

Behavioural research aims to identify the psychological and social factors—whether predisposing, determining or aggravating—that play a role in the causes, circumstances and consequences of accidents and the resulting injuries. As in other fields of research, there is less knowledge on accidents to children and old people than on accidents to adults (see Chapters 6 to 9).

Health services research

Health services research has a cardinal role to play in determining the needs for treatment services, particularly at the primary health care level, in order to optimize the utilization and quality of these services and to ensure that prevention technologies and research findings are applied by the health services at all levels within an intersectoral framework. The findings of the research need to be converted into appropriate action, especially at community level.

Safety policies

Research on safety policies has been given little attention up to now, but important aspects include the study of the policies, legislation and regulations in force in different countries, and comparison of the efficacy of particular policies at different times (before and after the introduction of new measures) or in different places (differences in regulations between provinces, between states, or between regions of countries with a federal structure) (see Chapter 12).

Specific types of accident

Some categories of accident, such as road accidents, have been very thoroughly studied. In these cases, the real issue is the wider dissemination and application of prevention techniques (seat-belts, helmets for riders of motorcycles, etc.).

On the other hand, knowledge about other types of injury, whose importance is far from negligible, is often incomplete; this group includes domestic accidents, such as burns, falls and poisonings, and some occupational accidents, especially among agricultural workers. The situation is even worse in developing countries, where knowledge of these problems is generally insignificant. In these countries there is a need to promote inexpensive research and action aimed at solving the predominant problems.

Finally, in view of the increasing spread of products and technology, especially from the industrialized countries to the developing countries, international cooperation is needed, not only to ensure appropriate transfer of knowledge, but also to try to ensure an equal level of safety for these products and to promote safety standards for the use of technologies in working environments, especially in industry and agriculture.

Conclusion

There is therefore tremendous scope for research on accidents and safety among young people, and teams of epidemiologists, psychosociologists, economists, engineers and environmentalists need to be encouraged to become actively involved in such research. In view of the importance of accident injuries as a public health problem in most countries of the world, this is a truly urgent matter. Even though enough is already known about some types of accident for appropriate action to be taken, studies are still needed to identify the obstacles, constraints and resistance that prevent knowledge from being converted into action for greater safety. Exchange of experience between countries at different levels of development and with contrasting sociocultural values may prove extremely useful.

References

1. JEANNERET, O. Les accidents liés á l'activité sportive en milieu scolaire; point de vue d'un épidémiologiste. *Archives françaises de pédiatrie*, **38**: 791–796 (1981).
2. MANCIAUX, M. & DESCHAMPS, J. P. La prévention des accidents chez les enfants. In: *Journées parisiennes de pédiatrie*. Paris, Flammarion Médecine Sciences, 1977, pp. 323–340.
3. FÉLIX, M. & TURSZ, A. *Les accidents domestiques de l'enfant*. INSERM, International Children's Centre.
4. ROMER, C. J. & MANCIAUX, M. Research and intersectoral cooperation in the field of accidents. *World health statistics quarterly*. **39**: 281–284 (1986).

Injuries and poisonings in Aquitaine: preliminary results of an epidemiological survey

L. TIRET

In order to obtain more knowledge about injuries and poisonings, the Regional Hospital Centre in Bordeaux, the Aquitaine Regional Health Monitoring Station (ORSA), and the French National Institute for Health and Medical Research (INSERM, Unit 164) joined forces in 1986 to conduct an epidemiological study in the Aquitaine region. This project attracted wide participation from hospital physicians, medical inspectors of health, medical advisers to social security agencies, the statistics section of the Regional Department for Health and Social Affairs (DRASS), engineers at the Centre for Technical Studies of Infrastructure (CETE) and representatives of the forces of law and order.

The objectives of the study were to evaluate the annual number and frequency of severe injuries and poisonings and to determine their consequences for the hospital and the individual.

Number and frequency of injuries and poisonings

The definition adopted for "injury or poisoning" was that given in the International Classification of Diseases (supplementary classification of external causes of injury and poisoning). However, the area of study excluded complications occurring during medical or surgical procedures and the adverse effects of drugs and biological substances used for therapeutic purposes.

Since it was found not to be feasible to make an inventory of all injuries and poisonings (whether the patient was seen by a doctor or not) on account of the extent of the problem and the difficulty of defining the study area precisely, it was decided to include only "severe" injuries and poisonings, i.e. those that led either to immediate death or to admission to hospital for at least one day. Two different procedures were adopted to obtain information on these two situations.

Injuries and poisonings leading to immediate death

These cases were listed on the basis of the death certificate. The study was carried out jointly by the *département* medical inspectors and

INSERM Joint Service No. 8 which is responsible for the coding of certificates. The list included all deaths notified in Aquitaine in 1986 that were attributed to an injury or a poisoning and for which the place of onset was not a public or private hospital.

A brief questionnaire was filled in for each death, indicating the date and place of death, the type and cause of the accident, the subject's sex, age and occupation, the *département* and commune of residence, and finally the nature of the injuries.

Injuries and poisonings leading to hospitalization

This part of the study was conducted on a representative sample of all injuries and poisonings that led to admission to a public or private hospital in Aquitaine for at least one day.

The sample was constructed on the basis of a survey of all public and private hospitals, which were divided into two categories. The first category included all public hospitals and any private hospitals that regularly dealt with injured patients. All these establishments were included in the sample. In the second category, which comprised all other private hospitals, half the hospitals in each *département* were drawn by lot.

In each hospital thus selected the survey lasted 13 weeks, divided into several periods in order to obtain representative data for the whole year:

- the regional hospital centre was surveyed every fourth week;
- the hospitals in the first category were surveyed for three periods, of 4, 4 and 5 weeks, spread over the year (to ensure that the whole year was covered by the study, the hospitals were divided into four groups of equal size and the groups entered the survey successively at four-week intervals);
- the hospitals in the second category were divided into two groups, which entered the survey 15 weeks apart and were surveyed for 13 successive weeks.

The timetable for the survey is summarized in Table A1.1.

The medical staff at the hospital filled in a questionnaire for each patient admitted, specifying:

- the characteristics of the accident,
- the characteristics of the patient,
- the functional assessment on arrival at the hospital,
- the nature of the lesions, in the case of injury,

Table A1.1. Timetable for the survey in the hospitals

Type of hospital	Duration of survey	Survey periods
Regional hospital centre	13 weeks	Weeks starting on: 9/12, 6/1, 3/2, 3/3, 27/3, 28/4, 26/5, 23/6, 21/7, 14/8, 15/9, 13/10, 10/11
Hospitals of first category		
First group	13 weeks	16/12 to 12/1 (4 weeks) 21/4 to 25/5 (5 weeks) 25/8 to 21/9 (4 weeks)
Second group	13 weeks	13/1 to 16/2 (5 weeks) 26/5 to 22/6 (4 weeks) 22/9 to 19/10 (4 weeks)
Third group	13 weeks	17/2 to 16/3 (4 weeks) 23/6 to 27/7 (5 weeks) 20/10 to 16/11 (4 weeks)
Fourth group	13 weeks	17/3 to 20/4 (5 weeks) 28/7 to 24/8 (4 weeks) 17/11 to 14/12 (4 weeks)
Hospitals of second category		
First group	13 weeks	2/6 to 31/8
Second group	13 weeks	15/9 to 14/12

— the nature of the agent, in the case of poisoning,
— the patient's condition 48 hours and eight days after the accident.

On the basis of the nature of the lesions, an index of severity was calculated for each subject with the aid of a computer program. The "injury severity score" (ISS), developed by the American Association for Automotive Medicine, was used for this purpose.

Consequences of injuries and poisonings

The second part of the study also comprised two sections. The first considered the consequences of the accident from the hospital viewpoint (level of care provided throughout the hospital treatment of the patient), while the second assessed the consequences for the individual (sequelae of the accident).

These two aspects were investigated in a longitudinal study on a subsample of subjects admitted to the Regional Hospital Centre in Bordeaux and the Hospital Centre in Mont-de-Marsan. This subsample contained three groups of patients:

- all patients who had sustained a major injury requiring intensive care, or who had suffered major poisoning, or who had burn injuries;
- all patients who had sustained a major injury not requiring intensive care who were admitted to hospital during 9 predetermined weeks out of the 13 survey weeks;
- patients who had sustained a minor injury or mild poisoning and were admitted to hospital during three weeks other than the 9 weeks for the previous group.

The hospital viewpoint

Each hospital department concerned completed a questionnaire for each subject in the subsample, recording the medical and paramedical procedures performed each day. By evaluating the average time devoted to these procedures it was possible to quantify the activity deployed.

The individual viewpoint

The subjects included in the subsample were seen again by the attending hospital physicians six months after their hospitalization in order to evaluate the medical, social and occupational consequences of the accident. A questionnaire was developed for assessing the sequelae in accordance with the three concepts recommended by the World Health Organization[a]—impairments, disabilities and handicaps—and for summarizing the main categories of the international classification which is at present still at the experimental stage and very complex to use.

Subjects displaying a functional disability due to the accident at the six-month check-up underwent a second check-up one year after the accident.

---

[a] *International classification of impairments, disabilities, and handicaps.* Geneva, World Health Organization, 1980.

Initial results

The first part of the survey (evaluation of the number and frequency of injuries and poisonings) was conducted during 1986. Hospital participation in the survey proved very high; of the 64 establishments included in the sample only five private hospitals did not agree to take part (giving an overall participation rate of 92%) (Table A1.2). The participation rate can also be calculated in terms of the activity of the establishments. If it is assumed that in the hospitals that did not take part in the survey the proportion of overall activities devoted to injuries and poisonings was equivalent to that observed in the hospitals that did agree to take part, it may be estimated that the refusals represent only 3%—in terms of activity—of all the injuries and poisonings treated in the region.

In the course of the survey 9531 persons were admitted to hospital following an accident; extrapolation from this figure suggests that there are 39 100 such hospital admissions in the region each year. If we add the 1330 deaths that occurred before admission, the annual number of severe injuries and poisonings in the Aquitaine region may be estimated at 40 400.

The longitudinal study conducted at the Bordeaux Regional Hospital Centre and at the Mont-de-Marsan Hospital Centre covered 1500 subjects. An initial provisional evaluation indicated that over 75% of the subjects were seen at the six-month check-up. About half of these displayed a functional disability due to the accident and therefore underwent the second check-up one year after the accident.

Table A1.2. Participation of hospitals in the survey

	No. invited	No. participating	Participation rate	
			Hospitals[a]	Activity[b]
Public hospitals	21	21	100%	100%
Private hospitals	43	38	88%	90%
Total	64	59	92%	97%

[a] Rate calculated in terms of the total number of hospitals.
[b] Rate calculated in terms of the amount of activity in the hospitals.

Annex 2
An experiment: supervised driving at age 16

M. SIMONET-PERVANCHON

In some countries, including the United States of America, the driving test can be taken at the age of 14 years. Young people in France have to wait until they are 18, and it seems unlikely that the rules regarding the age limit will be changed in the near future. In any case, lowering the age limit does not necessarily lead to improvements in terms of safety. What is important is to give people experience of driving under less hazardous conditions. In other words, it would be better if young drivers were already "experienced" when they become entitled to drive on their own.

An original experiment has been set up in France to show how a gradual learning process could take place, which would help to reduce the number of road accidents involving young drivers. This experiment, which the Ministry of Transport conducted initially in the French *départements* of Essonne and Yvelines, is in keeping with research and action strategies for reducing mortality risk in 16–18-year-olds.

It is well known that during the first two years after obtaining their driving licence, young drivers are 3.5 times more likely than other drivers to be involved in a fatal road accident. This excess risk for young people is associated partly with a lack of driving experience, partly with the psychological characteristics of adolescents, and partly with the fact that, in our society, the driving licence is an important symbol of adulthood and independence.

It was therefore felt essential to separate training from the actual obtaining of the licence. Early training ensures that the skills needed for driving a motor vehicle are acquired gradually. Accordingly, young people who have reached the age of 16 are offered the opportunity to undergo training in driving schools and after that to drive accompanied by an adult until they reach the age of 18, at which time a driving licence can be issued. The obligatory presence of an accompanying adult also lends continuity to the educational process, thus enhancing its value. This experiment is much more than a technical or sectoral project; it foreshadows a change in the relationship between the French and their cars, through the relationship between parents and adolescents. It offers an opportunity for better control of the transport machine: in short, a new and more responsible way of driving and behaving.

Besides young people, those involved in this system are:

- *Driving schools*: those taking part in the training have signed agreements with the State and the parents, setting out their educational responsibilities. The instructors have undergone two days' training at the Ministry's experimental unit.
- *Driving examiners*: they act as educational advisers and observers. They are seen as "consultants", which changes their image.
- *Driving supervisors*: these are generally the parents of the young people. They have a responsibility as "skipper" when the initial training is completed; they also provide a guarantee of good behaviour, and play an educational role.
- *Insurance companies*: most have agreed to extend their third party coverage to supervised driving without any increase in premium.
- *The Ministry of Transport*: it monitors the experiment by means of an instruction log book and trip cards.

The initial results after sixteen months were as follows:

- Almost 1000 young people were involved in supervised driving.
- After 800 000 km of supervised driving there had been five accidents resulting in material damage; in no case was a young driver held responsible by the insurance companies.
- 120 of the young people had reached the age of 18 and all but 12 had passed the driving test at the first attempt. All had driven more than 3500 km.
- Two-thirds of the young people registered in the scheme were boys.
- Three-quarters were at secondary school, mostly in the highest class; the others were undergoing occupational training.

There is great enthusiasm to take part in the experiment, the leading motives being to make young people act responsibly and to increase safety. The possibility of "testing" the young people over several months seems important, while they get over the initial desire to take undue risks. The trusting relationship required for this experiment is also seen by everyone concerned as a kind of enjoyable "conspiracy" to learn to drive and use the car.

In 1985, this experiment of "learning to drive early" was extended: it is now under way in 22 of France's 95 *départements*, and it is hoped that, after careful evaluation, the trial can eventually be extended to the whole country.

Annex 3
The "REACT" programme

M. J. RAMBEAU

France's present road safety policy is one of decentralization. Under the centralized system, the State played the leading role and local activities to heighten public awareness were modest compared with the regulations imposed directly by the State. These regulations, the best known of which concern speed limits, compulsory wearing of seatbelts, wearing of helmets by motorcyclists and the laws on drinking and driving, have proved their efficacy. From 1972 to 1978 there was a substantial drop in the number of accidents and also in the number of people killed. But after 1978 these figures levelled off, so other steps needed to be taken.

Under the new policy of decentralization, and with a view to attaining the Government's objective of reducing the death rate on the roads by one-third in five years, a number of action programmes were suggested to local government in 1982, including the REACT programme ("react" through surveys on serious accidents and through initiatives to prevent them). This is a programme of local political mobilization and local social communication, and includes a thorough technical investigation of every fatal accident. The investigation is ordered at *département* level by the State Commissioner, who is responsible for the programme, and is carried out by a multi-disciplinary team of road safety inspectors from the different groups concerned with road safety problems, such as: law enforcement (police), highway engineers, emergency medical and rescue services, and drivers' organizations. The purpose of each survey is to reconstruct the accident, not just in order to determine the apparent causes and the responsibilities, but also to identify the factors producing or aggravating the accident.

The surveys concern the various factors involved in accidents: infrastructure, environment, vehicle, and driver, whose psychological status at the time of the accident is determined. The programme also sets out to look into the relationships between these four factors and into ways of informing and educating politicians, the departments responsible for road safety, and the general public.

Each investigation should lead to proposals concerning each of the four factors, and these proposals are discussed by a technical group made up of the *département* road safety inspectors. Pooling the results of the various investigations may shed light on the circumstances, events or types of behaviour involved in a substantial proportion of cases, thus leading perhaps to new knowledge or to the development of new measures that can be applied throughout the country.

Some proposals or remedies are a matter for the State itself, but others can be carried out at local level, such as alterations to roundabouts, local speed limits, changes in road markings, or efforts to make the public aware of undesirable behaviour linked to the local environment.

List of contributors

Dr L. R. Berger, Albuquerque, New Mexico 87108, USA

Dr J. Greensher, American Academy of Pediatrics, Department of Pediatrics, Nassau Hospital, Mineola, NY 11501, USA

Dr (Mrs) F. Hatton, INSERM, 78110 Le Vésinet, France

Dr J. Havard, British Medical Association, London, England

Dr A. Hitchcock, Transport and Road Research Laboratory, Crowthorne, Berkshire, England

Professor J. R. Jordán, Higher Institute of Medical Sciences, Vedado, Havana, Cuba

Professor L. Köhler, Dean, Nordic School of Public Health, Göteborg, Sweden

Dr B.-Å. Ljungblom, Head, Children's Health Care in Blekinge County, Karlskrona, Sweden

Dr P. Maguin, INSERM, Paris, France

Dr M. Manciaux, Professor of Public Health, University of Nancy, Vandoeuvre-lès-Nancy, France

Professor D. Mohan, Centre for Biomedical Engineering, Indian Institute of Technology, New Delhi, India

Dr V. Nicaud, INSERM, Paris, France

Dr M. J. Rambeau, INRETS, Arcueil, France

Dr C. J. Romer, Injury Prevention Programme, World Health Organization, Geneva, Switzerland

Professor E. A. Sand, Director, Free University of Brussels, Brussels, Belgium

Dr M. Simonet-Pervanchon, Behavioural Psychology Laboratory, INRETS, Arcueil, France

Mrs A. R. Taket, Department of Health and Social Security, London, England

Dr L. Tiret, INSERM, Paris, France

Mrs A. Triomphe, Social Economics Laboratory, Teaching and Research Unit for Economic Analysis, Paris, France

Dr (Mrs) A. Tursz, INSERM, Paris, France

Dr F. Valdes-Lazo, Assistant Director, Institute of Growth and Development, Ministry of Health, Havana, Cuba

Professor J. A. Waller, University of Vermont, College of Medicine, Burlington, Vermont, USA

Ms S. Whitelaw, Executive Officer, National Safety Council of Australia, Bowden, South Australia

Dr B. Zeiller, INSERM, Montrouge, France